simple & delicious
RECIPES FROM THE HEART

PENGUIN BOOKS

PENGUIN BOOKS

Published by the Penguin Group
Penguin Books (South Africa) (Pty) Ltd, Block D, Rosebank Office Park,
181 Jan Smuts Avenue, Parktown North, Johannesburg, 2196, South Africa
Penguin Group (USA) Inc, 375 Hudson Street, New York, New York
10014, USA
Penguin Group (Canada), 90 Eglinton Avenue East, Suite 700, Toronto,
Ontario, Canada M4P 2Y3 (a division of Pearson Penguin Canada Inc)
Penguin Books Ltd, 80 Strand, London WC2R 0RL, England
Penguin Ireland, 25 St Stephen's Green, Dublin 2, Ireland (a division of
Penguin Books Ltd)
Penguin Group (Australia), 250 Camberwell Road, Camberwell, Victoria
3124, Australia (a division of Pearson Australia Group Pty Ltd)
Penguin Books India Pvt Ltd, 11 Community Centre, Panchsheel Park, New
Delhi – 110 017, India
Penguin Group (NZ), 67 Apollo Drive, Mairangi Bay, Auckland 1310, New
Zealand (a division of Pearson New Zealand Ltd)

Penguin Books (South Africa) (Pty) Ltd, Registered Offices:
Block D, Rosebank Office Park, 181 Jan Smuts Avenue, Parktown North,
Johannesburg, 2196, South Africa

www.penguinbooks.co.za

First published by Penguin Books (South Africa) (Pty) Ltd 2012

Copyright © Alida Ryder 2012

All rights reserved
The moral right of the author has been asserted

ISBN 978-0-14-352887-6

Cover by Flame Design, Cape Town
Printed and bound by 1010 Printing Int Ltd

Except in the United States of America, this book is sold subject
to the condition that it shall not, by way of trade or otherwise,
be lent, resold, hired out or otherwise circulated without the
publisher's prior consent in any form of binding other than that
in which it is published and without a similar condition including
this condition being imposed on the subsequent purchaser.

CONTENTS

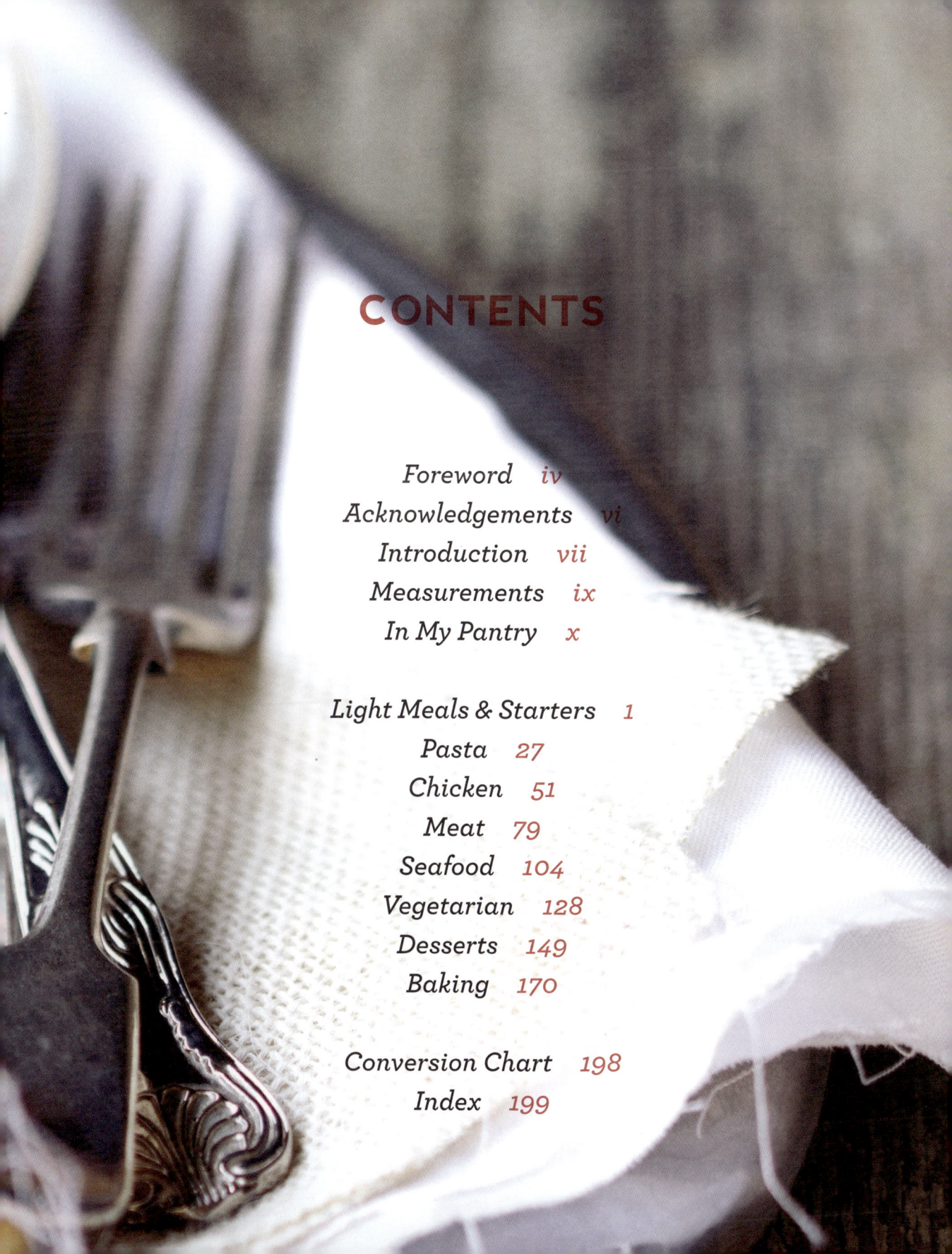

Foreword iv
Acknowledgements vi
Introduction vii
Measurements ix
In My Pantry x

Light Meals & Starters 1
Pasta 27
Chicken 51
Meat 79
Seafood 104
Vegetarian 128
Desserts 149
Baking 170

Conversion Chart 198
Index 199

FOREWORD

Unlike other brides, Alida never minded being photographed with a mouthful of wedding cake. I know this not because I attended her wedding, but because she once used it as a Twitter profile pic. You want to be friends with a girl who likes her food and is not ashamed of showing it.

I never quite understood the whole social media/ Twitter/ blog thing. That is until it happened to me. Until I started reading blogs and realised it was like reading somebody's diary, which I do admit appeals to the voyeur and snoop in me. And Google is a godsend when you can type in 'easy pork belly recipe' and hundreds of appropriate entries pop up; then you know you've come to the right place. Or when you find yourself returning to certain blogs, like *Simply Delicious*, because you know you'll always find inspiration in them when faced with the what-shall-I-make-for-supper dilemma. I also started making friends online: virtual friends who were uncomplicated in their affection and encouragement, friends who showed pictures of themselves with a mouthful of wedding cake. Friends I wanted to meet in person. Friends like Alida.

Before I met her, I, like other followers of her blog, knew quite a bit about her. I knew that she dated older boys at school because she was so much taller than the boys in her class. I knew that she loved clothes and make-up; that she fell in love with the man who is now her husband when she was 17 years old. And that she became a mother of twins in her early twenties. I knew that she loves her father and brothers very much and that not a day goes by that she doesn't miss her mother, a brilliant lecturer in criminology whose interest in food was not as passionate as her daughter's, but who left her with a collection of recipe books from which Alida bakes clementine cakes. I also knew that rooibos tea reminds Alida of her grandmother. I knew these things because Alida is such an honest writer; she knows that food and love and emotion are intimately connected, and so she, with open-hearted generosity, shares her life and her loves with us. She does the same with her recipes. Recipes that work. I know this because I've tried them. Successfully.

I've always liked Alida's enthusiasm for food, her generosity in preparing it and her authentic approach to the sometimes rather stuffy and pretentious world of the culinary arts. Having met her, I love her enthusiasm for life, her capacity for joy and her gratitude for the good things that come her way. And I know that this book, conceived, created, written, styled and photographed by Alida, is a reflection of herself. And that is recommendation enough.

Alida reminds me why I love food. Because the making of food is a gift. Because it tastes good. Because it always makes me feel better. And because, sometimes, it really is okay to want more.

Sam Woulidge
Confessions of a Hungry Woman

*To Aidan and Abigail, and
in loving memory of my mom,
Ronel and my gran, Alida.*

ACKNOWLEDGEMENTS

I am overcome with gratitude to every person who was involved in one way or another with this book. I have to start by thanking the one person who is always by my side and I can count on for absolutely anything: my husband Chris. This book belongs to you as much as it does to me, babe. You have put almost as much into it as I have, and I cannot say thank you enough. Thank you for being patient while I was raging, being calm while I was sobbing and for being absolutely the best father to our beautiful children. To my Aidan and Abi, thank you for being constant providers of joy and for your unconditional love.

To my dad, brothers and sister-in-law, thank you for eating all my flops with a smile on your face and for giving kind, constructive criticism. Thank you for supporting me, for always bringing me back to earth and for making me laugh.

To the rest of my family – my aunts, uncles and cousins – thank you for your honest and never-ending support of everything I do. I could not have asked for a better team of cheerleaders and I am humbled and genuinely grateful for being part of your family.

Then to my family-in-law, thank you for being eternally positive about all my endeavours and for being such eager guinea pigs.

My friends, you know who you are, thank you for being there to bounce ideas off, for being a shoulder to cry on, for listening to my rants and for giving me a cocktail when needed.

To my Penguin family, Reneé, Alison and Ellen, thank you for trusting me so much and for allowing me to be 100 per cent involved in this book. I could not have asked for a better publisher and I am so excited for our journey moving forward. A special thank you goes to Reneé for being by my side through all of this. Without you none of this would've been possible.

Thank you to Le Creuset for the use of their beautiful range of products. To Cecily Pohl from Feint Lifestyle Gallery in Duncan Yard for allowing me to use your beautiful space to do some of the shooting in. Another big thank you goes out to Ronel, one of my best friends' mom. Thank you for being so generous with your beautiful home and kitchen.

And I have to say a quick thank you to my mom and my gran. I know you are guiding me and holding my hand along the road, but I so wish you could be here in person. Thank you for making me the woman I am today and for teaching me that life is short and precious. I miss you every day.

And finally, thank you, the reader, for buying this book. May you be inspired to create beautiful dishes and share them with the people you love.

Alida

INTRODUCTION

I initially started my blog to allow myself the space to live out my creativity and get away from the everyday routine of raising twins. I always had an intense love for cooking and my family often asked me why I didn't go to chef school, but I just never thought that was the direction I was meant to go in. My husband then suggested I put my recipes online as friends and family were always asking for them.

My blog gained a loyal following rather quickly and I started getting comments like, 'You have changed the way I cook' and 'You've inspired me to get back into the kitchen again'. These comments put a spring in my step. I believe the reason for people leaving comments like that is the fact that I simply blogged about what my family eats for dinner. Sometimes it's something fancy pants and a little tricky, but most often it's simple, honest food, created with a big dose of love and enthusiasm and a pinch or two of creativity and curiosity.

You will see in my recipes that I very rarely stick to tradition, meaning that I am not a food purist or a food snob. I often add a splash of soy sauce to my curries or Bolognese, but if that thought makes you choke on your lamb chop, simply omit that step. I firmly believe that this adventurous (and often foolish) streak in me is the reason I'm a good cook today. I have added ingredients to recipes thinking I would create a masterpiece, only to find them inedible, and bless my family for not saying a word and masking the flavour with tomato sauce or washing it down with Coca-Cola. But I've also hit upon some truly amazing combinations and additions to dishes that I would never have thought of had I not lived on the dangerous side every now and then.

This adventurous spirit comes from my beloved mother. As I've mentioned on my blog numerous times, my mother loved the idea of cooking but I don't think she liked the practicality of it all that much. She was the ultimate express cook, although she did make some truly amazing food every now and then. Most weeknights saw her serving baked chicken with green beans and rice.

In spite of that, my mother's love for food, and adventurous food at that (Greek cuisine was her absolute favourite), was contagious and it was a bug I was very eager to catch. When my friends were eating macaroni and cheese, my mom would give us dolmades, taramasalata and crispy squid heads.

I am trying (and succeeding so far) to raise my own children with that same openness to new foods and now they ask for Kalamata olives and wasabi peas before sweets and chips (and yes, of course they do still ask for sweets and chips now and then; they're human after all).

If you are new to cooking – and even if you're not – I suggest that you go slowly and taste ingredients before adding them to dishes. Add a few teaspoons at a time and taste your food constantly as you go. You will soon become comfortable and learn what works for you and what doesn't. I also urge you to explore your supermarket aisles more. Go down those aisles with the foreign ingredients that you would never have dared to add to your shopping basket and have a look at what's on offer. Just read the labels and learn the names; maybe one day you'll build up enough courage to buy that nam pla (fish sauce) or ketjap manis (sweet, thick soy sauce).

Another option is to venture into the world of food markets. There is nothing like speaking to the producers of a product and learning where it's come from, how it's been made and the best way to eat it and cook with it. Their passion for their craft will most definitely inspire you. Buy a small amount of an ingredient you're intrigued by, and cook with it and taste it in every way possible. You will learn something new and possibly find something you love.

If I only achieve one thing with this book, I hope it is to inspire people to get back into their kitchens. I hope that you will think twice about buying something ready-made at the supermarket or visiting that drive-through again; that you will learn to love cooking and that you will not think about it as 'just another chore'.

I hope that you will enjoy cooking from this book as much as I have enjoyed creating, cooking and tasting the recipes. May your kitchen become your new playground!

MEASUREMENTS

When it comes to cooking, I very rarely (read: almost never) weigh the ingredients I use. I always go on feel and taste (as you will too as you become more comfortable with cooking). In this book I have used cups (250 ml), tablespoons (15 ml) and teaspoons (5 ml).

But when it comes to baking, I always, and I mean always, weigh the ingredients. This is the only way to make sure you have complete accuracy, which is necessary when you want a successful end result, and I'm pretty sure that's what you're after. I always struggle to convert imperial measurements to metric, so I choose not to do it; however, most electronic scales nowadays have settings for both systems. Sometimes in baking there are obscure measurements like 75 g or 83 g. In these cases, I have included this measurement but also, in brackets, I have included a tablespoon or teaspoon measurement to make things easier for you. I suggest you invest in an electric scale (you can find good-quality, relatively cheap ones at all homeware stores), glass measuring jugs (the ones that give measurements for cups, millilitres and fluid ounces are great), and measuring cups and spoons if you are interested in baking. It will make your life much easier, I promise.

NOTES FROM THE AUTHOR

- I use free-range, organic meat and chicken. I am not here to preach to you; I just prefer using meat from animals that have had a life outside of a factory. The quality of meat is much better and there is no hiding the fact that the flavour cannot even be compared.
- I use extra-large, free-range eggs.
- When frying foods, I choose to use canola oil. The flavour is unobtrusive and it is a healthier choice than sunflower oil. I also often use this instead of olive oil to sauté with for no other reason than it is easier to reach in my cupboard.
- Most of the recipes in this book serve 4 (possibly 6 if your family and friends aren't as greedy as mine). However, there is a serving size included with every recipe for your convenience.
- You will see in some of my baking recipes I use bicarbonate of soda. This is sometimes called baking soda in other countries.
- When using tinned tomatoes, I always add 1 teaspoon sugar to counteract the tartness tinned tomatoes often have. If you don't want to add sugar, feel free to substitute or omit it.
- For more information about the products and ingredients I like to use, refer to the Pantry List on page xii.

IN MY PANTRY

Listed here are all the ingredients and products that make my life a whole lot easier. Without these staples (and there are a lot of them), I wouldn't be able to cook the food that I love. If you don't have some (or any) of these products in your kitchen at the moment, buy a few at time, cook with them and see if they're things you'd like to use again. These are the things that I love and you might not like some or you might have a much more impressive pantry than I do, but personalise this list to suit you, your household and your budget.

PANTRY LIST
Canned goods

Tomatoes • *Chopped, whole, purée and paste. I find the imported Italian varieties to be both the cheapest and the best quality.*
Beans and legumes • *Red kidney beans, cannellini beans, butter beans, lentils, chickpeas.*
Fish • *Tuna in spring water, crab, smoked mussels and oysters.*

Starches

Pasta • *Linguini, spaghetti (also wholewheat), penne, macaroni, fusilli.*
Rice • *Arborio or Carnaroli (for risotto), basmati, jasmine, brown and wild rice.*
Other • *Couscous, pearl barley.*

Oil, vinegar and condiments

Oil • *Olive oil (for cooking), extra virgin olive oil (for salad dressings and drizzling over foods), canola oil, sesame oil, flavoured oil (chilli, garlic, herb).*
Vinegar • *Aged balsamic vinegar, white balsamic vinegar, white spirit vinegar, white wine vinegar, sherry vinegar, infused balsamic reductions.*
Condiments • *Dijon mustard, wholegrain mustard, hot English mustard, tomato sauce, chutney, sweet chilli sauce, soy sauce, oyster sauce, chilli sauce (hot sauce), good mayonnaise, Bovril, Marmite.*
Sweet condiments • *Honey, maple syrup, golden syrup, strawberry jam, apricot jam, peanut butter.*

Flavourings, stocks and spices

Stock • *When I don't have home-made stock, I rely on NoMU's concentrates. They are very flavoursome.*
Flavourings • *Salt (I use a variety, including table salt, Maldon Sea Salt and smoked salt), white pepper, black pepper, mustard powder, cayenne pepper.*
Spices • *I have a huge assortment of spices. I suggest that you buy whole spices and toast and grind them yourself if you won't be using them too often as ready-ground spices lose their flavour if not used within a month. Spices I always have in the house are: coriander, cumin, cloves, nutmeg, cinnamon, mustard seeds, star anise, turmeric, paprika, smoked paprika, cardamom pods, chilli powder, chilli flakes, good-quality garam masala and good-quality dukkah. I also always have a really good-quality spice and herb mix on hand (something like roasting spice or braai spice). Try to get a spice mix where you can see the actual*

dried spices and herbs (again, I rely heavily on NoMU's all-for-one spice rub here). I also always have a good-quality Thai curry paste and Indian curry paste in the fridge.

Cereals and snacks

Cereal • *I always have one or two different kinds of wholegrain (not sugar-laden) cereals available for my kids. It makes an easy breakfast when paired with some yoghurt and fruit.*
Oats • *Organic rolled oats are my favourite but I also have the instant kind in the pantry.*
Snacks • *Wholegrain crackers (Pro-Vita), rice or corn cakes, nuts, crackers and popcorn.*

Baking

Flour • *Cake flour (all purpose), bread flour (strong/ 00), cornflour.*
Sugar • *White sugar (granulated), caster sugar, icing sugar (powdered/ confectioner's), light-brown sugar, muscavado sugar (treacle sugar).*
Other • *Baking powder, bicarbonate of soda (baking soda), cream of tartar, vanilla extract, cocoa powder, caramel treat (tinned caramel), condensed milk, chocolate.*

Other pantry staples

Aluminium foil, cling wrap, baking paper, wax paper, zip seal bags in all sizes, kitchen towels and paper serviettes.

FRIDGE LIST

The ingredients in my fridge include everything from fresh dairy products, opened condiments, fruit and veg that will go off if left in the veg drawer or fruit bowl, and leftovers.

Dairy

Milk • *Low fat/ 2 per cent.*
Cream • *Reduced fat and single (pouring) cream.*
Crème fraîche • *Similar to sour cream but milder in taste.*
Butter and shortening
Yoghurt • *Greek, fat-free natural and small containers of flavoured yoghurt.*
Cheese • *Mature Cheddar, Gouda, feta, pecorino/ Parmesan and occasionally others such as goat's cheese, Camembert and talleggio.*

Fruit, vegetables and herbs

This really is an assortment of seasonal fruit and veg. I always have salad ingredients and the basics.
Fruit • *Seasonal, including for example berries, nectarines, plums, melon and pineapple.*
Vegetables • *Lettuce, rocket, watercress, cucumber, cherry tomatoes, mushrooms, peppers, avocados, aubergines, fresh corn, asparagus, green beans, sugar snap peas, broccoli.*
Herbs • *Flat-leaf (Italian) parsley, basil, thyme, sage, mint, chives.*

FREEZER LIST

Meat and fish • *Most often whole chickens, chicken breasts, chicken livers, bacon, sausages, stewing beef and lamb. I try to buy fresh fish as often as possible but I do like to have frozen mussels or crab stocked and I also always have good-quality fish fingers in the freezer for quick lunches for the kids.*
Pastry • *Ready-made puff pastry and shortcrust pastry.*
Vegetables • *Frozen baby peas and corn.*
Bread • *I often buy fresh bread in bulk and freeze it immediately as we have a big household and a loaf of bread doesn't last more than a day. I also like freezing leftover bread to make into fresh breadcrumbs or, if I'm feeling less lazy, I'll make the leftover bread into breadcrumbs first and then freeze them.*
Stock • *When I make stock I try to make quite a bit (more than 4 litres) and then freeze it in 1 litre containers. If I don't have time to make the stock then and there, I freeze the chicken bones from a roast to make into stock later on. The same goes for beef bones, etc.*
Ice cream • *I'm not an ice cream fan but it's handy to have on hand when you need to whip up an easy dessert.*
Fruit • *I'm not crazy about frozen fruit, but having berries in the freezer is great. They can be used for smoothies, compotes (great over flapjacks) and in baking.*

OTHER KITCHEN STAPLES

Fresh bread • *I always have sliced white bread and wholegrain bread in the house. I also like to have more artisanal breads like ciabatta and baguette in the house for easy lunches, croutons, etc.*
Eggs • *I keep my eggs in a basket in my kitchen. I like to have them at room temperature.*
Vegetable drawer • *Fresh garlic, ginger, onions (red and brown), chillies, potatoes, butternut, sweet potatoes.*
Fruit bowl • *Again, seasonal fruit like clementines (naartjies), oranges, grapefruit, apples, pears, mangoes, bananas and kiwi.*

LIGHT MEALS & STARTERS

If you are on diet, skip this page. If, like me, you are a shameless cheese addict, you will be in heaven when you eat this, and I cannot be held responsible for what you might do to your diet if you read further.

Cheese on its own is delicious, but when it's coated in breadcrumbs and deep-fried, you have a little piece of heaven. Before I leave you with the recipe (and most probably a drool stain on this page), let me say it's important to serve this with a deeply flavourful sauce as mozzarella doesn't have an awful lot of flavour on its own. I like this tomato sauce as it cuts through the fattiness of the fried cheese nicely and adds just the right amount of flavour.

Now go!

FRIED MOZZARELLA WITH ROASTED TOMATO SAUCE

Makes approximately 12 fried mozzarella balls

- 300 g bocconcini (small mozzarella balls)
- 1 cup flour, seasoned with salt
- 2 eggs, beaten
- 2 cups breadcrumbs, seasoned with 1 teaspoon salt and 1 teaspoon smoked paprika
- oil for frying

Tomato sauce

- 1 tin cherry tomatoes
- 1 red onion, chopped
- 2 garlic cloves
- 1 teaspoon sugar
- 1 teaspoon salt
- ½ cup fresh basil leaves, roughly chopped

1. To make the tomato sauce, pre-heat the oven to 220 °C.
2. Combine all the sauce ingredients except for the fresh basil in a small roasting dish and allow to roast for 20–25 minutes until the tomatoes are soft and have started to colour slightly. Add the fresh basil and pulse in a food processor to break up any big lumps.
3. For the fried mozzarella, place the seasoned flour, egg and breadcrumbs in separate bowls and heat the oil in a saucepan.
4. Remove the bocconcini from the liquid they come in and pat dry with kitchen paper.
5. Cover the bocconcini first in flour, then in egg and finally in the breadcrumbs before frying in the hot oil for 3–5 minutes until the breadcrumbs are crisp and golden.
6. Remove from the oil and drain on kitchen paper.
7. Serve immediately with the roasted tomato sauce.

Pesto is by no means a new thing on the foodie scene but I have fallen so deeply in love with it all over again and use it as often as I can with almost everything I cook. Its strong flavour goes incredibly well with pasta, chicken, vegetables and in salad dressings.

More and more supermarkets are stocking really good-quality pesto and I often buy a few bottles, but there is no question in my mind that home-made is best. I know that the ingredients are expensive, but you will get a bigger quantity of pesto (which in my case is more cost effective as I can easily use a whole tub on one meal) if you make it yourself and the taste will be far superior.

Parmigiano reggiano (Parmesan) is normally used for pesto but I prefer the nuttiness of pecorino romano (in fact I prefer pecorino to Parmesan in most cases). Make sure that the basil you buy (if you don't have it growing in your garden) is bright green and fresh.

If you want to make a big quantity of pesto, I suggest you freeze it in ice cube trays. This way it's much easier to add that delicious pesto flavour to dishes because you can just pop a few cubes into a sauce or defrost it quickly. Many people suggest you omit the cheese if you are going to be freezing the pesto, but I just leave the cheese in and freeze as is.

BASIL PESTO

Makes 1 cup pesto

- 50 g toasted pine kernels, cooled
- 80 g fresh basil leaves, stems removed
- ½–¾ cup pecorino, grated
- 1 garlic clove, sliced
- salt to taste
- 1–1½ cups olive oil

1. Place all the ingredients except for the oil and salt in a food processor and process until you have a fine-textured mixture.
2. With the processor running, drizzle in the oil. You could also make the pesto with a pestle and mortar in exactly the same way.
3. Test the pesto for seasoning and adjust. I find that the pecorino gives it enough saltiness and I normally don't need to adjust the seasoning.
4. Store the pesto with a layer of oil on top, in a covered jar in the fridge, for up to 10 days.

Like most cooks, I have recipes that I come back to time and time again. This is one of them. Whether it is for breakfast, lunch or an easy dinner, I eat this so often my husband says my second name should've been Bruschetta. And I have to be honest, I wouldn't mind if it was! I just love saying it (and I imagine myself to be quite the Italian signora when I do).

For me, there are two options when making this. You can either rub the bread with olive oil and garlic and place it under the hot grill to become toasted and crisp, or you can fry it in butter until it becomes toasted and crisp (and very buttery). There is no right or wrong way in my book; it all depends on how much time you have and how many calories you'll allow yourself. The buttery version, although incredible, is very rich and I can only ever eat a small amount of it, whereas the olive oil grilled version is much lighter and I can eat a lot of it. And I mean a lot.

Use any artisanal bread of your choice. I use anything from baguette or sourdough to French boule (which is my favourite but I don't often find it).

The amounts I give in this recipe aren't specific, as I insist you taste as you go. This also makes it easier when you're feeding more than one – just slice more bread and chop more tomatoes as you need them.

BRUSCHETTA WITH FRESH TOMATOES

bread of your choice, sliced
ripe tomatoes, roughly chopped
fresh basil, torn
salt and pepper to taste
olive oil, for rubbing the bread
1 garlic clove, halved

1. Heat the grill and place one of the oven racks higher up so it's closer to the grill.
2. Combine the tomatoes with the fresh basil and season to taste. Set aside.
3. Rub the sliced bread first with some olive oil and then with the halved garlic clove.
4. Place the bread under the grill and allow it to become toasted and golden. You'll have to keep watching it as it can go from gloriously toasted to horribly burnt in a second.
5. Flip the bread and allow the other side to become toasted.
6. Remove from the oven and place spoonfuls of the tomato mixture on top. Add some more salt and pepper before serving

This is a great, easy lunch recipe that can be made with things from your pantry and fridge. I always have ready-made puff pastry in my freezer and often reach for it when I need to whip up something for lunch.

What I love most about this tart is that it is incredibly versatile and you can substitute the tomato for almost anything you can think of. Any vegetables will work and to make it more pizza-like, you can add bacon, chicken or chorizo.

Serve warm with a zesty salad.

TOMATO AND PESTO TART

Makes 1 tart (feeds 2–6, depending on appetites)

- 1 roll ready-made puff pastry, defrosted
- ½ cup basil pesto
- ½ cup crème fraîche
- 4 large, ripe tomatoes, thinly sliced
- salt and pepper to taste
- 1 egg yolk

1. Pre-heat the oven to 220 °C and line a baking tray with baking paper.
2. Place the pastry onto the baking paper and score a 1 cm border around the edge of the pastry.
3. Combine the pesto and the crème fraîche and spread it onto the pastry (not onto the border).
4. Arrange the tomato slices on top and season to taste.
5. Brush the border of the pastry with the egg yolk and place in the oven.
6. Bake the tart for 15–20 minutes until the pastry is crisp and cooked through and the tomatoes are soft. Remove from the oven and slice.
7. Serve warm with a side salad.

My mom wasn't a massive fan of spending hours in the kitchen, but there were certain things she made, and she made them very well. One was chicken liver pâté.

My chicken liver pâté is not exactly the same as my mom's (for the simple reason that I can't find her recipe), but I have to say, it's pretty close. I don't think she ever added apple to hers and I know this might seem like a very strange addition, but trust me, it works. The apple's sweetness just balances out the richness of the butter and the cream and adds lots of flavour without making the pâté too sweet. Also, frying it beforehand with the onions and garlic allows all the flavours to mingle. My mom always added brandy to her chicken liver pâté but I've found that sherry and cognac also work well.

To keep the pâté fresh, it's important to pour some clarified butter (or ghee) on top of the pâté before refrigerating. Some specialist stores stock clarified butter/ ghee but if you can't find it, you can make your own. Place the (unsalted) butter in a saucepan and melt. Allow to sit for a few minutes until the milk solids separate from the fat. Skim the foam off of the top and slowly pour the fat off the milk solids, which would have settled at the bottom of the saucepan. You can also pass the melted butter through a fine sieve that has been lined with damp cheesecloth. Clarified butter will last for 3-6 months in the refrigerator.

CHICKEN LIVER PÂTÉ

Makes 2-3 cups chicken liver pâté

- 2 tablespoons butter
- 750 g chicken livers (3 small tubs)
- 2 onions, chopped
- 2 apples, peeled and chopped
- 1 garlic clove, sliced
- 1 tablespoon fresh sage, finely chopped
- 100 ml cream
- 150 g butter, room temperature, cubed
- 150 g clarified butter/ ghee

1. Melt the 2 tablespoons of butter in a large frying pan and fry the chicken livers until golden brown.
2. Remove from the pan and set aside.
3. In the same pan, fry the onions, apples, garlic and sage for 5 minutes before adding ½ cup water.
4. Allow the water to evaporate. When the water has evaporated, allow the mixture to fry for another 5 minutes until golden brown and soft.
5. Add the chicken livers back into the pan and fry for another 5 minutes with the apple and onion mixture.
6. Place the chicken livers and onion mixture in a food processor and process until fine.
7. Add the cubed butter and cream and process for another 2 minutes until very smooth.
8. If you want the mixture to be even smoother, pass it through a sieve.
9. Place into a bowl and pour the clarified butter/ ghee over the top.
10. Place in the fridge and allow to set for at least 6 hours.

There are only three main components to these beautiful little tarts and because of this I recommend you use the best-quality ingredients you can afford. Good, all-butter puff pastry and a good-quality chevin (little logs of goat's cheese, available at any supermarket) will make these tarts unforgettable.

I love serving them for lunch with a simple salad made with rocket, watercress, avocado slices and a lemony dressing. Not forgetting an ice-cold glass of Chenin blanc, of course!

CARAMELISED ONION AND GOAT'S CHEESE TARTS

Makes 4 tarts

- 2 red onions, finely sliced
- 1 tablespoon balsamic vinegar
- 2 tablespoons sugar
- 1 roll ready-made puff pastry
- 100 g log of chevin, cut into 4 thick circles
- fresh thyme
- 1 egg yolk, beaten

1. Pre-heat the oven to 180 °C.
2. In a frying pan, sauté the onions until soft and translucent. Add the balsamic vinegar and sugar and allow to caramelise for 5 minutes. Remove from the heat and set aside.
3. Roll the pastry out slightly and using a round cutter or drinking glass (about 10 cm in diameter), cut 8 circles out of the pastry. Place 4 of the circles on a baking sheet lined with baking paper.
4. Now use a glass or cutter that is approximately 8 cm in diameter to cut a hole in the remaining 4 circles of pastry (what you want is a ring of pastry, of sorts).
5. Brush the edges of the pastry on the baking sheet with egg yolk and place the 'ring' of pastry on top of that (creating a border).
6. Place a tablespoon of caramelised onion into the hollow of each pastry topped with a thick slice of chevin.
7. Brush the pastry with more egg yolk and place a sprig of thyme on each little tart.
8. Place in the oven and bake for 10 minutes until the pastry is golden brown and the chevin has softened slightly.
9. Allow to cool for 5 minutes and serve warm with salad.

These are perfect for a light lunch with buttered rye bread or as an hors d'oeuvre at a party. Smoked salmon can be very expensive so you may want to use smoked trout, which tastes almost exactly the same but is quite a bit cheaper.

SMOKED SALMON CREAM CHEESE ROLLS

Makes 6–8 rolls

200 g smoked salmon

100 g cream cheese, room temperature

50–100 g rocket

1 lemon, sliced into wedges

cracked black pepper, to serve

1. Lay the smoked salmon out in front of you. If it is not already cut then slice it into long strips about 4–5 cm wide.
2. Place 2 teaspoons of cream cheese at the one end of a strip of smoked salmon.
3. Add a few sprigs of rocket, a squeeze of lemon juice and some black pepper.
4. Roll the salmon up and around the cream cheese and rocket.
5. Place on a platter and serve immediately.

Smooth, velvety and subtly flavoured, this soup is the perfect thing to start off a dinner party. It's equally perfect to eat with stacks of buttered toast all on your lonesome in front of the TV (well it is for me anyway)!

Serving it with crispy bacon makes it extraordinarily good.

CAULIFLOWER SOUP WITH BACON

Serves 2–4, depending on serving size

1 onion, chopped
1 garlic clove, sliced
300 g cauliflower florets
2 large potatoes, peeled and chopped
1 bay leaf
3 cups chicken or vegetable stock
150 ml cream
salt and pepper to taste
crispy bacon, to serve

1. Fry the onion and garlic in a large saucepan until soft and translucent.
2. Add the cauliflower, potato and bay leaf and allow to sauté for 5 minutes.
3. Pour in the stock and allow to simmer, covered, for 20–25 minutes until the cauliflower and potato are soft.
4. Transfer the soup to a blender and blend until smooth and velvety.
5. Pour the blended soup back into the saucepan and add the cream.
6. Season to taste and serve with crispy bacon.

*Not much needs to be said about this soup. If you like mussels, you will **love** this soup. It's simple, delicious and perfection when served with lots of buttered bread.*

MUSSEL SOUP

Serves 4

- 3 tablespoons olive oil
- 1 onion, finely chopped
- 2 garlic cloves, crushed
- 2 teaspoons smoked paprika
- ½ cup white wine
- 2 cups fish or vegetable stock
- 1 cup cream
- 500–700 g mussels, in the half shell
- juice of ½ lemon
- handful fresh parsley, chopped
- salt and pepper to taste
- buttered bread, to serve

1. In a large saucepan, sauté the onion and garlic in the olive oil until soft and translucent. Add the smoked paprika and fry for 30 seconds.
2. Pour in the wine and allow to reduce for 5 minutes before adding the fish or vegetable stock and cream.
3. Allow to simmer for 10 minutes before adding the mussels and then simmer for another 10 minutes until the mussels are cooked.
4. Add the lemon juice and parsley, and season to taste.
5. Serve hot with buttered bread.

Quiche is the ultimate easy and satisfying meal. The combinations for fillings are endless and if you use pre-made pastry, it really is a breeze.

I love the combination of salty biltong and blue cheese with the slight sweetness of the caramelised onions. To make it even easier, you can use onion marmalade instead of caramelising the onions yourself, but be sure only to use a tablespoon or two, as shop-bought marmalade tends to be very sweet.

I prefer using pre-made shortcrust pastry for quiches, but you could of course make your own shortcrust pastry. When using pre-made pastry, ensure it's thoroughly defrosted before rolling it out.

BILTONG AND BLUE CHEESE QUICHE

Makes 1 standard-size quiche

1 onion, sliced
1 teaspoon sugar
1 roll pre-made shortcrust pastry, thawed
200 g sliced biltong
100 g blue cheese, crumbled
5 eggs
1 cup cream
200 ml milk
½ teaspoon salt
black pepper to taste
½ cup fresh parsley, finely chopped

1. Pre-heat the oven to 180 °C.
2. Start by frying the onions in a frying pan until soft and translucent. Add the sugar and allow to caramelise.
3. On a floured counter, roll the pastry out to fit into your quiche dish and lay it in the dish, pressing it up the sides.
4. Spread the caramelised onion on top of the pastry.
5. Add the biltong, making sure it's well spread out. Follow with the crumbled blue cheese.
6. Combine the eggs, cream, milk, salt and pepper and beat well.
7. Gently pour the mixture over the biltong, blue cheese and onion.
8. Scatter over the chopped parsley and place in the pre-heated oven for 15–20 minutes until the pastry is just set but still slightly soft in the middle.
9. Remove from the oven and allow to cool slightly before lifting the quiche out of the dish.
10. Serve at room temperature with a green salad.

This is the perfect breakfast dish to make when you have a crowd of people to feed before 11 am (which is madness in my opinion, but sometimes needs to be done). What I love most about it is that you can fry the bacon and leeks the night before and put them in the ramekins, then 10 minutes before serving just crack the eggs on top of each one, pour in some cream, season to taste and pop them into the oven. The more guests you have to feed, the more ramekins you add, so this recipe doubles, triples and quadruples very easily.

I like serving these with 'soldiers' made from buttered sourdough bread, but any good-quality bread will do. And of course, you can swop the bacon and leeks for any ingredients you have in the fridge or pantry.

EGGS EN COCOTTE WITH LEEKS AND BACON

Serves 4

4 large leeks, washed and finely sliced
250 g streaky bacon, sliced
2 garlic cloves, finely chopped
4 extra-large, free-range eggs
100 ml cream
salt and pepper to taste
sourdough 'soldiers', to serve

1. Pre-heat the oven to 160 °C and grease four ramekins.
2. Fry the bacon and leeks in a large frying pan until the bacon starts to crisp and the leeks are soft. Add the garlic and fry for another minute.
3. Place a few spoonfuls of the bacon and leek mixture into the bottom of each greased ramekin.
4. Break an egg into each ramekin and pour in 25 ml cream. Season to taste.
5. Place the ramekins in the oven and allow to bake for 7–10 minutes depending on how you would like your eggs cooked.
6. Serve immediately with sourdough 'soldiers'.

I've never been to Mexico, but I absolutely love Mexican food. Or should I say I love the idea of Mexican food. Chillies, limes, beans, tacos, enchiladas, tequila – of course, there is much more to Mexican cuisine than these ingredients, but these are some of my favourites.

Finding authentic Mexican food in South Africa is unfortunately very difficult (though there are a few restaurants that get it right). I like to think that the Mexican food I prepare at home for my family is pretty good – besides, even if it's not, they don't know the difference! The only thing that matters is that they enjoy it and that they have an open mind about the meals I prepare for them.

One such dish is huevos rancheros. My family was quite hesitant the first time I made this. It took some convincing but I finally got them all to taste it and within minutes their plates were empty and they were asking for more. Eggs baked in a rich and flavourful tomato sauce might sound strange, but believe me, it's to die for. The chilli is optional (the version I serve to my kids is spice-free) but instead of leaving it out, I suggest you add just a small amount. It really does transform the dish into something magnificent.

You can serve the eggs with tortillas but I prefer it with thick toast made from sourdough bread.

HUEVOS RANCHEROS

Serves 4

- 1 red onion, finely chopped
- 3 garlic cloves, finely chopped
- 2 tins chopped tomatoes
- 1 tablespoon tomato paste
- 1 teaspoon sugar
- 2 teaspoons dried oregano
- 1–2 red chillies, deseeded and finely chopped
- salt to taste
- 4–8 eggs (1–2 per person)
- fresh coriander, to serve
- bread or tortilla wraps, to serve

1. In a large frying pan, fry the onion and garlic until soft and translucent.
2. Add the chopped tomatoes, tomato paste, sugar, oregano and chillies, and cook for 5 minutes until slightly reduced and thick. Season to taste.
3. Carefully break the eggs into the tomato sauce and turn the heat down. Cover the pan with a lid and allow the eggs to cook to your liking.
4. Serve the huevos rancheros with fresh coriander and toasted bread or tortilla wraps.

This salad has become one of my favourite recipes and is now a stand-by for whenever I need a substantial and delicious side dish or a quick and easy light meal. I've always been a fan of perfectly steamed, seasonal vegetables and paired with salty feta, it's a winner.

Even though I mostly serve this straight away, it's also good made an hour or so ahead so the steamed vegetables absorb the dressing.

The addition of chilli is optional but it really adds to the flavour. If you're not a fan of very spicy foods, simply remove the seeds and chop the chillies very finely – this way you'll just get a hint of tongue-tingling spice.

WARM SPRING VEGETABLE SALAD

Serves 4–6
It is not necessary to follow the quantities to the letter. If your shop sells beans in 250 g packets, use that. It's most definitely not necessary to make up the other 50 g.

150 g sugar snap peas
300 g green beans, topped and tailed
350 g courgettes, thinly sliced
2 cups baby peas
200 g asparagus tips
1 cup feta cheese, crumbled

Dressing
5 tablespoons olive oil
5 tablespoons lemon juice
1 teaspoon crushed garlic
1 teaspoon Dijon mustard
2 chillies, finely chopped
½ teaspoon sugar
salt and pepper to taste

1. Steam all the vegetables until slightly tender. You want them to still be bright green and pleasant to eat, not too soft and limp but also not raw and hard.
2. Combine the steamed vegetables with the feta cheese.
3. Mix together all the dressing ingredients and pour over the salad. Toss to combine and serve warm or at room temperature.

This salad is made all the more charming when you see how few ingredients are required (not counting the ingredients needed for the aioli), though you can add some extra salad goodies if your heart desires. There is nothing better than eating the prawns piping hot from the pan – a quick dunk into the garlicky, silky-smooth aioli makes it a heavenly mouthful.

Served with crusty bread and lots of white wine, this salad makes for a perfect Saturday lunch.

CAJUN PRAWN SALAD WITH AIOLI

Serves 4

Aioli

2 free-range egg yolks

1 garlic clove, peeled and roughly chopped

1 teaspoon Dijon mustard

1 teaspoon sugar

1–1½ cups (250 ml–300 ml) canola oil

1 tablespoon lemon juice

salt and pepper to taste

Cajun prawn salad

12–16 king prawns (3–4 per person), deveined and shells removed (I prefer to leave the tails on as they look so pretty)

2–3 tablespoons Cajun spice of your choice

1 teaspoon salt

100 g fresh rocket

2 ripe avocados

fresh lemon wedges, to serve

1. Start by making the aioli. I would suggest you use a hand-held blender as this produces a thicker aioli, but if you have a food processor the process is the same.
2. Using a tall container, add the egg yolks, garlic, Dijon and sugar. Blend all the ingredients together until the mixture goes slightly frothy and light.
3. With the blender running, slowly drizzle in the oil, moving the blender up and down to incorporate air (if you're using a food processor, allow it to blend at maximum speed while drizzling the oil in).
4. You might not need all of the oil. The more oil you add, the thicker the aioli will be.
5. When the aioli is thick, add the lemon juice and season to taste. If you want it a bit sweeter, add a teaspoon or two of honey and blend again. Set aside until you are ready to use it.
6. Coat the prawns in the Cajun spice and salt.
7. Heat a frying pan and fry the prawns in olive oil or butter until cooked, approximately 1–2 minutes per side.
8. Slice the avocado and arrange with the rocket on 4 plates. Top with the cooked prawns and drizzle over some of the aioli. Serve with a wedge of lemon.

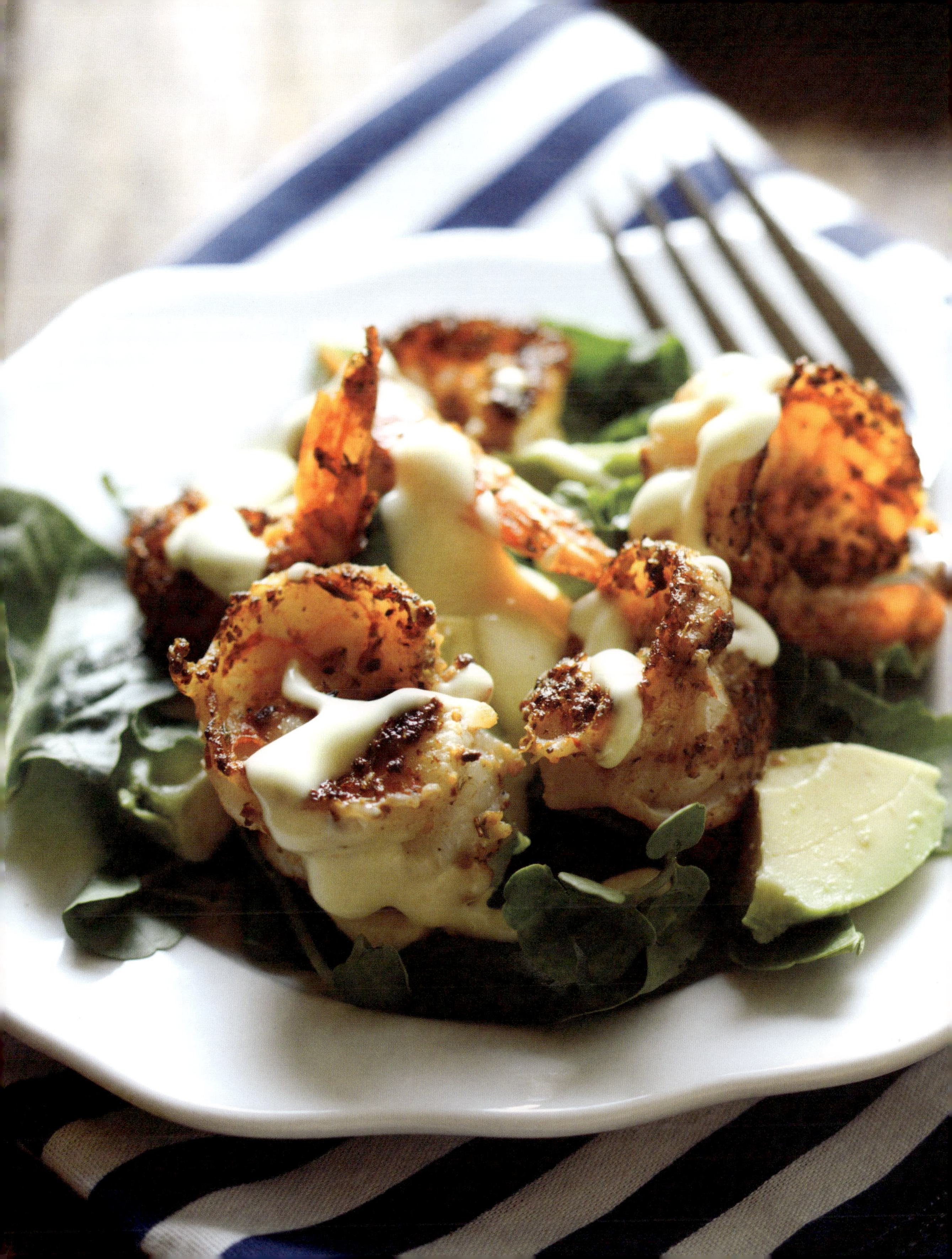

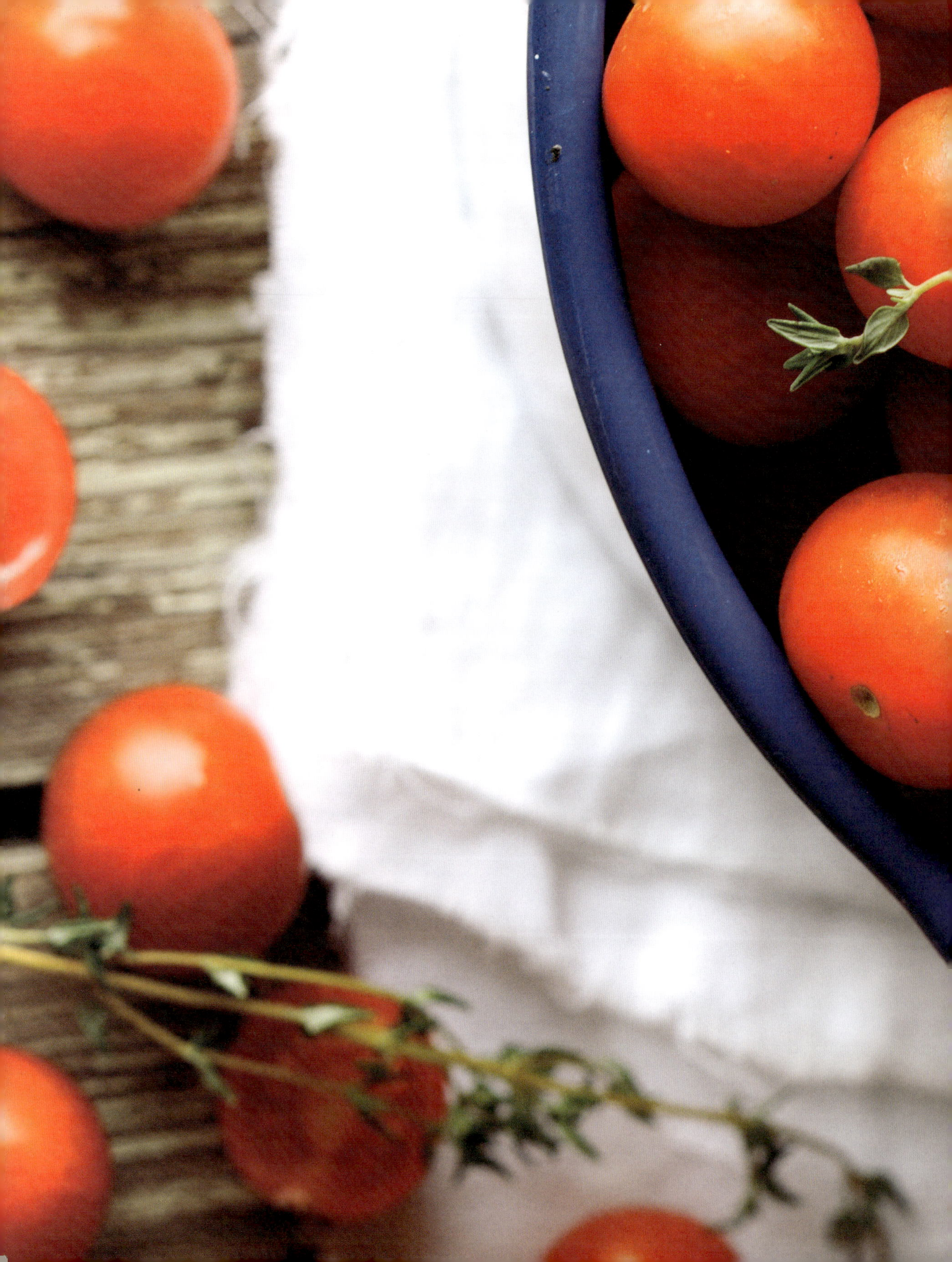

PASTA

When I first started cooking vegetarian food, I never thought it would last very long as I didn't know how versatile vegetables could be. But it turned out that the more I did it, the more ideas came to me. It's very easy to create a filling and delicious meal without meat when you have pasta as a base to work from. And the beauty of it is that you can go really intricate or really simple.

During the warmer months, my craving for pasta doesn't go away but my need for something lighter and healthier calls for fresh, seasonal vegetables paired with fresh herbs and luscious cheese to add just that touch of indulgence.

The key to making this dish a success is to use the best ingredients you can find or afford. Sweet cherry tomatoes roasted with a splash of balsamic vinegar, creamy ricotta cheese and a garlicky basil pesto, combined with al dente pasta, makes it one of my favourite meals ever.

PASTA WITH ROASTED CHERRY TOMATOES, RICOTTA AND PESTO

Serves 4

- 400 g cherry tomatoes
- 2 tablespoons balsamic vinegar
- 1 tablespoon olive oil
- 1 teaspoon sugar
- ½ teaspoon salt
- ½ teaspoon black pepper
- 500 g pasta of your choice (I use spaghetti)
- 300 g ricotta cheese, crumbled
- 4 tablespoons basil pesto thinned out with 2 tablespoons olive oil

1. Pre-heat the oven to 220 °C.
2. Toss the cherry tomatoes with the balsamic, oil and seasonings and transfer to a roasting tray.
3. Roast for 15–20 minutes until the tomatoes are blistered and the skin starts coming loose. Keep watching the tomatoes because the oven will be very hot and you don't want them to burn.
4. Meanwhile, cook the pasta in plenty of salted water until al dente. Drain and combine with the tomatoes (and all their pan juices), ricotta and basil pesto.
5. Serve with extra ricotta and basil pesto.

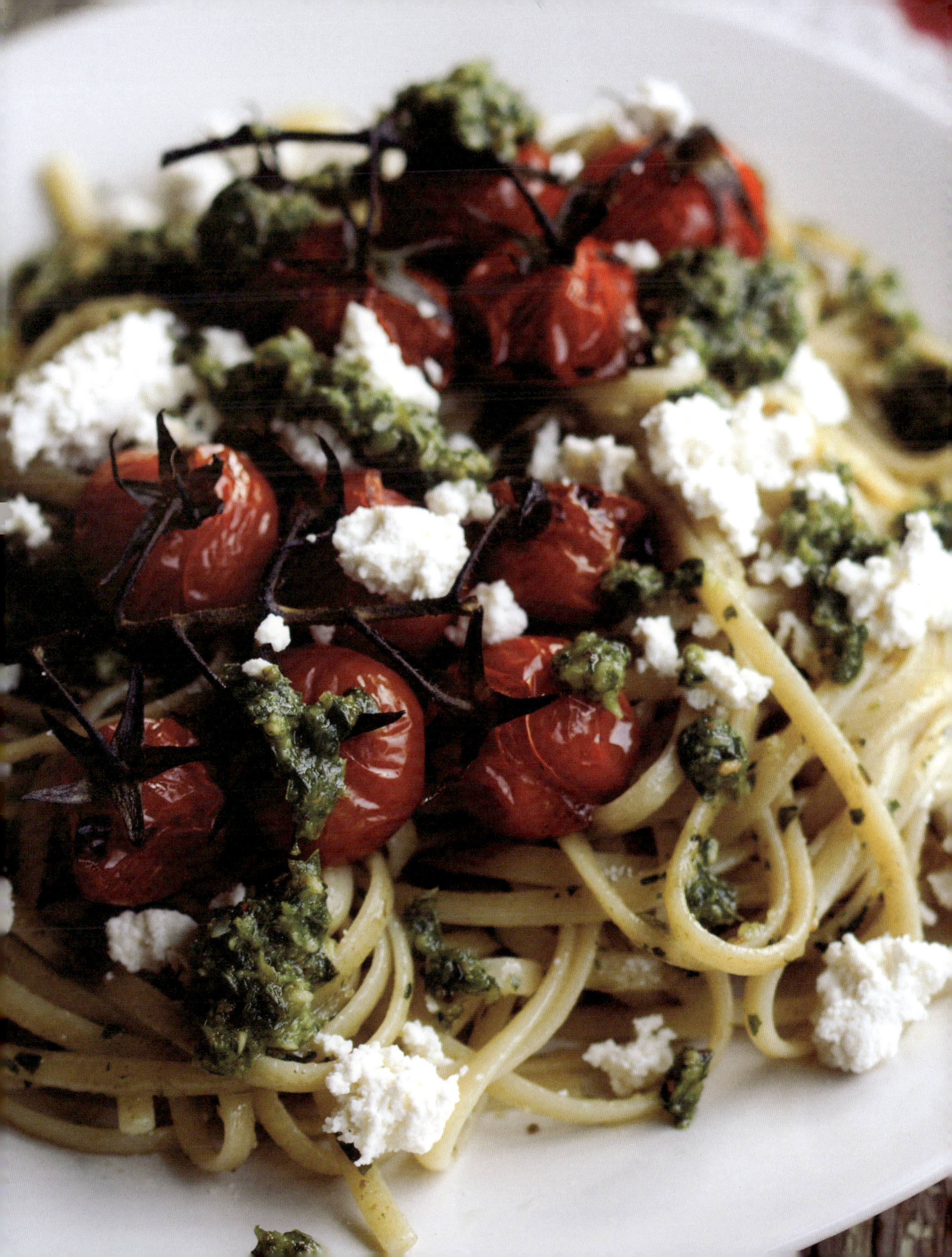

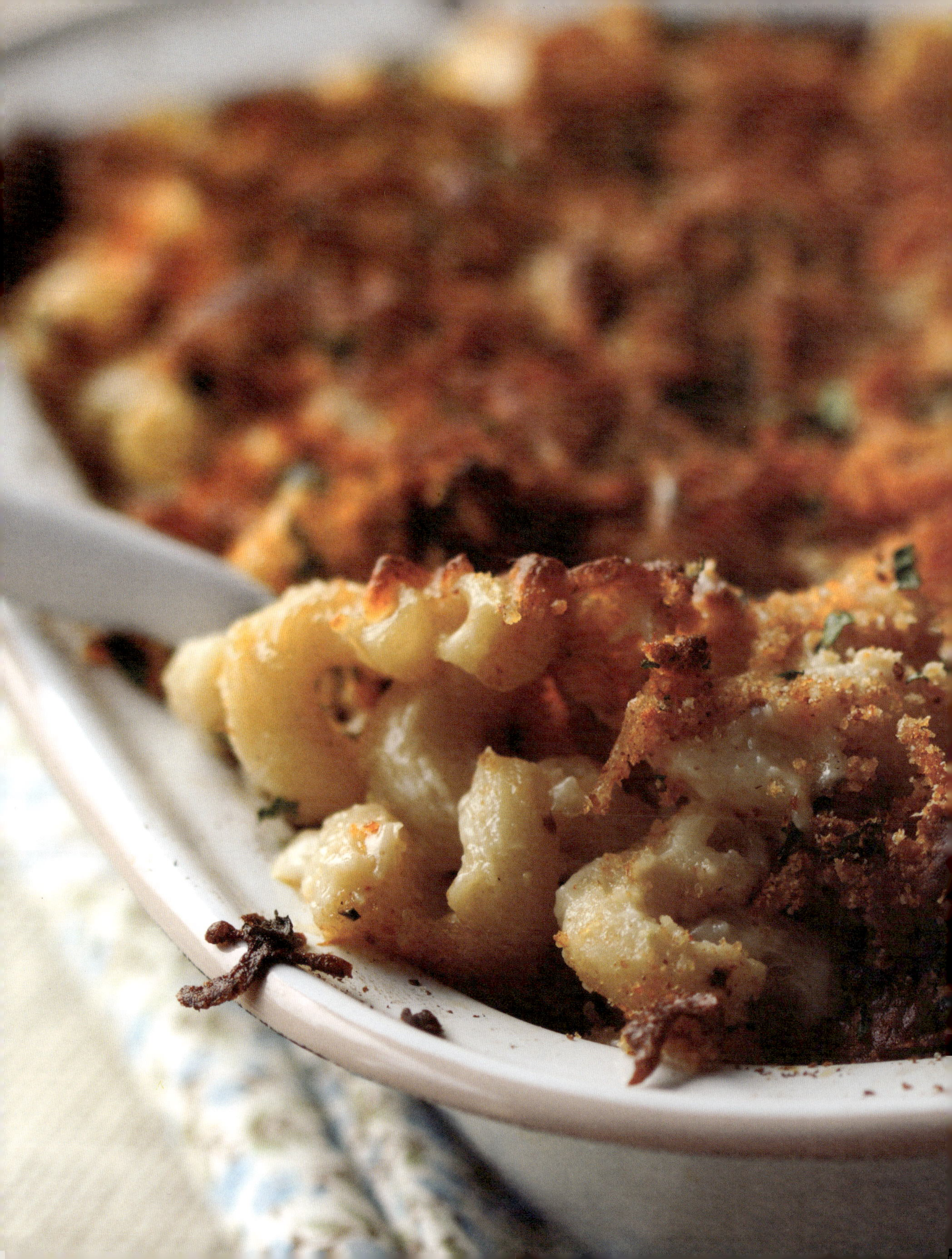

Macaroni and cheese is definitely the working mother's stand-by. It's easy, cheap and I've never come across a child who doesn't eat it. The problem with the average mac 'n cheese is that it can be very bland and you either end up covering it in tomato sauce to add flavour or need to add tons of cheese, which not only increases the price but also the fat content.

My solution is to add small amounts of three or four different cheeses. I try to use the best strong cheese I can find. Extra-mature Cheddar, gorgonzola, goat's cheese and Gruyère are all good, as well as pecorino and Parmesan. To add texture you can add chunks of feta or haloumi. I finish all the cheesiness off with a crust made from grated mozzarella and fresh breadcrumbs.

Some people like adding bacon, mince and vegetables to mac 'n cheese, and feel free to do so. Sometimes I add some sliced tomatoes or caramelised onion and peppers, but most often I like it left plain and simple. Serve with a mixed salad and some garlic bread and it's transformed from an easy weekday dish into a filling and satisfying meal.

I use the leftovers for lunch the next day or I freeze them for another time.

FOUR-CHEESE MAC 'N CHEESE

Serves 8

- 150 g butter
- 1½–2 cups flour
- 1 litre milk mixed with 2 cups chicken stock
- 2–3 cups grated cheese of your choice
- ½ teaspoon nutmeg
- 1 teaspoon paprika
- 2 teaspoons Dijon mustard
- salt and pepper to taste
- 1 kg macaroni, cooked according to the packet instructions
- 1–1½ cups grated mozzarella cheese

1. Pre-heat the oven to 180 °C and grease a baking dish about 30 cm in diameter.
2. In a large saucepan, melt the butter. Add the flour and whisk until a roux (thick paste-like mixture) is formed. Allow to cook for 1 minute.
3. Slowly start adding the milk mixture and whisk continuously. Allow to simmer gently until the sauce is thick and the flour has cooked through.
4. Take off the heat and add the mustard, cheeses and spices. Allow the cheese to melt and check the seasoning. Don't add salt before you've tasted as the cheese might be salty enough.
5. Mix the sauce with the cooked macaroni and transfer to the prepared baking dish. Scatter over the grated mozzarella and bake for 15–20 minutes at 180 °C until the cheese is golden.
6. Allow to stand for 5 minutes before serving.

The idea for this pasta came to me one night while I was standing in front of the fridge with nothing but vegetables (needing to be used immediately before they went off) staring back at me. No fish, chicken or meat in sight – just the vegetables. For me this is not an issue, but the men in my family tend to resist a bit when presented with a meat-free meal.

I knew the easiest way to use up all the vegetables would be with a pasta dish of sorts and decided on keeping things fresh and simple by just steaming them, followed by a quick pan-fry before coating them in a creamy, lemony sauce. To add some protein, I served the pasta with softly poached eggs. If, like me, you hate the thought of poaching an egg, one of those great egg-poacher contraptions makes life a lot easier, or simply boil them until the white is set and the yolk is still beautifully oozy. Serve them on top of the pasta.

SUMMER VEGETABLE PASTA WITH POACHED EGGS

Serves 4

- 500 g summer vegetables, trimmed or sliced according to your preference (I use a variety of vegetables such as asparagus, green beans, summer squash like patty-pans and courgettes, sugar snap peas and broccoli)
- 2 garlic cloves, finely chopped
- 150 ml cream
- juice of ½ lemon
- salt and pepper to taste
- 500 g tagliatelle or pappardelle, cooked according to the packet instructions
- grated pecorino, to serve
- 4 eggs, poached, to serve

1. Place the vegetables in a steamer and steam for 10 minutes until they are just tender but still bright green.
2. Fry the garlic in 1 tablespoon butter and add the vegetables. Fry for a minute before adding the cream and lemon juice.
3. Allow to simmer for 5 minutes. Season to taste and toss with the cooked pasta.
4. Serve warm topped with the poached eggs and grated pecorino.

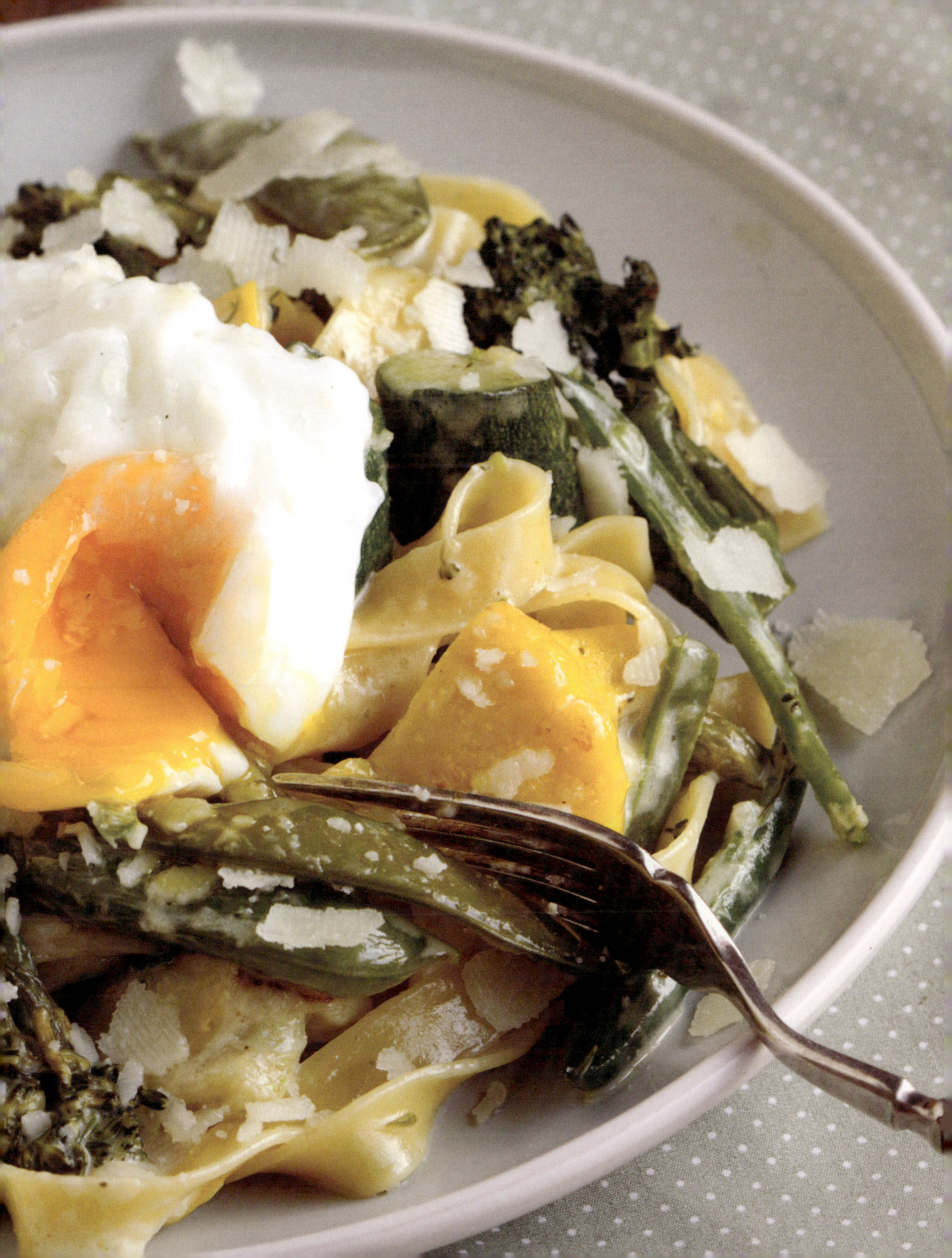

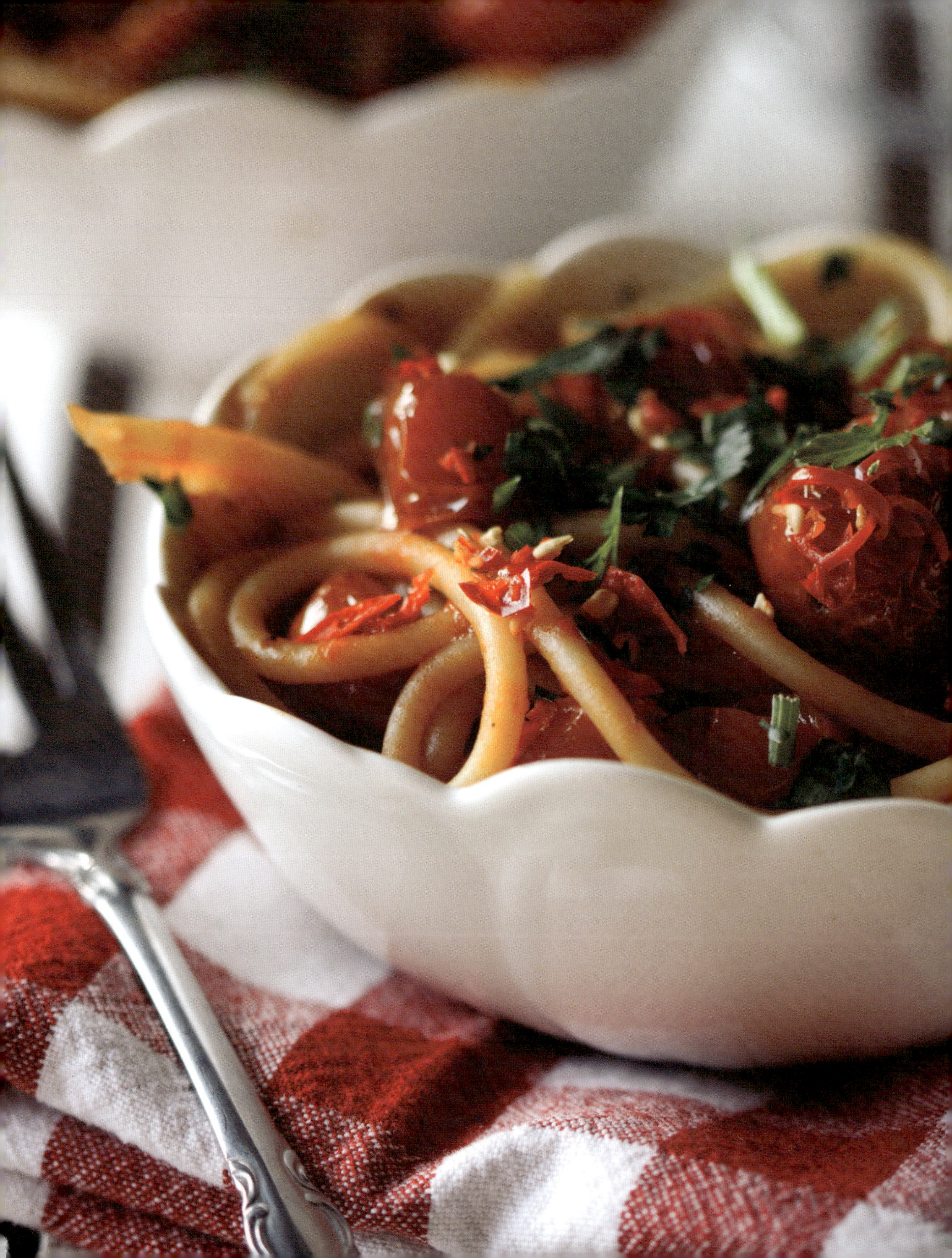

We all know the feeling. You've had a miserable day at work and all you want to do is sit back, have someone massage your feet and bring you food and wine. But the reality is you have kids to bath and feed, a dog that wants attention and a partner who wants to offload about their miserable day at work.

On days like that, the last thing you need is to stand in the kitchen for more than, oh, 10 minutes? Keep this recipe for those nights; you can thank me later.

What I love about spaghetti arrabiata is that without the chilli, it's technically a spaghetti Napolitano, which is perfect for kids. So what I always do is add my freshly chopped chillies (or minced chillies from a jar) after the sauce has cooked and I've dished for the kids. I allow it to simmer for another 2 minutes and then the adult version is ready.

If you have the energy, this is delicious served with a green salad, some crusty bread and a good grating of Parmesan. But if you don't, simply serve it in bowls in front of the TV and allow the comfort-inducing properties of pasta to soothe you.

SPAGHETTI ARRABIATA

Serves 4

- 500 g spaghetti
- 1 red onion, finely chopped
- 2 garlic cloves, thinly sliced
- 2 tins chopped tomatoes (or cherry tomatoes)
- 1 small tin (about 50 g) tomato paste
- 1 teaspoon sugar (optional)
- 2 teaspoons dried oregano
- 2 chillies, finely chopped (or 2 teaspoons minced chillies from a jar)
- salt and pepper to taste
- fresh basil, to serve
- grated Parmesan, to serve

1. Fill a large pot with water, add 1 tablespoon salt and place on a high heat.
2. In a medium saucepan, fry the onion and garlic until soft and translucent and add the tinned tomatoes and tomato paste.
3. Add the sugar and dried oregano and simmer for 10 minutes.
4. Meanwhile, cook your pasta in the salted water according to the packet instructions until al dente.
5. Add the chillies to the tomato sauce and season to taste. Allow to simmer for another 2 minutes.
6. Combine the sauce with the cooked pasta and serve with fresh basil and grated Parmesan.

This is a great vegetarian, weeknight pasta bake (and I assure you the meat eaters in your house won't even miss the meat). I like to add different cheeses (I normally just use whatever I have in the fridge) and I've found that ricotta, goat's cheese and chunks of feta all work really well. Serve this with warm garlic bread and your family will sing your praises, guaranteed.

BAKED PENNE WITH AUBERGINE, COURGETTE AND SUN-DRIED TOMATO

Serves 4–6

- 1 onion, finely chopped
- 2 garlic cloves, thinly sliced
- 350 g courgettes, thickly sliced
- 2 aubergines, cubed
- 5 sun-dried tomatoes, chopped
- 1 tablespoon thyme leaves
- 2 x 400 g tins chopped tomatoes
- 1 cup cheese of your choice, crumbled or grated
- 500 g penne, cooked
- 1 cup breadcrumbs
- 1 teaspoon salt
- 1 cup grated mozzarella cheese
- handful fresh parsley, finely chopped

1. Pre-heat the oven to 180 °C.
2. In a large saucepan, fry the onion until translucent in a couple of tablespoons of olive oil.
3. Add the garlic and the courgettes, aubergines and sun-dried tomatoes. Sauté for 10 minutes until they start to soften.
4. Add the thyme leaves and chopped tomatoes. Allow to simmer for 10 minutes until the vegetables are cooked.
5. Combine the sauce with the pasta and the grated or crumbled cheese and transfer to an ovenproof baking dish.
6. Combine the breadcrumbs, salt, mozzarella and chopped parsley and scatter over the pasta.
7. Place the pasta in the oven and bake for 15 minutes until the topping is crisp and golden.

This is one of the most delicious pastas I've ever had the pleasure of eating, if I say so myself. There's something about pairing prawns with courgettes that just works so well. If you are not keen on prawns, you can use chicken breasts instead and it will be just as delicious.

FETTUCCINI WITH PRAWNS AND COURGETTES

Serves 4

1 leek, washed and finely chopped
2 garlic cloves, minced
2 large courgettes, washed and sliced
500 g fettuccini
500 g prawn meat
150 ml cream
juice of ½ lemon
salt and pepper to taste

1. Fill a large pot with water and place on a high heat, for the pasta.
2. While the water is coming to the boil, fry the leek and garlic in a little olive oil in a saucepan until soft and fragrant.
3. Add the courgettes and allow to sauté for 5–10 minutes until they are just tender.
4. At this point the water for the pasta should be boiling. Add a few tablespoons of salt to the water (the Italians say the water should be as salty as the Mediterranean!) and carefully drop in the pasta. Allow to cook until al dente.
5. Add the prawn meat to the saucepan and fry for 2 minutes before adding the cream and lemon juice. Allow to simmer for 5 minutes.
6. Once the pasta is cooked, reserve 1 cup of the pasta water and drain the pasta.
7. If the sauce needs to be thinned out a bit, add the reserved pasta water and stir. Season the sauce with salt and pepper.
8. Serve the prawn and courgette sauce with the cooked fettuccini.

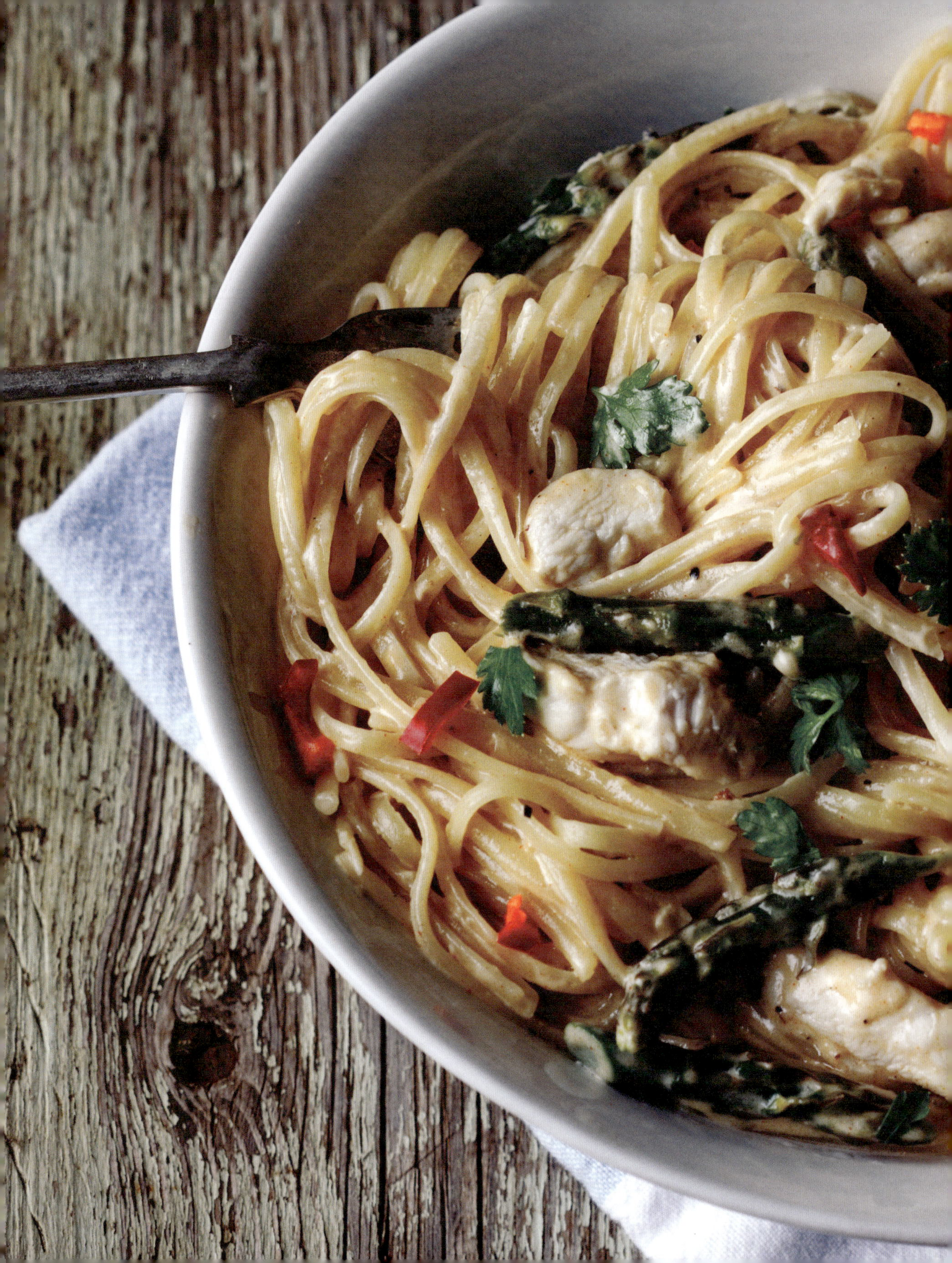

Yet another one of my stand-by recipes when asparagus is in season. Green beans, broccoli and sugar snap peas all work well as substitutes.

I love effortless pasta dishes like this where the sauce is made as the water for the pasta reaches boiling point. A squeeze of lemon, a pinch of salt, the delectable way the cream soothes everything as it is poured in – it's the small things in life that make me happiest.

CHICKEN AND ASPARAGUS PASTA

Serves 4

- 2 large chicken breast fillets, sliced
- 2 garlic cloves, finely chopped
- 100 ml chicken stock
- 100 ml cream
- ½ teaspoon paprika
- 500 g linguini or long pasta of your choice
- juice of ½ lemon
- 200 g asparagus, washed and woody ends snapped off*
- salt and pepper to taste
- extra lemon juice and finely chopped chillies, to serve (optional)

1. Bring a large pot of salted water to the boil for the pasta.
2. In a saucepan, sauté the chicken in olive oil until golden and cooked through. Add the garlic, chicken stock, cream and paprika and allow to simmer gently.
3. By this time, the water for the pasta should be boiling. Add the pasta to the water and allow to cook according to the packet instructions.
4. Add the lemon juice and the asparagus to the sauce and allow to cook for 5 minutes. Season to taste and remove from the heat.
5. When the pasta is cooked, drain thoroughly and toss with the sauce.
6. Serve with extra lemon juice and finely chopped chillies.

* Bend the asparagus ends until they snap and break off. The snapped-off piece will be tough and stringy.

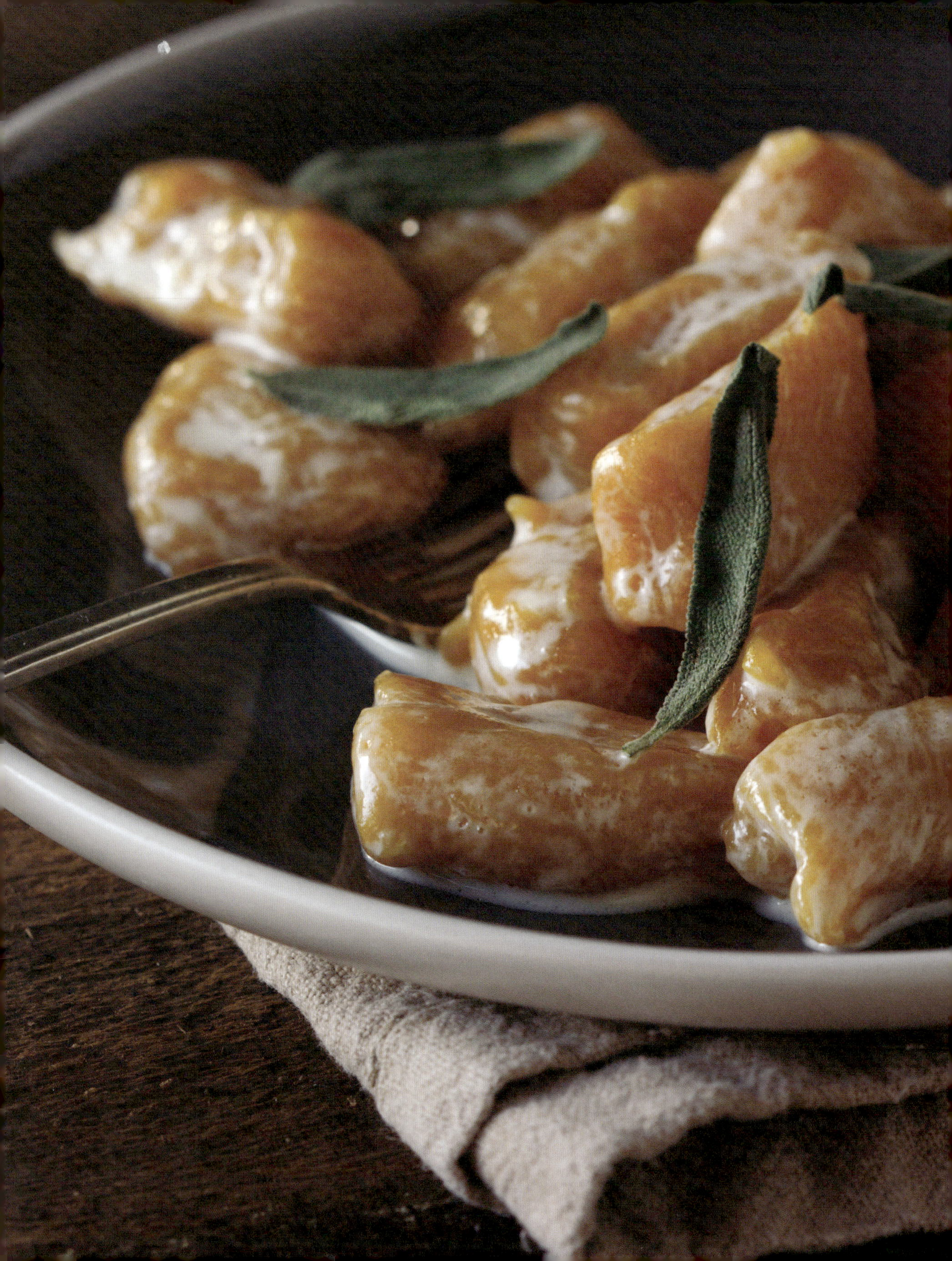

Making your own gnocchi might seem daunting but it really isn't as scary as you think. With butternut gnocchi, the key is to make sure the butternut is completely dry. The way I do this is to roast the butternut until cooked, purée it and then place it in a muslin-lined colander to drain for 20 minutes, to make sure there is no excess moisture. Excess moisture results in your having to add more and more flour to the mixture to make it less sticky and this in turn results in very tough gnocchi.

Butternut gnocchi is also absolutely delicious served with burnt butter and crispy sage.

BUTTERNUT GNOCCHI WITH SAGE CREAM

Serves 4

- 1 large butternut, peeled, deseeded and cubed
- 1–2 cups flour
- 1 teaspoon salt
- ½ teaspoon nutmeg

Sage cream

- 1 cup cream
- 1 garlic clove, whole
- 2 tablespoons fresh sage, thinly sliced
- salt and pepper to taste

1. Pre-heat the oven to 200 °C.
2. Place the butternut onto a roasting tray, drizzle with olive oil and roast for 25–30 minutes until it is fully cooked.
3. Remove the butternut from the oven and allow to cool slightly before puréeing.
4. Place the puréed butternut in a muslin-lined colander and allow to drain for 20 minutes until the butternut is dry.
5. Place the drained butternut in a mixing bowl and add the flour. Add a cup at a time until you have stiff but still soft, workable dough. Add the salt and nutmeg.
6. On a floured surface, roll a quarter of the dough into a long sausage shape and cut into 2 cm pieces. Place on a floured tray and continue with the rest of the dough.
7. To cook the gnocchi, bring a large pot of salted water to the boil. Gently drop the gnocchi into the boiling water and once they float to the surface, remove them immediately.
8. To make the sage cream, simply bring the cream, garlic clove and fresh sage to the boil and allow to simmer gently for 20 minutes until the cream has reduced. Season to taste. Remove and discard the garlic clove before serving.
9. Serve the cooked gnocchi with the sage cream.

Being a busy mom, spaghetti Bolognese is on our menu more often than I'd like to admit. It is truly one of the meals I can make with my eyes closed, but I like to inject it with loads of flavour and nutrients. Fortunately, I have been blessed with children who enjoy vegetables, so I don't have to hide them in their food, but I know many mothers whose kids who will only eat spag Bol for dinner.

There is a very quick and easy solution to this problem. Add as many grated vegetables to the sauce as you possibly can. When I make regular spaghetti Bolognese, onion, garlic, carrot and celery are always in the ingredients, but with this version I take it up a notch or two and add grated courgettes, finely diced peppers, super-finely chopped broccoli, cauliflower, mushrooms and spinach. To make things easier for myself, I pop the vegetables into my food processor and whizz it until they're really finely chopped.

If your child will pick out the grated veg (even though by the end of cooking it won't be recognisable), purée the vegetables and add them to the sauce. It's exhausting having to fight with children to eat their food (let alone their vegetables), but this way of cooking your child's favourite eliminates all of that. And if you serve it with a good grating of cheese over the top, you know they'll wolf down the entire bowl!

VEGETABLE-LOADED SPAGHETTI BOLOGNESE

Serves 4

- 500 g lean beef mince
- 1 onion, finely chopped
- 2 garlic cloves, minced
- 2 carrots, finely chopped
- 2 celery sticks, finely chopped
- 2 cups (about 300 g) assorted vegetables of your choice, finely chopped
- 1 tin chopped tomatoes
- 1 tin beef stock (using the tomato tin)
- 1 small tin (50 g) tomato paste
- 1 bay leaf
- 2 thyme sprigs
- salt and pepper to taste
- 500 g spaghetti, to serve
- grated Cheddar, to serve

1. Brown the beef mince in a medium pot in batches in a few tablespoons of olive oil to allow it to fry rather than stew. Remove and set aside.
2. In the same pot, sauté all the fresh vegetables for 10 minutes until soft and fragrant.
3. Add the mince back into the pot and add the tinned tomatoes, stock, tomato paste and herbs.
4. Stir to combine everything and simmer, covered, for 15–20 minutes.
5. Cook the spaghetti in a large pot of salted water. When you put the spaghetti into the water, remove the lid from the Bolognese sauce pot and turn the heat up. Allow the sauce to reduce for as long as it takes the pasta to cook (about 10 minutes).
6. Serve the cooked spaghetti with the Bolognese sauce and a good grating of cheese.

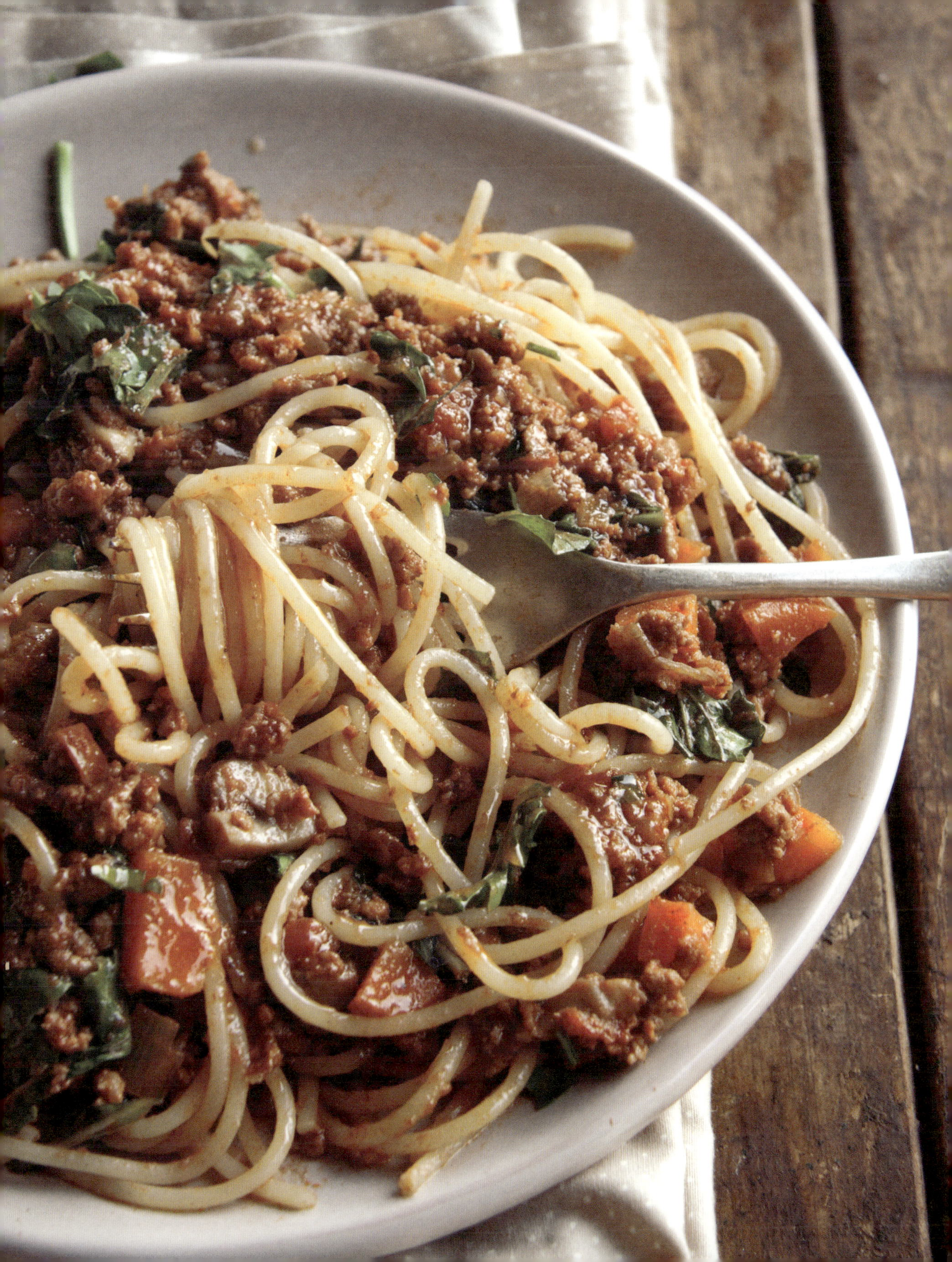

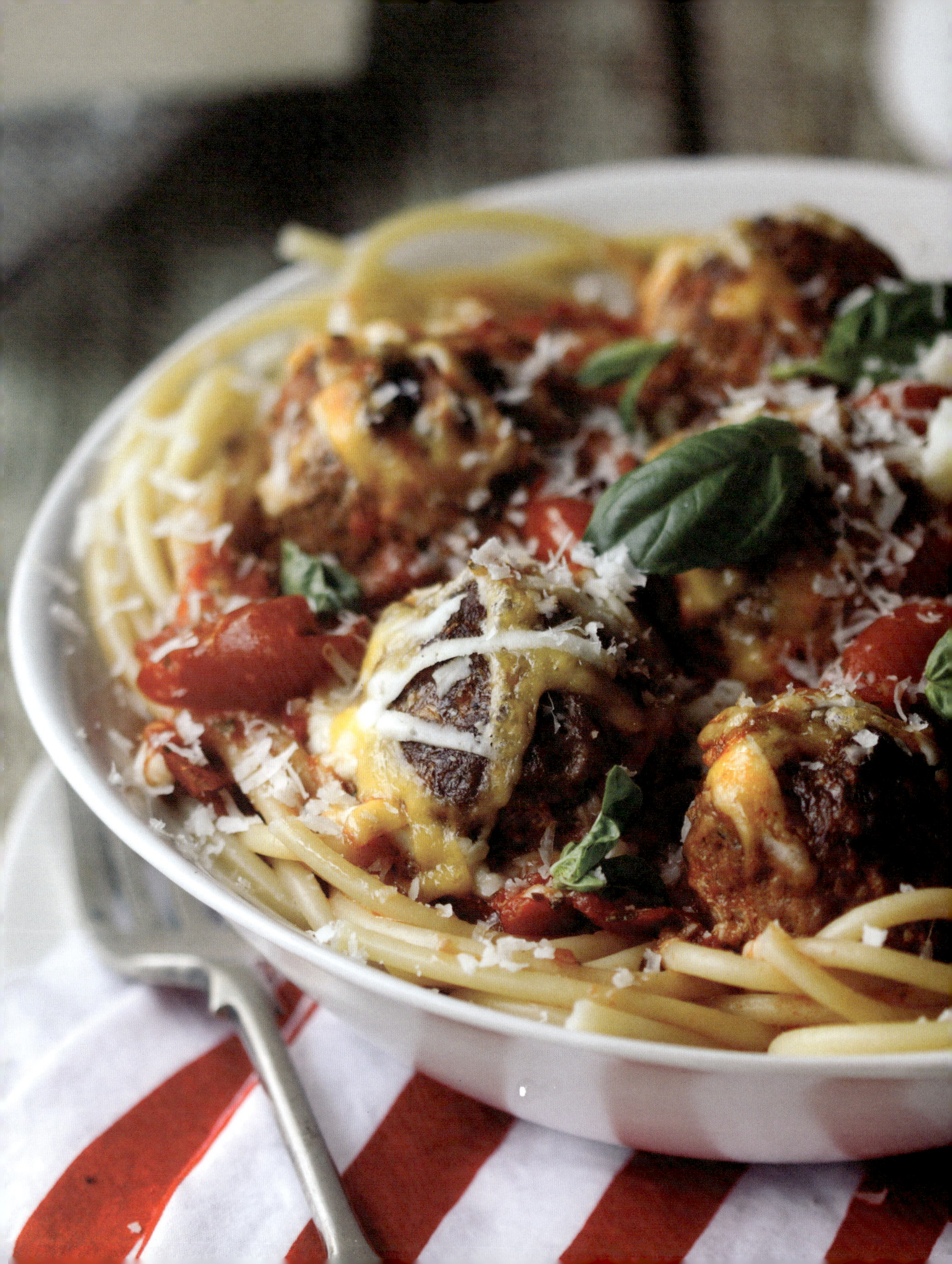

A meal of spaghetti and meatballs conjures up images of little Italian ladies feeding their massive families, with their sons just glowing in their love of 'Mama's' cooking! I so hope to be one of those ladies one day. Although I'll never be little, or Italian!

I use lamb mince for my meatballs but any mince is delicious. You could also make your own tomato sauce, but using a few tins of tomato purée and tinned chopped tomatoes just makes it so much quicker. And the versatility doesn't end there – these little meatballs are so yummy wrapped in a roti or stuffed into a fresh baguette. But sticking to tradition, I usually serve this with spaghetti (or sometimes linguini or tagliatelle) and lots of garlic bread.

CHEESY MEATBALLS BAKED IN TOMATO SAUCE

Serves 4

Sauce

2 x 400 g tins chopped tomatoes
1 x 400 g tin tomato purée
1 teaspoon sugar
1 tablespoon dried oregano
salt and pepper to taste

Meatballs

500 g lamb mince
1 onion, finely chopped and fried
2 garlic cloves, crushed
1 teaspoon ground coriander
½ teaspoon cumin
½ teaspoon ground cloves
1 egg
1 cup grated Parmesan or pecorino
squeeze of lemon juice
salt and black pepper to taste

2 cups grated Cheddar cheese
500 g spaghetti, cooked according to the packet instructions

1. Pre-heat the oven to 180 °C.
2. Combine all the sauce ingredients and pour into a deep roasting or casserole dish.
3. In a bowl, mix all the meatball ingredients. Form medium-sized meatballs and place them in the roasting tray on top of the sauce. Do not mix through.
4. Place the dish in the oven and bake for 10–15 minutes.
5. Sprinkle over the Cheddar cheese and bake for another 10 minutes until the meatballs are firm but still juicy and the cheese is melted and golden.
6. Serve the meatballs on top of the spaghetti and spoon over some of the tomato sauce.

Sometimes all I need is a bowl of comforting, perfectly cooked pasta. I don't mind what sauce I have on it – even something as simple as garlic butter is perfect. But alas, my family expect more of me than garlic-butter spaghetti, so I have to give them something slightly more substantial while keeping it easy peasy and low fuss.

I add a touch of reduced-fat cream to this sauce but if you don't have it or you don't want to add it, then just reserve some of the pasta's cooking water to loosen everything up a bit once combined. It's probably the easiest thing I've ever cooked and my family all love it.

LINGUINI WITH GARLIC AND MUSHROOMS

Serves 4

500 g linguini
500 g portabellini mushrooms, sliced
2 large leeks, finely chopped
4 garlic cloves, thinly sliced
½ cup reduced fat cream (optional)
juice of ½ lemon
salt and pepper to taste
fresh oregano, to serve (optional)
cracked black pepper, to serve

1. Bring a large pot of water to the boil and add the linguini. Cook according to the packet instructions until al dente.
2. Meanwhile, fry the mushrooms and leeks in a large saucepan until all the liquid from the mushrooms has evaporated and they have started to brown (about 5–7 minutes). Add the garlic and fry for another minute.
3. Add the cream and lemon juice and season to taste.
4. Drain the linguini and toss through the sauce. Serve with extra cracked black pepper and a few oregano leaves.

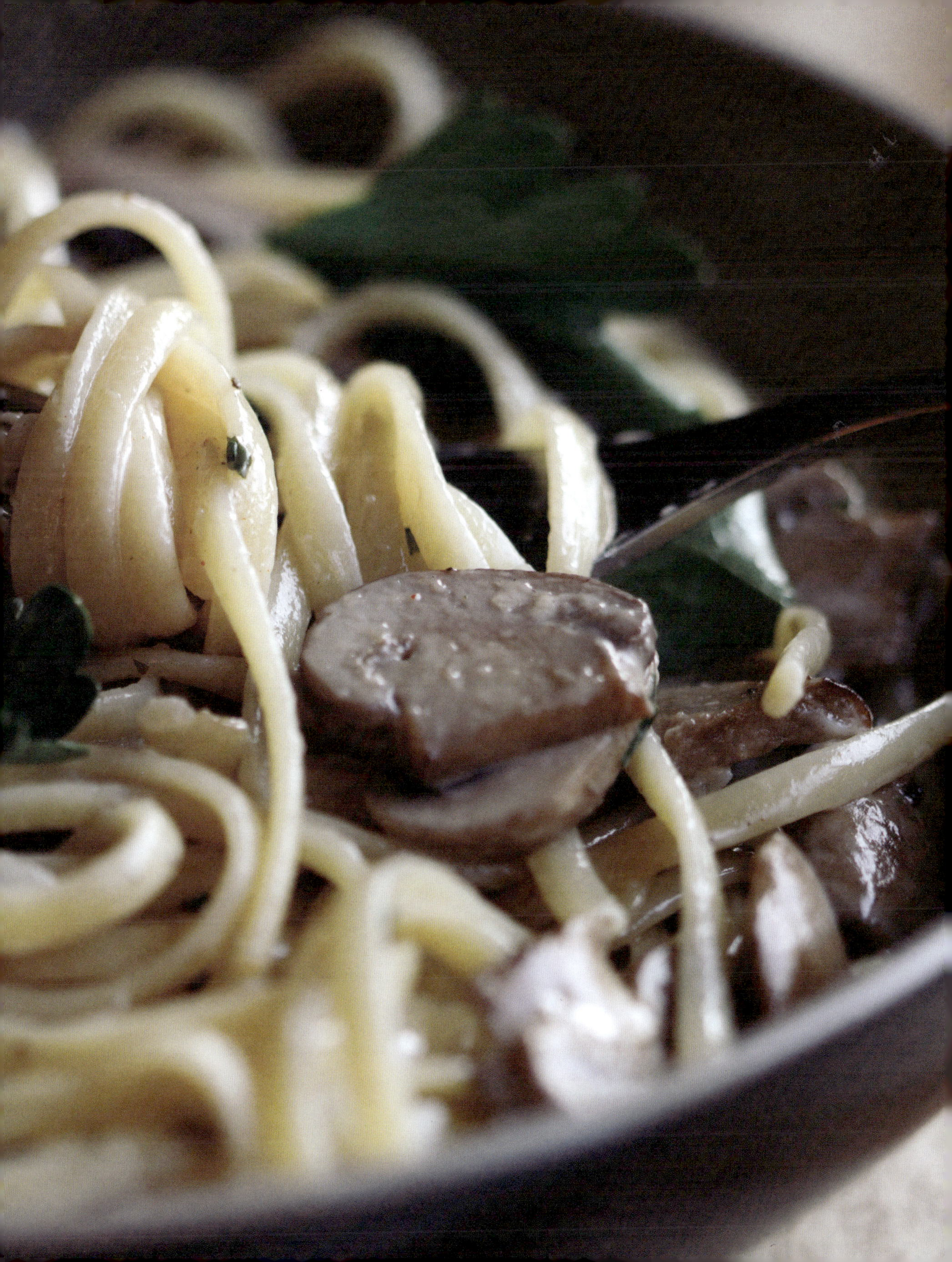

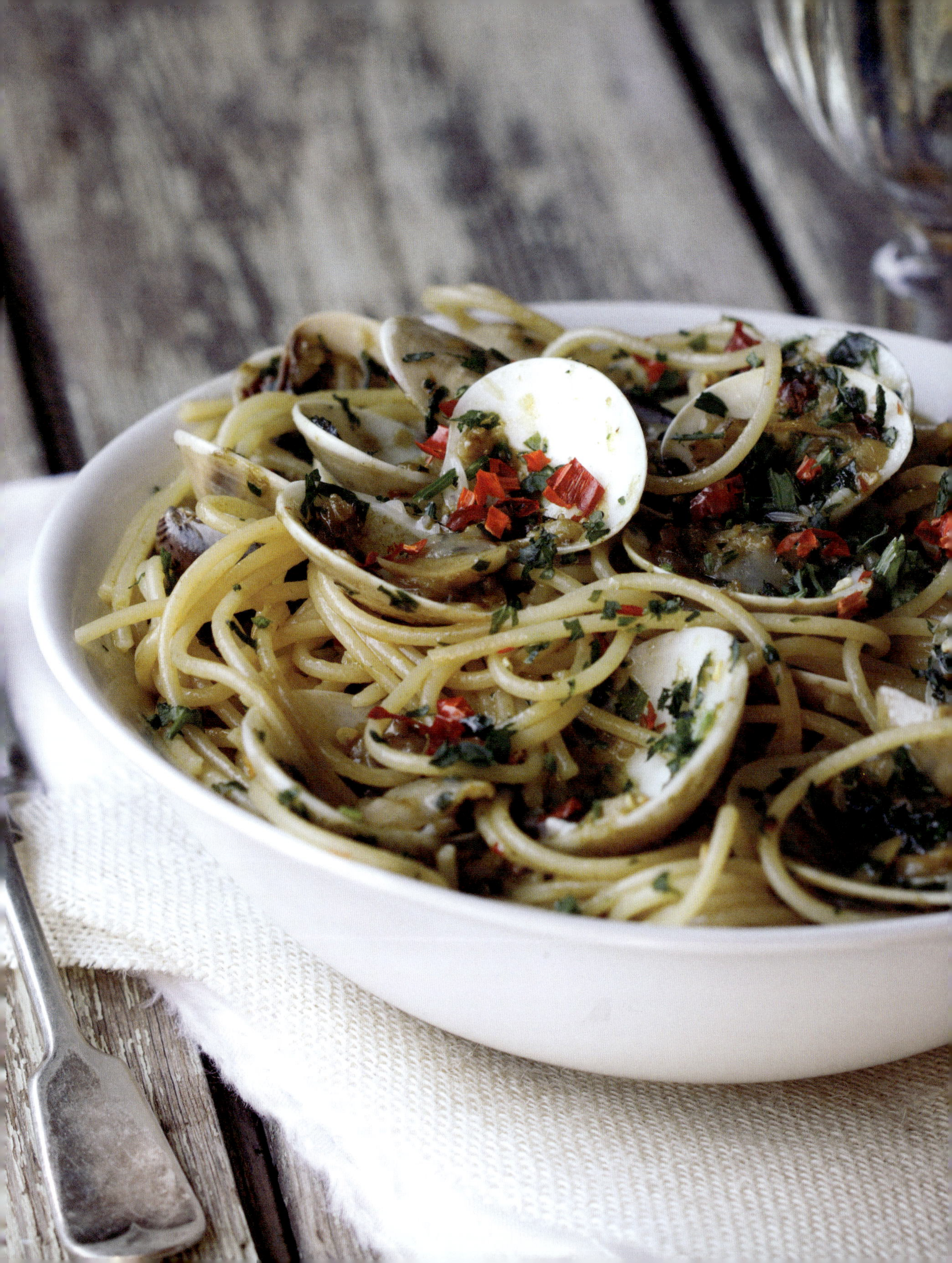

This is just perfect for those holidays where you spend time at the coast and you have beautiful fresh seafood at your fingertips daily. If you don't have fresh clams available, clam meat can be purchased at any fishmonger.

If you are using fresh clams it's important that you clean them very well as they contain quite a lot of sand and grit. I soak the clams in fresh, cool water for at least an hour and then rinse each one individually. I then steam them with a few cups of water and discard that liquid if it has any grittiness or sand in it. Your clams should then be clean and sand-free.

I love this pasta for the fact that it takes a couple of minutes to throw together but tastes like it took hours to make. Creamy, lemony and just a bit spicy. Perfect summer fare.

SPAGHETTI WITH CLAMS AND CREAM

Serves 4

1 onion, finely chopped
3 garlic cloves, minced
½–1 teaspoon dried chilli flakes
4 big handfuls fresh clams in the shell (approximately 200 g clam meat)
200 ml cream
1 large handful chopped parsley
juice and zest of 1 lemon
salt and pepper to taste
500 g spaghetti, cooked according to packet instructions

1. Fry the onion and garlic in olive oil until soft and translucent.
2. Add the chilli flakes and the clams and allow to cook for 4 minutes.
3. Add the cream, parsley and lemon juice and zest and simmer for 10 minutes until the sauce has reduced slightly and the clams are cooked.
4. Season to taste and serve with the cooked spaghetti.

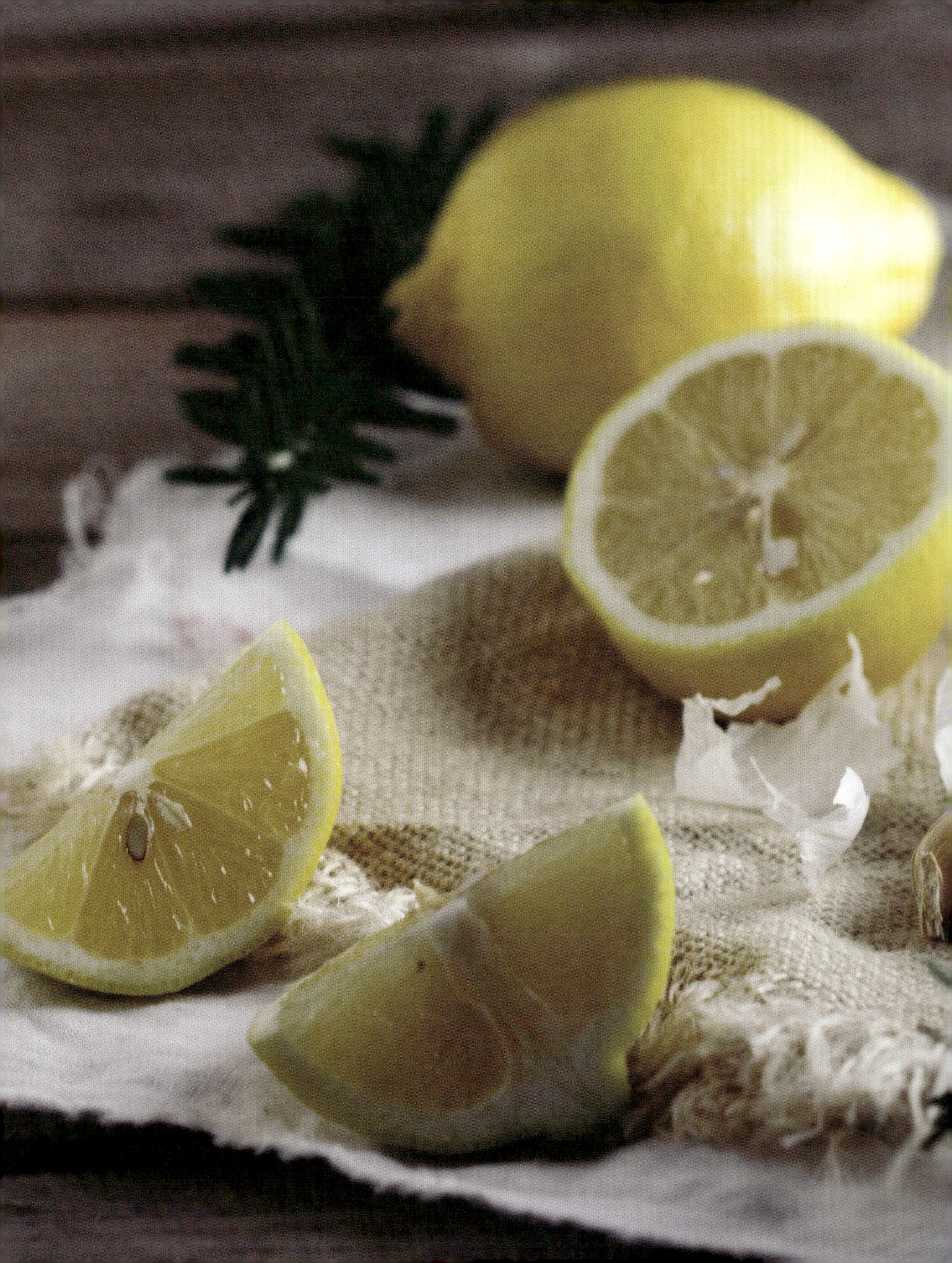

CHICKEN

With this recipe, I'm combining two of my favourites: butter chicken, which is a relatively mild but very aromatic chicken curry, and a bunny chow, which is definitely one of my favourite ways of eating curry. I was planning on making butter chicken for dinner one night and started the curry before I checked whether we had any basmati rice in the pantry. By the time I wanted to put the rice on, I realised we had none. I happened to have bread dough rising on the window sill and quickly decided to convert my traditional butter chicken into a bunny chow. It was absolutely delicious. Of course, basmati rice, poppadoms or roti would be equally scrumptious.

BUTTER CHICKEN BUNNY CHOW

Serves 6–8

Bread

600 g bread flour

400 ml luke-warm water

20 g yeast

1 tablespoon white sugar

2 teaspoons salt

extra flour for dusting

Butter chicken

1 kg chicken breasts, cut into bite-sized chunks

100 ml plain yoghurt

1 red chilli

1 bay leaf

½ teaspoon ground cloves

½ teaspoon ground cinnamon

2 teaspoons garam masala

2 cardamom pods

1 teaspoon salt

2 teaspoons white sugar

6 tomatoes, peeled (or 1 x 400 g tin chopped tomatoes)

small tin (50 g) tomato paste

thumb-sized piece ginger, grated and chopped roughly

3 garlic cloves, crushed

1 tablespoon vinegar

50 g butter

2 large onions, sliced

50 ml cream

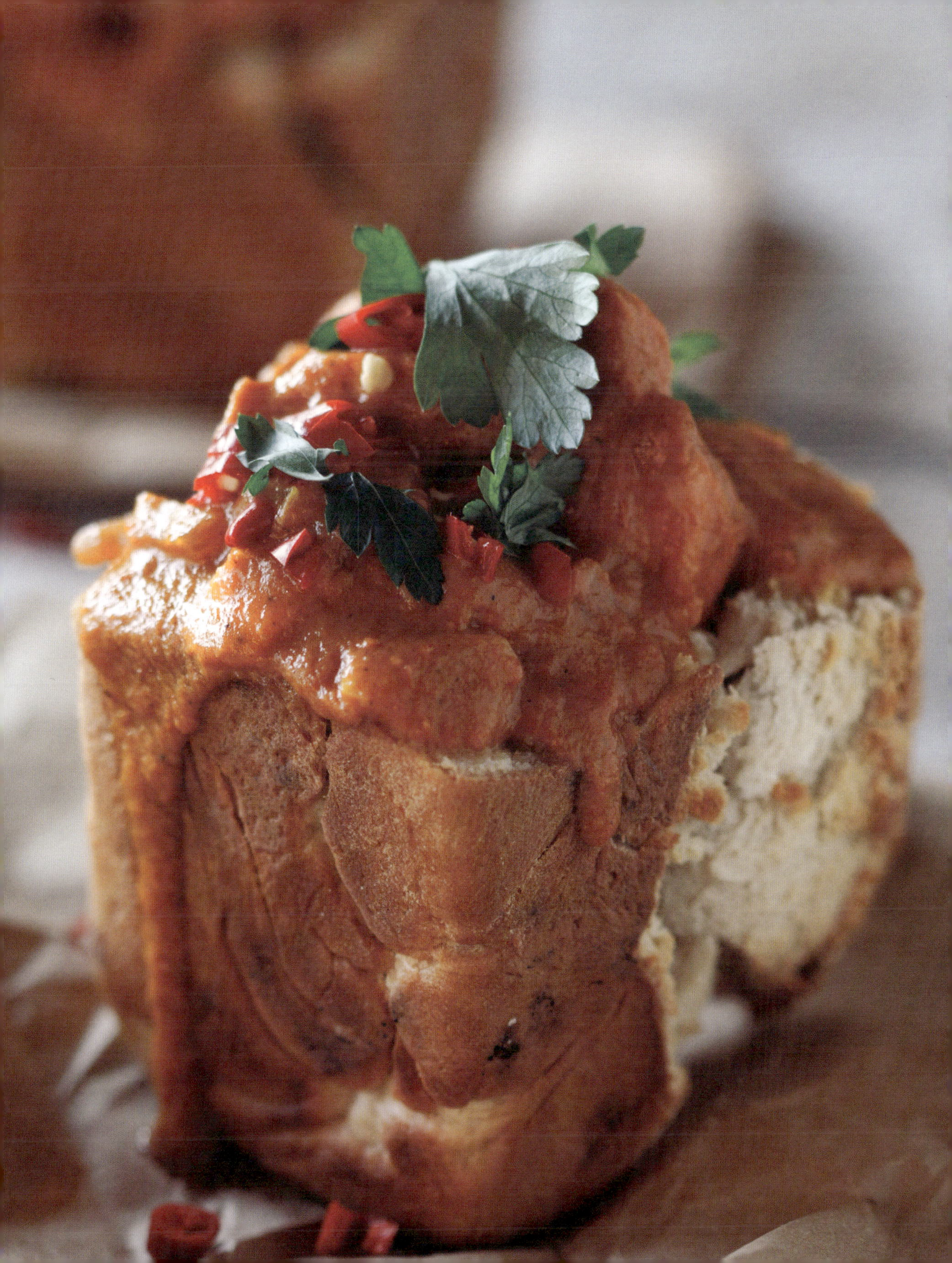

Bread

1. Start by putting all the bread flour into a pile on your working surface. Make a large well in the centre. Pour in half of the water, followed by the yeast, sugar and salt.
2. Stir with a fork until the water, yeast, sugar and salt are all combined then slowly start bringing some of the flour in with the fork. When the mixture is thick and porridge-like, add the rest of the water. Repeat the process of bringing the flour slowly into the paste until the mixture is thick enough so the water won't run all over the place. Now you can start working the dough with your hands.
3. Gently start working the dough into a ball and knead for about 5–7 minutes until it becomes soft and smooth. Also remember that, depending on the water and the type of flour, you might need a bit more water or a bit more flour to get the dough smooth and soft.
4. When you've finished kneading the dough, place it into an oiled bowl and cover with cling wrap or a damp tea towel. Allow to rise (prove) for about 45 minutes to an hour. Make sure the dough is left in a relatively warm place.
5. When the dough has risen, knock it down by punching it and then transfer it to the greased bread tin. Once again, allow to rise again for about 30 minutes. Pre-heat the oven to 180 °C.
6. Gently place your bread in the oven. Bake for 1 hour, but check after 45 minutes as ovens vary. You can check whether it is cooked by tapping the bottom: if it sounds hollow, the bread is cooked.
7. Allow your bread to cool on a wire rack for at least 30 minutes.

Butter chicken

1. In a blender, process the yoghurt, spices, tomatoes, tomato paste, ginger, garlic and vinegar until fine. Pour over the chopped chicken and allow to marinate (I leave mine for about 2 hours).
2. Melt the butter in a large, hot pot and fry the onions until soft and golden.
3. Add the chicken and the marinade and allow to come to the boil. Lower the heat and simmer for 30–45 minutes until the chicken is fully cooked and the sauce has thickened.
4. Add the cream and check to adjust the seasoning.
5. Serve the butter chicken in the hollowed-out bread.

Sometimes you need to take out all the stops to impress a dinner guest. Whether it is your boss or your mother-in-law, everyone needs a recipe in their repertoire they know will impress. This is one of mine. And what I love about it most is that, even though it looks like I've spent hours cooking, it's so very easy to assemble.

You could use any cheese for the filling but I like the subtle smokiness the mozzarella adds. I imagine goat's cheese would be equally delicious though.

I like to serve this with creamy mashed potatoes and steamed greens for an elegant and delicious dinner.

CHICKEN ROULADE WITH SMOKED MOZZARELLA AND ROCKET

Serves 4

- 4 large skinless chicken breast fillets
- 200 g smoked mozzarella, grated
- 40 g fresh rocket
- juice of 1 lemon
- salt and pepper to taste
- tin foil for roasting
- olive oil for drizzling

1. Pre-heat the oven to 180 °C.
2. Flatten the chicken with a mallet between two sheets of cling film or baking paper. You want the chicken to be approximately ½ cm thick.
3. Place a square of tin foil slightly bigger than the flattened chicken in front of you and place the flattened chicken on top.
4. Scatter a quarter of the grated mozzarella over the chicken, followed by a few rocket leaves, a drizzle of lemon juice and season with salt and pepper.
5. Using the tin foil, roll the chicken up and tuck in the sides of the foil to create a little rolled parcel.
6. Continue with the other chicken breasts and place on a roasting tray.
7. Place in the oven and allow to cook for 15 minutes until the chicken feels firm.
8. Remove from the oven and remove the chicken from the foil.
9. Place the chicken back onto the roasting tray, drizzle with olive oil and place back in the oven to roast for another 5 minutes until golden brown.
10. Serve with mashed potatoes and steamed greens.

During winter, curry is on our menu at least twice a week, but during the hotter months when a blow-your-head-off curry just seems too unbearable, I often revert to biryani. I love lamb best but chicken comes a close second. Not only is it cheaper, but it also requires less cooking time.

Food purists might frown at my shortcuts, but I make no excuses for them. The idea of standing in front of a stove on a hot day is just too much to bear, so I use alternatives that save me time but don't compromise the flavour. One of these shortcuts is the use of spices in two forms. I use a mild curry paste packed with coriander, cumin, cinnamon, turmeric, garlic, ginger and onions, and then I also use ground versions of the spices. I assure you it works and the curry is not too spicy, especially because it is layered with jasmine or basmati rice and fried potatoes. If you don't have all the spices in your pantry and you don't want to buy all of them, use a good-quality curry paste and curry powder or garam masala instead.

Never serve this without the buttermilk raita. It complements the biryani perfectly and without it, even though still delicious, the biryani tends to be a bit dry.

CHICKEN BIRYANI

Serves 6–8

Biryani

2 kg skinless chicken breast fillets
2 onions, finely chopped
3 garlic cloves, crushed
2 cm piece fresh ginger, grated
2 tablespoons curry paste (I use a mild one), optional
2 teaspoons ground coriander
2 teaspoons ground cumin
2 teaspoons ground turmeric
1 teaspoon ground cinnamon
½ teaspoon each ground nutmeg and ground cloves
2 tablespoons hot garam masala
2 bay leaves
1 tin chopped tomatoes
1 teaspoon sugar
2 cups chicken stock
salt to taste

To assemble

4 large potatoes, peeled and cubed
3 cups cooked jasmine or basmati rice
1 cup chicken stock

Buttermilk raita

1 cup buttermilk
1 teaspoon ground cumin
1½ teaspoons ground coriander
½ teaspoon turmeric
½ teaspoon chilli powder
1 tablespoon lemon juice
1 teaspoon salt

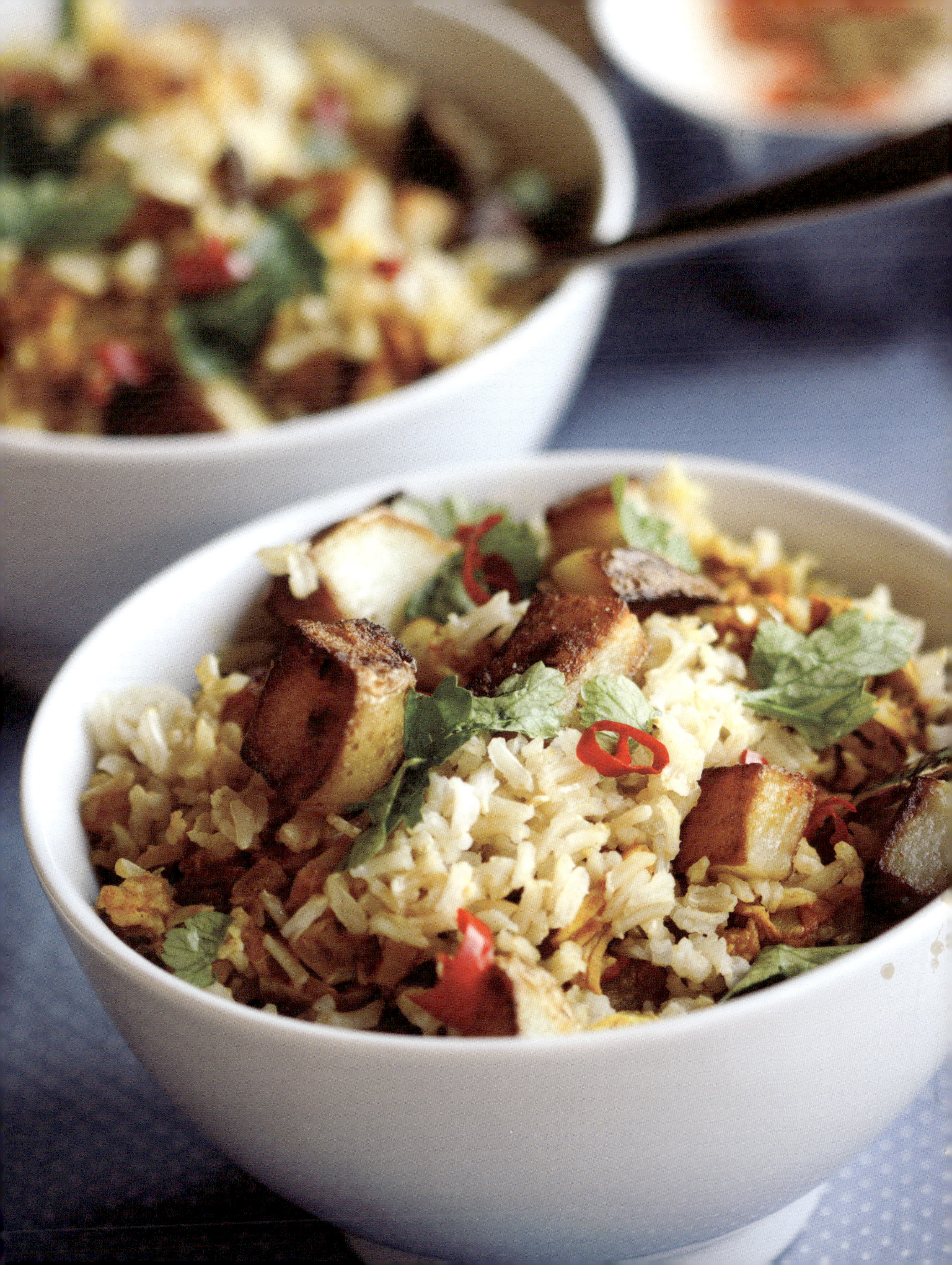

1. Pre-heat the oven to 180 °C.
2. Heat 3 tablespoons oil in a large pot.
3. Cut the chicken breasts into large chunks and fry in the oil until they start to brown. Remove and set aside.
4. Fry the onions, garlic and ginger for 2 minutes before adding the curry paste and spices. Allow to fry for another minute and add the chicken back into the pot.
5. Stir to coat the chicken in all the spices and add the tomatoes, sugar and chicken stock.
6. Lower the heat and allow to simmer for 15 minutes.
7. Heat ½ cup oil in a large frying pan and fry the potatoes until golden and crisp. Season with salt and set aside.
8. To assemble the dish, layer one-third of the rice at the bottom of a greased ovenproof dish. Next, cover the rice with the chicken curry but reserve some of the sauce. Follow with the rest of the rice and spoon over the remaining sauce. Finally, cover the rice with the fried potatoes. Pour over the chicken stock and cover with foil (or a lid if your dish has one).
9. Place in the oven for 25–30 minutes.
10. To make the raita, combine all the ingredients in a bowl and mix well.
11. Serve the biryani with the buttermilk raita and fresh coriander leaves.

This is a great mid-week soup that allows you to use up all the leftover vegetables in your fridge (I love adding all types of vegetables). If you don't have leftover chicken to use, I suggest you buy a ready-cooked chicken from your supermarket and simply shred it into the soup. Serve with a cooling avocado salsa and cheesy quesadillas (follow the recipe for cheese, corn and bean quesadillas on p 140 but only use mature Cheddar and add sliced spring onions).

SPICY CHICKEN SOUP WITH AVOCADO SALSA

Serves 4–6

1 large onion, finely chopped
2 large carrots, peeled and finely chopped
2 celery sticks, finely chopped
3 garlic cloves, crushed
2 teaspoons ground coriander
2 teaspoons ground cumin
1 teaspoon smoked paprika
1 red chilli, finely chopped (remove the seeds if you want less heat)
2 tins chopped/ cherry tomatoes
1 teaspoon sugar (optional)
500 g chicken, shredded
3 tins chicken stock (using the tomato tins)
1 bay leaf
salt and pepper to taste
cheese quesadillas, to serve

Avocado salsa

1 ripe avocado, peeled and finely chopped
1 red onion, finely chopped
handful fresh parsley, finely chopped
juice of 1 lemon
salt and pepper to taste

1. In a large pot, fry the onion, carrots and celery until soft and translucent (approximately 10 minutes).
2. Add the garlic and spices and allow to fry for another minute before adding the tomatoes and sugar.
3. Allow to simmer for 5 minutes.
4. Add the chicken, stock and bay leaf and allow to simmer for 20 minutes uncovered until the soup has thickened slightly.
5. Season to taste.
6. To make the avocado salsa, combine all the ingredients and mix well.
7. Serve the chicken soup with the avocado salsa and cheese quesadillas.

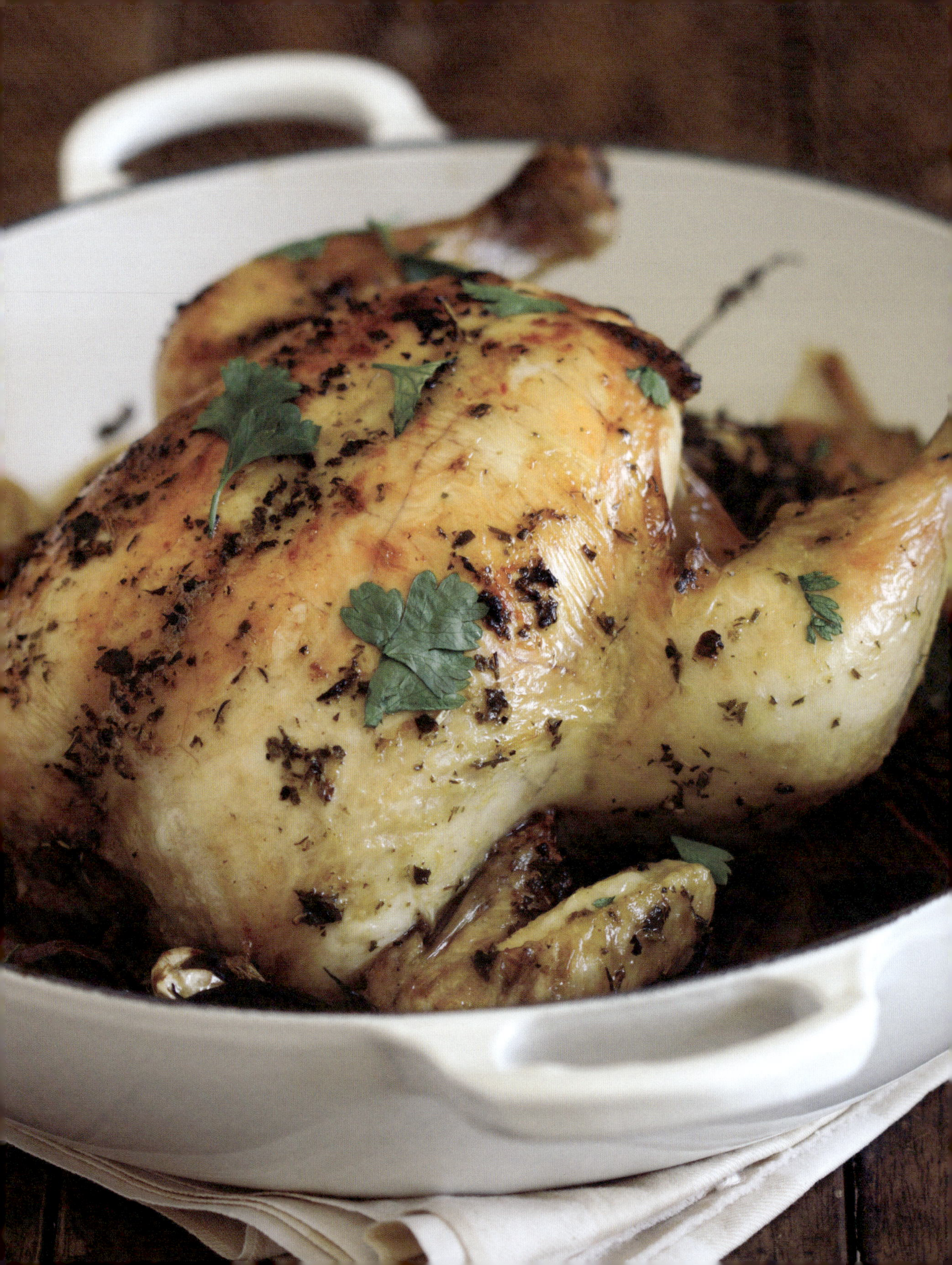

Very few people can resist the charm of a simple roast chicken. It is synonymous with home for me and nothing is as inviting as the smell of roast chicken making its way through the house.

Whether you serve it as an old-fashioned Sunday lunch with all the trimmings, shredded between two slices of thick bread, or as leftovers in a simple salad of greens and Parmesan shavings, a roast chicken is one of the most versatile things you can cook. And you can be assured that there won't be any wastage.

My favourite way of roasting a chicken is to add lots of roasting spice to the skin along with some butter and lemon juice. I also put the lemon halves in the cavity to flavour the chicken meat from inside. The lemon acts as a tenderiser for the meat so what you are left with is a succulent and juicy bird filled with amazing flavour.

LEMON ROASTED CHICKEN

Serves 4–6

- 1 x 1½–2 kg free-range chicken, innards removed
- 100 g butter, softened
- 1 lemon, halved
- 2 tablespoons roasting spice
- 2 teaspoons salt
- 1 teaspoon pepper
- 2 onions, quartered
- 2 large carrots, chopped into large chunks
- 3 thyme sprigs
- 1 head garlic, halved

1. Pre-heat the oven to 180 °C.
2. Smear the butter all over the chicken with your hands. Squeeze over the lemon juice and season with the roasting spice.
3. Using 1 teaspoon salt and ½ teaspoon pepper, season the outside of the bird and use the remainder to season the inside cavity.
4. Place the squeezed-out lemon halves inside the cavity.
5. Place the onion, carrot, thyme and garlic in a roasting tray and drizzle with olive oil. Place the chicken on top of the vegetables and place in the oven.
6. Allow the chicken to roast for 30 minutes per 500 g, so for a 2 kg bird, this will be 2 hours. To check if the chicken is cooked, make an incision where the leg is joined to the body. If the juices run clear, the chicken is cooked.
7. When the chicken is cooked, remove from the oven and cover with foil. Allow to rest for 10–15 minutes before carving and serving.

Chicken livers are something I have in my freezer most of the time. They are versatile, cheap and incredibly nutritious. I know many people will not eat them but I believe that everyone should try a well-cooked chicken liver at least once in their lives. (I only buy free-range chicken livers as the quality just cannot be compared to that of a battery chicken liver.)

Even though I adore chicken livers in a pâté or in a rich peri-peri sauce, I sometimes want something different. As pasta is such a staple in our home, I thought I'd try using the chicken livers in a pasta sauce. It all really just happened, like most good recipes do. I had some mushrooms in the fridge and decided to use them along with fresh cream to make what is now one of my all-time favourite pasta sauces.

CHICKEN LIVERS IN CREAMY MUSHROOM SAUCE

Serves 4

500 g free-range chicken livers (make sure they are properly cleaned)
1 large onion, finely chopped
4 cloves garlic, crushed
250 g portabellini mushrooms, chopped
½ cup sherry
1 cup cream
1 cup chicken stock
2 bay leaves
½ teaspoon dried thyme
salt and black pepper to taste
500 g cooked pasta of your choice, to serve

1. In a large hot pan or wok, fry the chicken livers until brown and almost cooked. Remove from the pan and set aside.
2. Wipe the pan clean and add more oil. Fry the onion and garlic until soft and add the mushrooms. Sauté for another 5 minutes and add the sherry.
3. Allow to reduce a little and add the cream and chicken stock. Allow to simmer for 10 minutes until reduced slightly.
4. Return the livers to the pan and add the seasonings. Allow to cook for about 10 minutes on a low heat until the chicken livers are cooked and the sauce has thickened slightly.
5. Serve the sauce over cooked pasta of your choice.

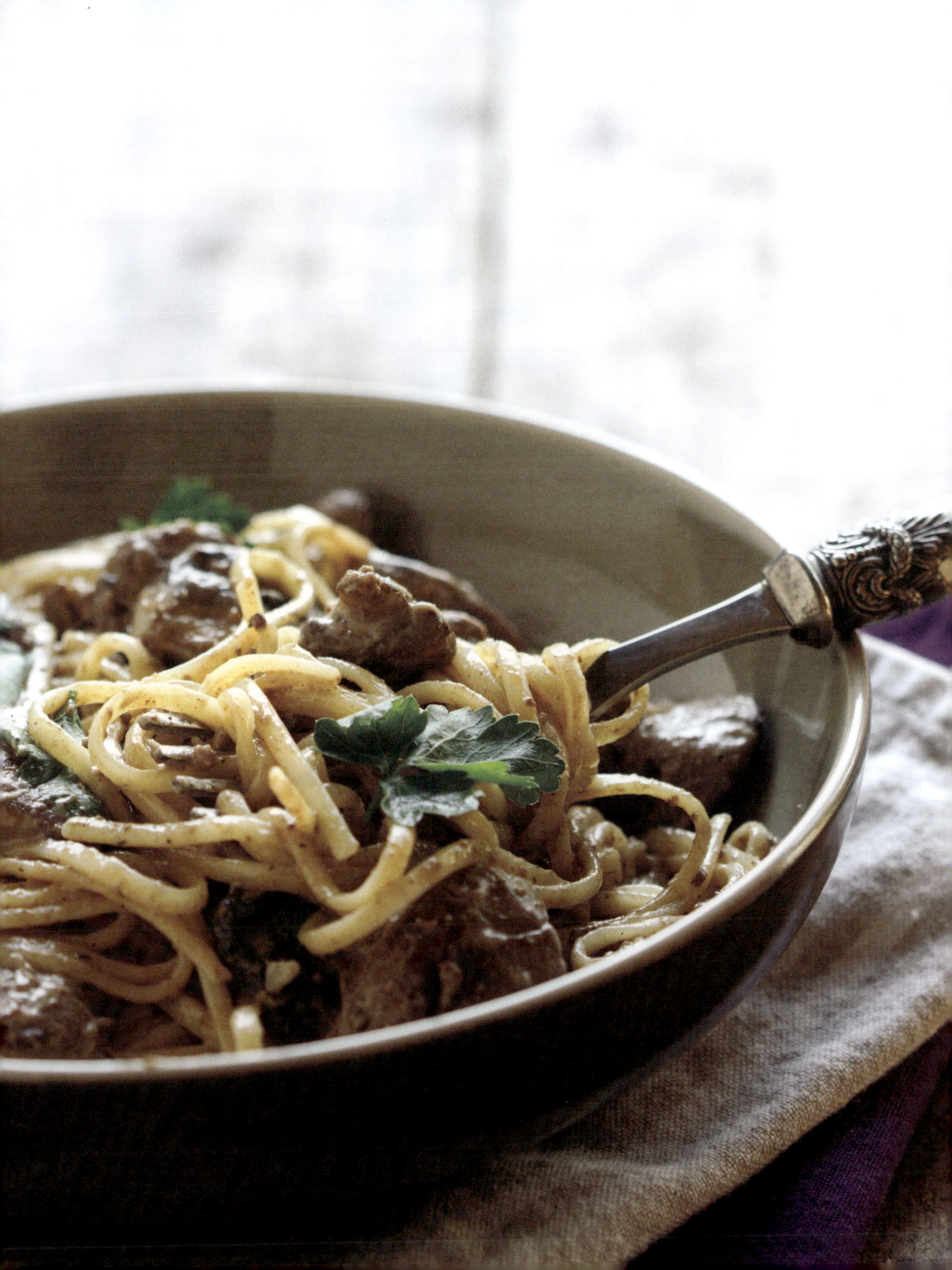

I make sure I poach the chicken with loads of vegetables to create that delicious depth of flavour and I never leave out the nutmeg or cloves. When I'm having a very lazy day I use shop-bought cooked chicken, but the flavour isn't as rich and deep as that of the chicken you poach yourself – and of course if you make it yourself you'll have some home-made stock for soup or risotto.

I sometimes buy ready-made béchamel or I simply combine 1 cup crème fraîche, 1 cup mascarpone, 1 teaspoon salt and 1 tablespoon flour. This will give you a creamy and delicious sauce without all the fuss of making béchamel.

CHICKEN PIE

Makes 6 individual pies or one large one

Chicken

2 large chickens, cleaned
4 large carrots, roughly chopped
2 large onions, halved
1 head garlic, halved
3 cloves
3 bay leaves
1 tablespoon whole peppercorns
1 sprig thyme
1 sprig rosemary

Filling

2 cups béchamel (white sauce)
2 cups vegetables of your choice, finely chopped and sautéed
½ teaspoon grated nutmeg
½ teaspoon ground cloves
½ cup mature Cheddar, grated
juice of ½ lemon
salt and pepper to taste

Pie

2 rolls puff pastry, rolled out
2 eggs, beaten

1. Combine all the poaching ingredients in a large pot with water and allow to come to the boil. Turn down the heat and simmer gently for 45–60 minutes until the chickens are cooked.
2. Remove the chickens from the stock and set aside to cool slightly.
3. Strain the stock and reserve 1 cup for the filling. Freeze the remaining stock for risotto or soup.
4. Remove the skin from the chicken and shred the meat.
5. Mix with all the filling ingredients.
6. Spoon into separate pie dishes or one big dish of your choice.
7. Cut the pastry to fit over the top of the dish you have chosen.
8. Crimp the edges of the pastry and brush with beaten egg.
9. Place in the oven at 180 °C for 20–30 minutes until the pastry is golden and crisp.
10. Serve with a side salad.

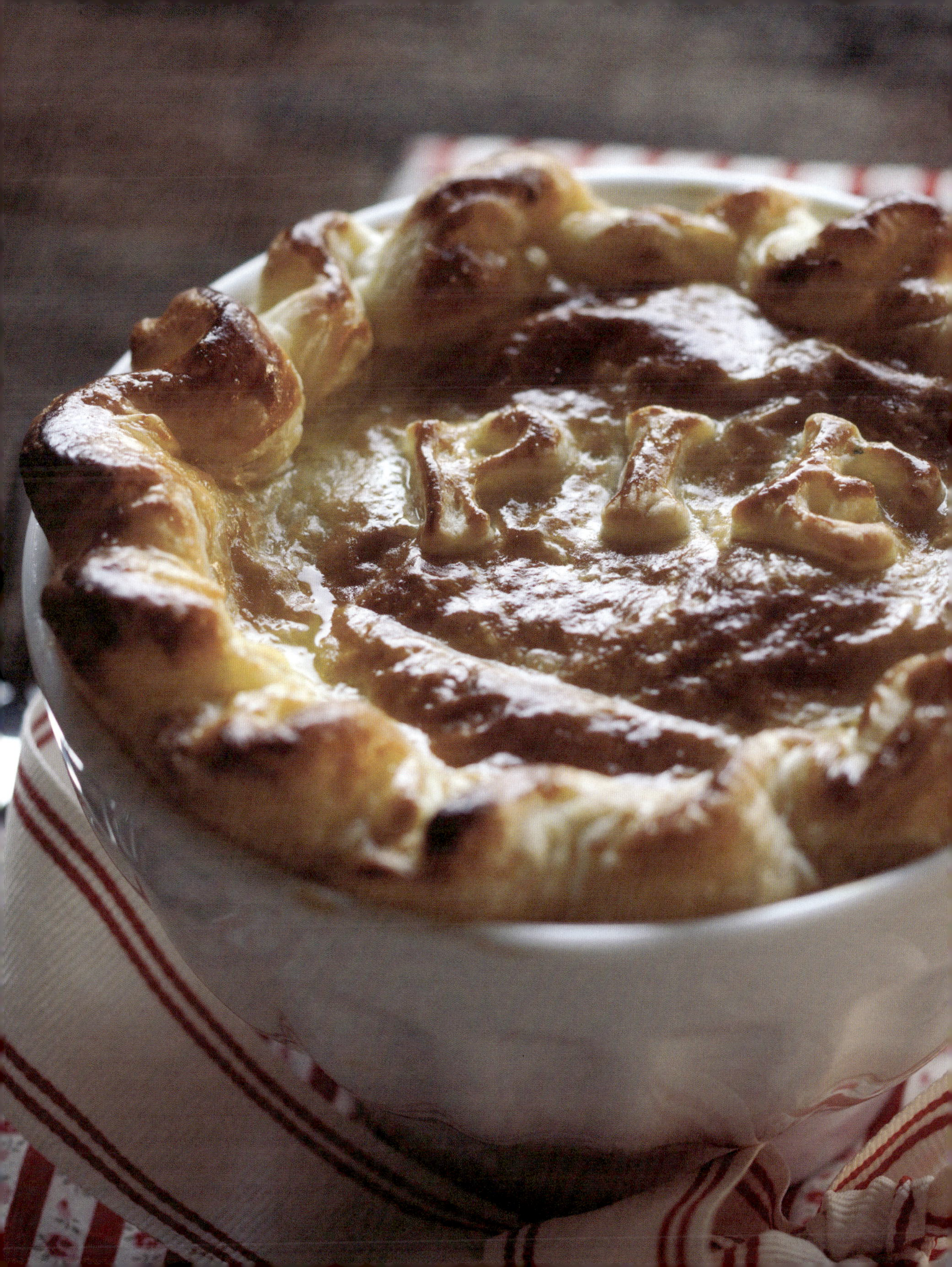

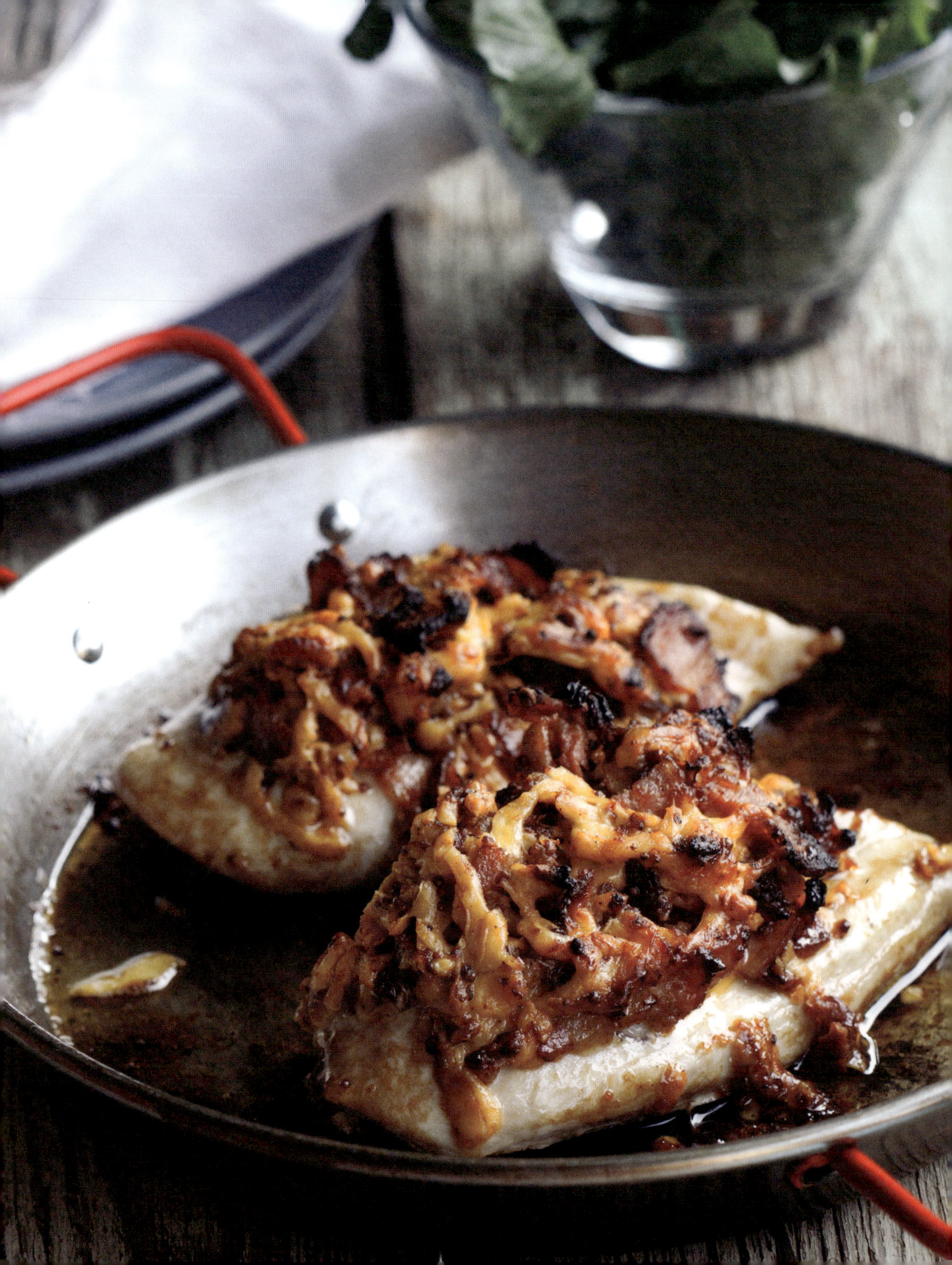

This is a really great way to add some life to chicken breasts, which can easily be dry and bland. Don't let the idea of 'stuffing' a chicken breast put you off; you simply make a slit on top of each breast and stuff in a few spoonfuls of the bacon mixture. Easy as pie! Serve with some crispy potato wedges and a salad for a great, easy supper.

BACON AND CHEESE STUFFED CHICKEN BREASTS

Serves 6

- 250 g bacon, chopped
- 1 cup mature Cheddar, grated
- ½ cup mozzarella, grated
- 2 garlic cloves, finely chopped
- ½ cup fresh parsley, finely chopped
- ½ cup cream
- ½ teaspoon pepper
- 6 large, free-range, skinless chicken breast fillets
- juice of 1 lemon
- salt, to season the chicken
- ½ cup chicken stock

1. Pre-heat the oven to 200 °C.
2. Fry the bacon in a hot pan until crisp.
3. Remove, drain of oil on kitchen paper and allow to cool slightly before combining with the cheeses, garlic, parsley, cream and pepper. There is no need to add extra salt to the stuffing as the bacon and cheese are salty already.
4. Make a deep incision into the top of each chicken breast (be careful not to cut right through the breast).
5. Squeeze over the lemon juice and season lightly with salt.
6. Place spoonfuls of the bacon and cheese stuffing into the slit on top of each breast.
7. Place in a baking dish and pour in the chicken stock. Cover the tray with foil and place in the oven.
8. Allow the chicken to cook for 8–10 minutes until the chicken is cooked throughout but still juicy.
9. Serve immediately with potato wedges and a salad.

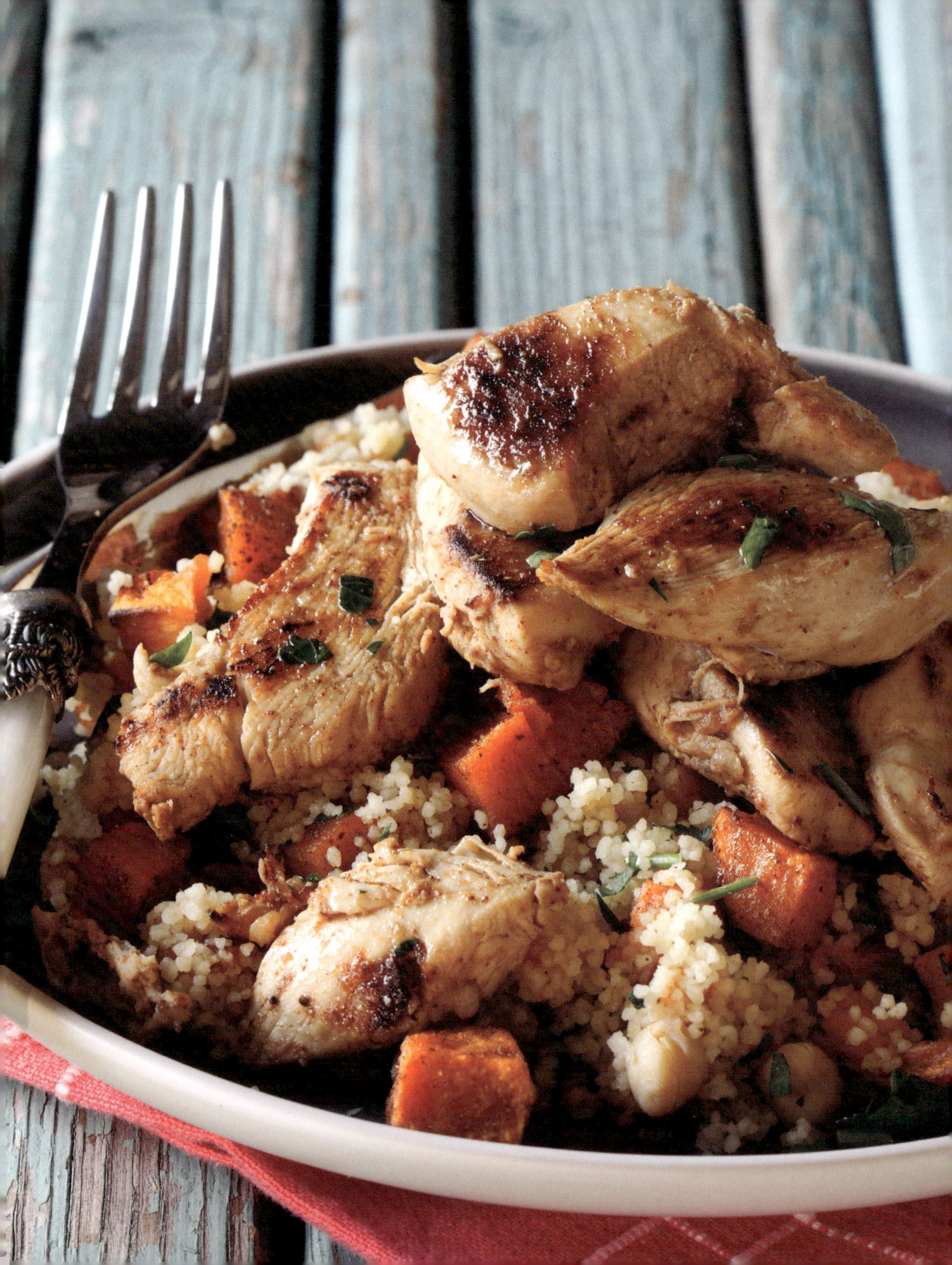

I just love this dish on those days when I need good food but I've had an exhausting day and I need dinner to be done in a flash.

To save time, I chop the butternut for the couscous into very small cubes so they roast in no time. I then soak the couscous while I get going on the chicken breasts. I make a quick marinade that I cook the chicken in to make sure it stays succulent and juicy. When the chicken is thoroughly cooked, the butternut should be done and can just be combined with the couscous plus a drizzle of olive oil and a scattering of fresh parsley. Quick, delicious and perfect for busy weeknights.

MOROCCAN CHICKEN ON BUTTERNUT COUSCOUS

Serves 4

Butternut couscous

- 1 medium butternut, peeled and chopped into small cubes
- 2 tablespoons oil
- 2 teaspoons sugar
- 1 teaspoon ground cinnamon
- 1 teaspoon salt
- 2 cups quick-cooking couscous
- 3 cups chicken stock
- 2 tablespoons oil
- handful fresh parsley, finely chopped
- salt to taste

Moroccan chicken

- 500 g skinless chicken breast fillets
- 2 tablespoons oil
- juice of 1 lemon
- 1 teaspoon ground coriander
- 2 teaspoons ground cumin
- 1 teaspoon paprika
- 2 teaspoons salt

1. Pre-heat the oven to 220 °C.
2. Place the butternut in a roasting tray and add the oil, sugar, cinnamon and salt. Mix everything together with your hands, making sure the butternut is coated in the spice and seasoning.
3. Place in the oven and roast for 10–15 minutes until the edges are caramelised and the butternut is cooked.
4. Remove from the oven and set aside.
5. Meanwhile, place the couscous in a bowl and add the stock and oil. Stir with a fork and cover with cling film. Allow to soak for 10 minutes.
6. When the couscous has absorbed all the stock, add the parsley and salt, and fork everything through. You want the couscous to be light and fluffy.
7. Mix the butternut into the couscous.
8. Slice the chicken breasts into thin strips and combine with the oil, lemon juice and spices.
9. Fry the chicken in a hot frying pan until golden brown and cooked through.
10. Serve the chicken on top of the butternut couscous.

If you love a good burger as much as I do, then you have to try these. The crunch and spiciness of the chicken patty is so perfectly complemented by the fresh, soft bread roll and the cooling home-made aioli. I like to add thinly sliced cucumber and fresh watercress to the burgers for a fresh element. At my house they are always served with an ice cold beer. Perfection!

CRISPY CHICKEN BURGERS WITH HOME-MADE AIOLI

Serves 4

600 g chicken breasts, roughly chopped, or chicken mince
3 cups fresh breadcrumbs
1 large egg
1 teaspoon paprika
1 teaspoon salt
2 chillies, finely chopped (optional)
black pepper to taste
2 large eggs, beaten
1 cup flour mixed with 1 teaspoon salt
fresh bread rolls, to serve
peeled and sliced cucumber, to serve
fresh watercress, to serve
aioli, to serve

Mayo/ aioli

3 large egg yolks
1 teaspoon Dijon mustard
2 tablespoons lemon juice
salt to taste
1 garlic clove
250–300 ml oil (I use canola)

1. To make the chicken patties, pulse the chicken breasts in your food processor (if using whole chicken breasts). Make sure that you don't leave the food processor running as the chicken will just become a purée.
2. Mix the chicken with 1 cup of the breadcrumbs, the egg, paprika, salt, chillies and pepper. Form patties with your hands and place on a plate or tray lined with wax paper. Refrigerate for 30 minutes.
3. Coat the burgers first with the seasoned flour, then dip into the beaten egg and coat in the remaining breadcrumbs. Fry in very hot oil for 1–2 minutes a side until the breadcrumbs are crisp and golden. Place in a roasting tray and then in a 180 °C oven for 15–20 minutes until the burgers are cooked all the way through.
4. Serve on fresh bread rolls with cucumber, watercress and aioli.
5. For the aioli, mix the egg yolks, Dijon mustard, lemon juice, salt and garlic together in a food processor. The mixture should be smooth and pale.
6. With the food processor running, slowly drizzle in the oil until the mixture is thick and pale. Taste and adjust the seasoning.
7. Serve straight away or transfer into a sterilised jar and refrigerate.

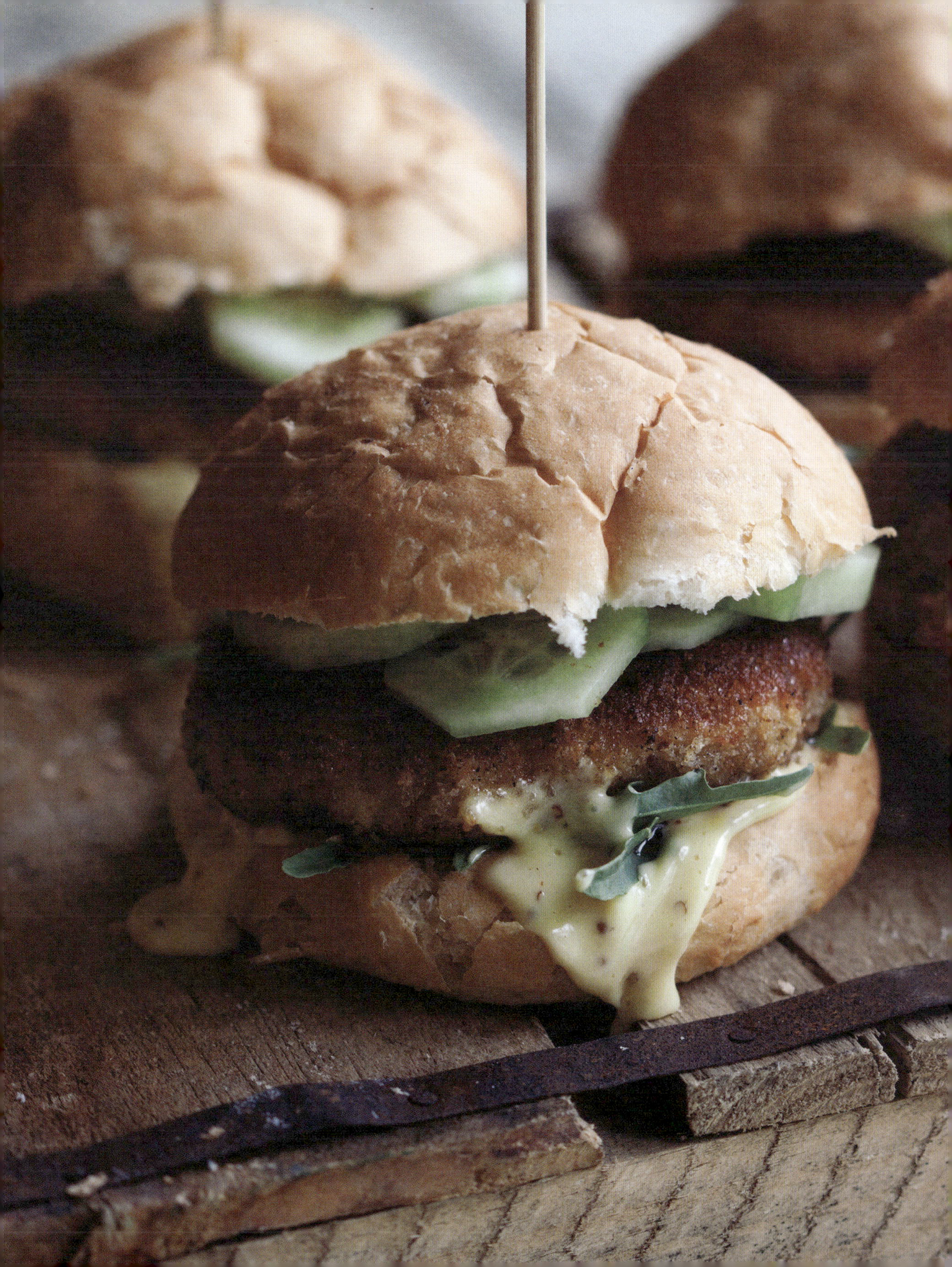

Like many parents I sometimes opt for takeaways when I need to feed my kids and I've run out of time, but knowing how much salt, fat and empty calories one little takeaway chicken nugget contains (not to mention the stuff we don't know about) makes me feel very guilty when I buy them for my kids. When you make them yourself, you don't have to worry about any of that. If you use fresh, free-range chicken, free-range eggs and bake the nuggets instead of deep-frying them, it's actually a pretty healthy snack or meal if paired with baked potato wedges and tomato sauce.

I suggest you get a little assembly line going in your kitchen. One child can be responsible for dunking the chicken pieces in flour, another child does the egg and another does the breadcrumbs. Just be sure not to allow the children to fry the chicken nuggets themselves if you won't be baking them.

I make my own breadcrumbs using stale bread that I process in my food processor and freeze in freezer bags ready for use, but you can also use fresh or dried breadcrumbs from the shops.

HOME-MADE CHICKEN NUGGETS

Makes approximately 20 nuggets

- 4 large, free-range skinless chicken breast fillets
- 1 cup flour seasoned with ½ teaspoon salt and 1 teaspoon paprika
- 4 eggs, beaten
- 2 cups breadcrumbs, seasoned with ½ teaspoon salt
- oil for frying (optional)
- tomato sauce, to serve

1. If you are going to be frying the nuggets, heat about 2 cm oil in a large frying pan. If you are going to be baking them, pre-heat the oven to 200 °C.
2. First, get your assembly line together. Place the seasoned flour, beaten eggs and seasoned breadcrumbs in separate bowls suitable for dipping and dunking the chicken (wide, shallow bowls work best).
3. Next, cut your chicken breasts into large chunks. I usually get 5–6 chunks out of each chicken breast.
4. First coat the chicken in the seasoned flour, then dunk it into the beaten egg.
5. Finally coat each nugget in the seasoned breadcrumbs before placing them carefully into the hot oil or onto a greased baking dish.
6. Fry the chicken for 1–2 minutes per side before draining on kitchen paper. If you are baking the nuggets, bake them for 20 minutes until golden brown and crisp.
7. Serve the nuggets with baked potato wedges and tomato sauce.

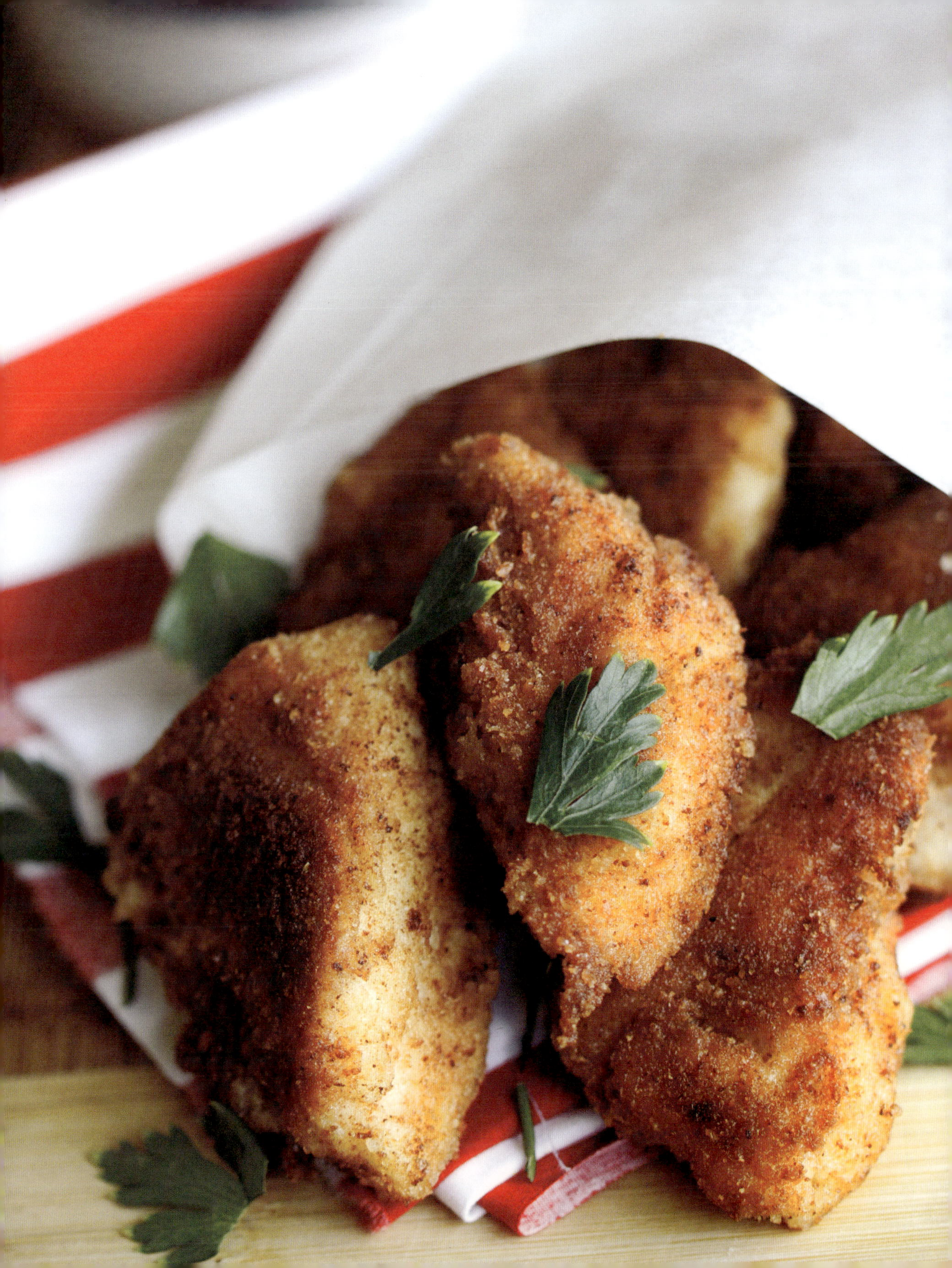

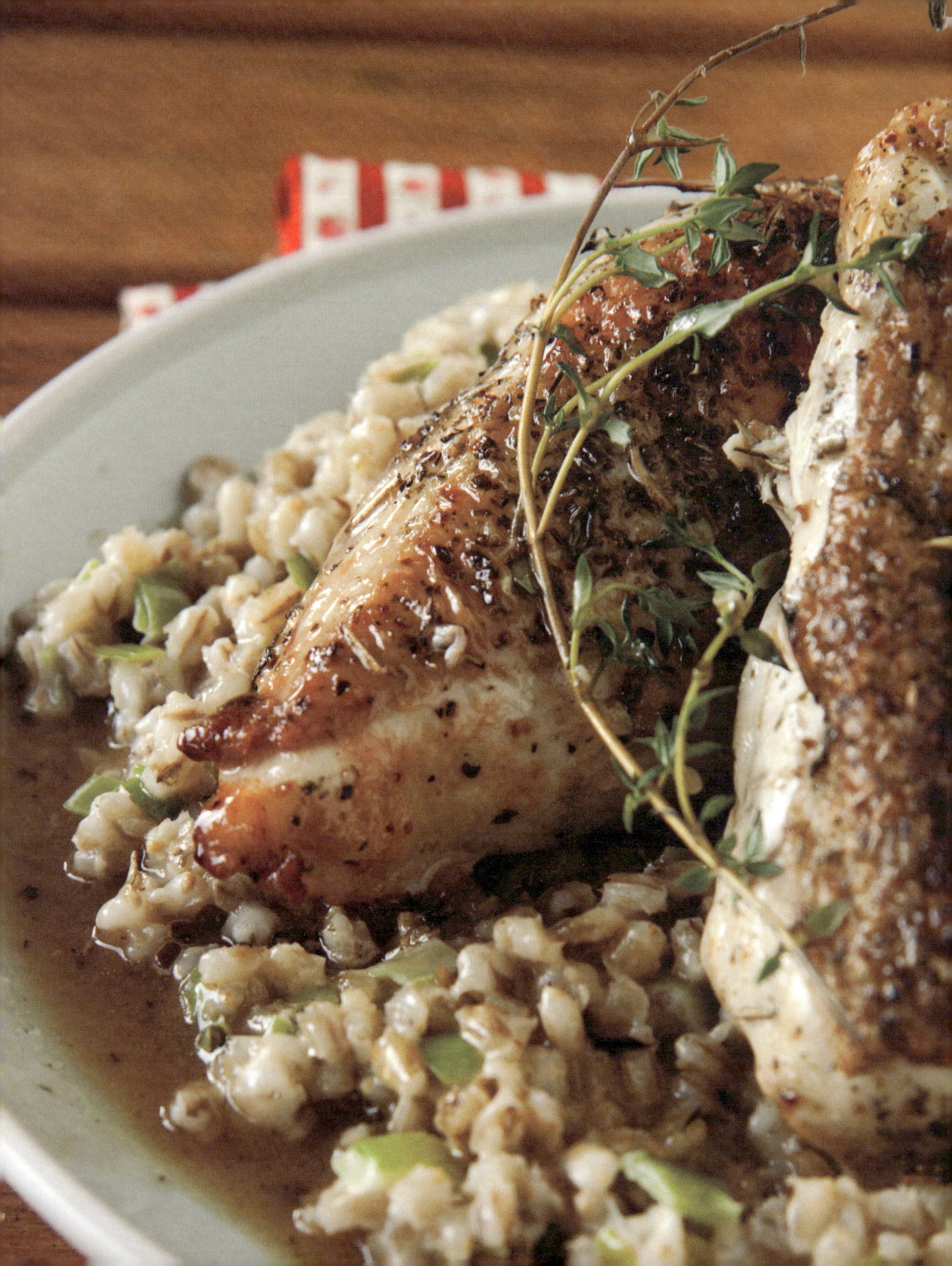

I know barley is not synonymous with risotto but believe me, it works. I am normally not a fan of barley – I find it very bland and dry – but this way of cooking it results in creamy and delicious barley that complements roast chicken just perfectly.

If you don't like chicken breasts, chicken thighs or a whole chicken can be used.

I like to serve this with a simple salad of watercress and rocket with a sharp, lemony dressing. Beautiful, simple comfort food!

ROAST CHICKEN BREASTS ON BARLEY RISOTTO

Serves 4

Barley risotto

1 cup pearl barley

8 cups (2 litres) water

2 leeks, washed and finely chopped

2 garlic cloves, crushed

2 cups chicken stock

½ cup cream

salt and pepper to taste

Chicken

4 chicken breasts, on the bone with the skin on

juice of 1 lemon

2 tablespoons roasting spice

1 teaspoon salt

1½ cups chicken stock

1. Pre-heat the oven to 200 °C.
2. To get the risotto going, boil the barley in the water for 20–25 minutes until softened but still chewy in the middle.
3. In a frying pan, brown the chicken on both sides and place in a roasting dish. Drizzle with the lemon juice and season with the roasting spice and the salt. Pour in the chicken stock and cover with foil. Place in the oven and roast for 20–25 minutes until cooked throughout but still moist. Remove from the oven and allow to rest in a warm spot.
4. Drain the barley once cooked and set aside.
5. In the same pot you cooked the barley in, fry the leeks and garlic until soft and fragrant then add the barley. Stir to combine and add half of the chicken stock.
6. Stir the barley and chicken stock together and allow the stock to get absorbed. When the stock has been absorbed, taste the barley. If it still feels too firm for you, add the rest of the stock and repeat.
7. When the barley is cooked to your liking, add the cream and season with salt and pepper.
8. Serve the barley with the roasted chicken, its pan juices and a side salad.

This is great for those days when you have leftover chicken and potato in the fridge from a previous meal and you have no idea what to do with them. Combine them with fresh rocket and watercress, some feta cheese if you wish and toss with fresh pesto dressing. Of course you could make this from scratch as well, and in that case I suggest you poach the chicken to ensure it's succulent and juicy. Halve the baby potatoes, toss with olive oil, salt and pepper, and roast in a very hot oven for 15–20 minutes until they are just cooked. Simple and delicious.

WARM CHICKEN AND POTATO SALAD WITH PESTO DRESSING

Serves 4

2 cups cooked chicken, cut into large chunks

2 cups cooked baby potatoes, halved

1 packet fresh rocket

1 packet fresh watercress

feta cheese, crumbled (optional)

Dressing

3 tablespoons fresh basil pesto

2 tablespoons olive oil

½ tablespoon lemon juice

1 teaspoon salt

1. Combine the chicken and potatoes with the rocket and watercress. Crumble over the feta cheese.
2. To make the dressing, simply mix together the ingredients and drizzle over the salad.
3. Serve immediately.

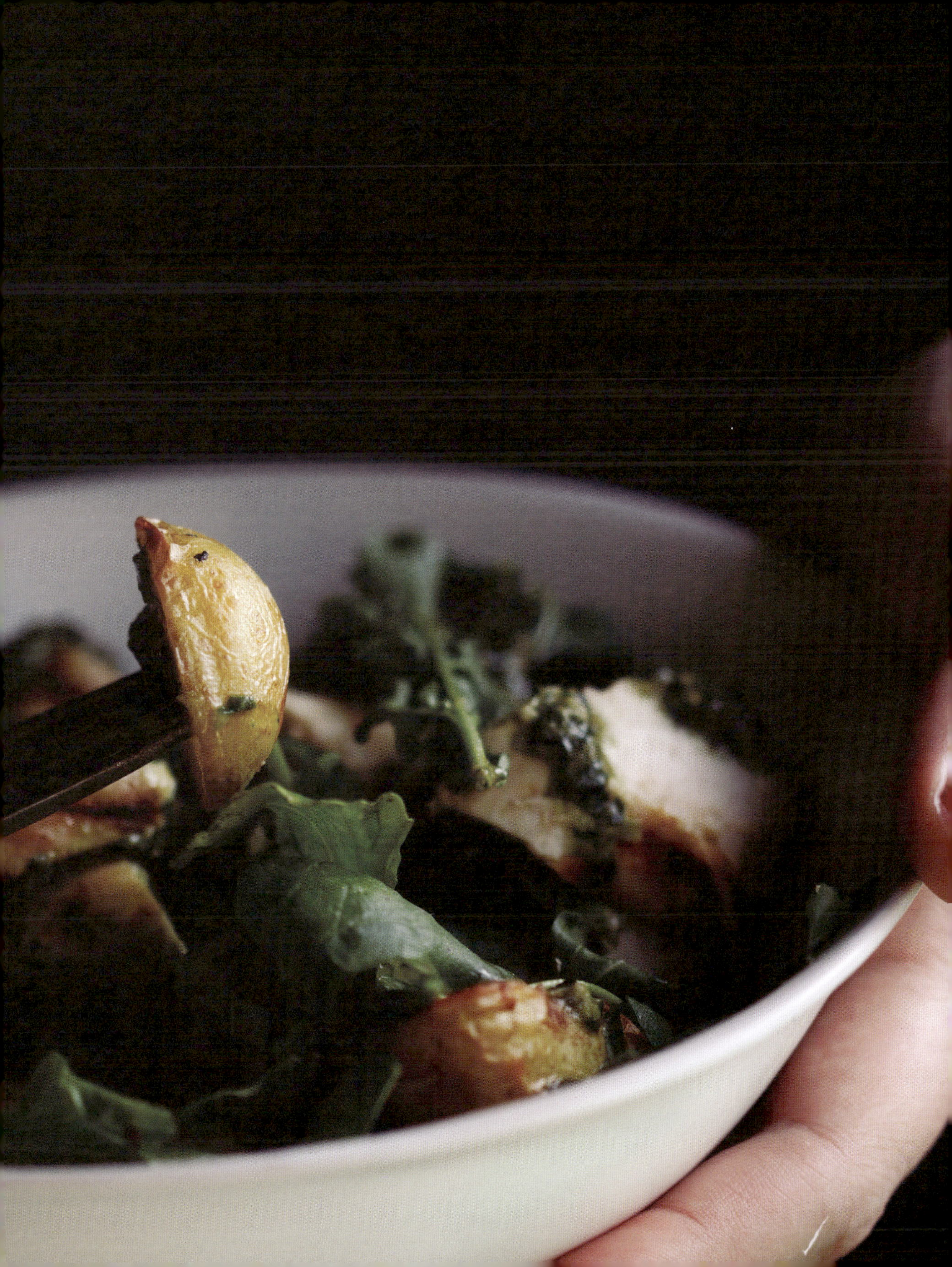

You would think that these would be loved only by children but I often find that the adults look at a platter of pint-sized burgers more longingly than the kids do – so these are great to serve with drinks at a party!

Using chicken sausages makes for easy assembly and all you need is cocktail burger buns, small squares of cheese and a few sliced cherry tomatoes to make this a delicious little burger.

MINI CHICKEN BURGERS WITH SWEET POTATO FRIES

Makes approximately 12–15 mini chicken burgers

1 onion, finely chopped (I use my food processor)

2 garlic cloves, crushed

800 g chicken sausage

1 egg yolk

½ teaspoon salt

handful fresh parsley, chopped

To assemble

cocktail burger buns

mayonnaise

cheese, sliced into small squares

lettuce

cherry tomatoes, sliced

Sweet potato fries

4 large sweet potatoes, peeled and sliced into fries

3 tablespoons oil

2 teaspoons salt

1. Pre-heat the oven to 200 °C.
2. To make the chicken burgers, first fry the onion and garlic until soft and translucent.
3. Squeeze the sausage meat from the casings and combine with the fried onion and garlic, egg yolk, salt and parsley.
4. With wet hands, shape the patties and place on a paper-lined baking tray. Place in the refrigerator for 20 minutes.
5. To make the sweet potato fries, combine the sliced sweet potatoes with the oil and salt and place in a large roasting tray.
6. Place in the oven and allow to bake for 20–25 minutes until cooked and golden.
7. When the chicken patties have firmed up slightly, fry them in batches in a large frying pan until browned on both sides and cooked through.
8. To serve, slice the cocktail buns in half, layer the mayonnaise, lettuce, chicken patties, cheese and cherry tomatoes on the sliced cocktail buns. To hold everything in place, push a cocktail bamboo skewer through each burger.
9. Serve with the sweet potato fries.

MEAT

LAMB SHANK PIES

Serves 4

2-4 lamb shanks, depending on size

1 large onion, finely chopped

2 garlic cloves, crushed

2 tins chopped tomatoes

2 tablespoons tomato paste (one small tin)

2 cups lamb or beef stock

few sprigs of fresh thyme

2 bay leaves

2 teaspoons sugar

1 teaspoon salt

black pepper to taste

1 roll ready-made puff pastry, defrosted

beaten egg yolk

1. Pre-heat the oven to 160 °C.
2. In a large, ovenproof pot fry the lamb shanks in olive oil until browned all over. Remove from the pot and set aside.
3. Fry the onions and garlic until soft and translucent. Add the tomatoes, tomato paste, stock, herbs and seasoning and allow to simmer for 5 minutes.
4. Place the lamb shanks in the sauce, coat the shanks in some of the sauce and place a lid on top.
5. Place the pot in the oven and allow to cook for 2-3 hours until the meat falls from the bone and the sauce has reduced.
6. Remove the pot from the oven and remove most of the meat from the bones.
7. Turn the oven up to 180 °C.
8. Mix the meat with the sauce and transfer to a baking dish.
9. Arrange the bones in the sauce so that they are facing upwards.
10. Push the pastry over the bones (so that the bones stick out of the pastry). To make this easier, hold the pastry above the bones and mark where the bones will be coming through, then cut a slit into each spot.
11. Press the pastry onto the sides of the baking dish. If there are any holes in the pastry, simply cut off some of the pastry from the sides of the dish and patch them up.
12. Brush the pie with the beaten egg yolk and place in the oven.
13. Bake for 20-25 minutes until the pastry is golden brown and cooked throughout.
14. Remove from the oven and allow to stand for 5 minutes before serving.

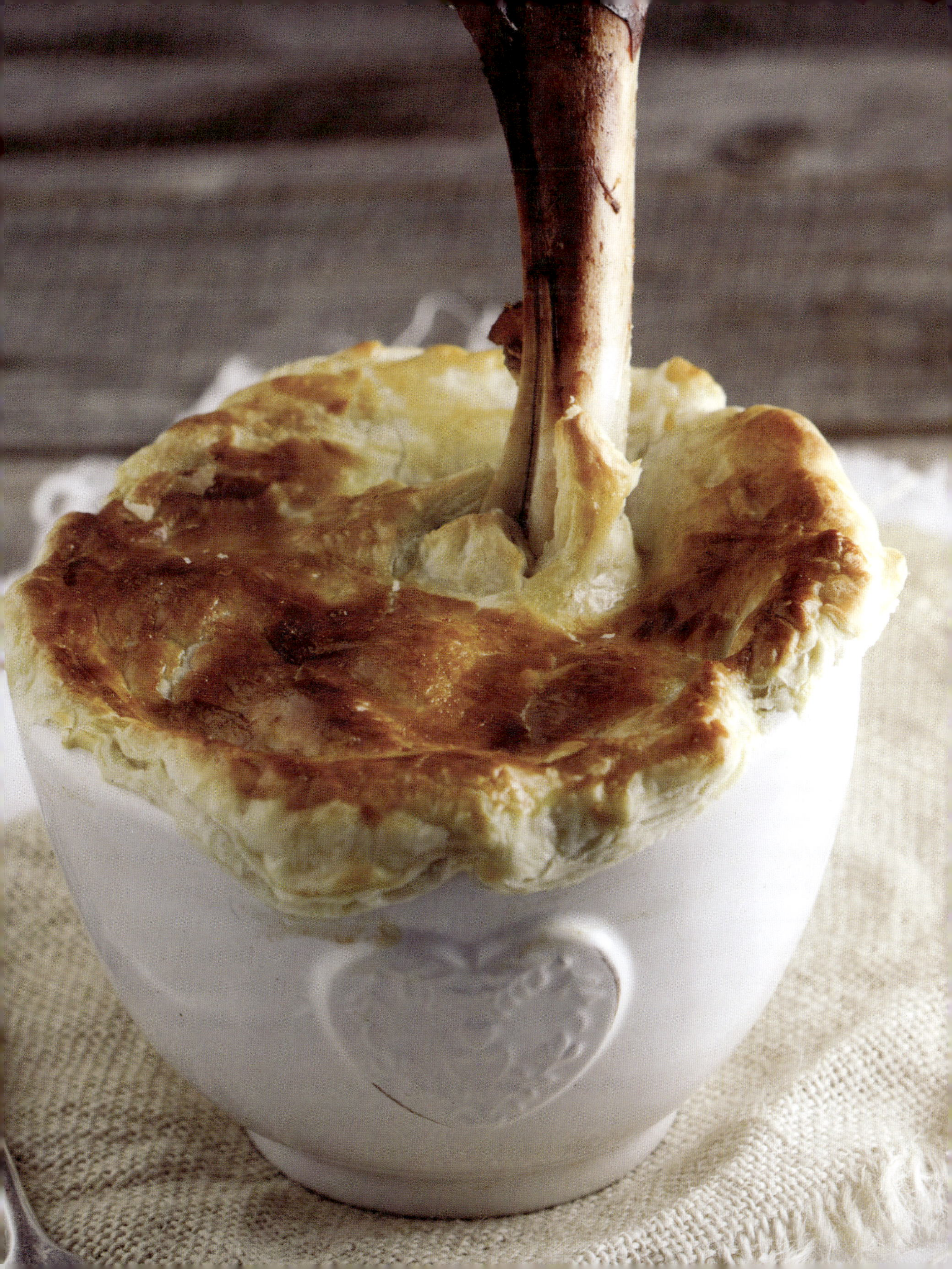

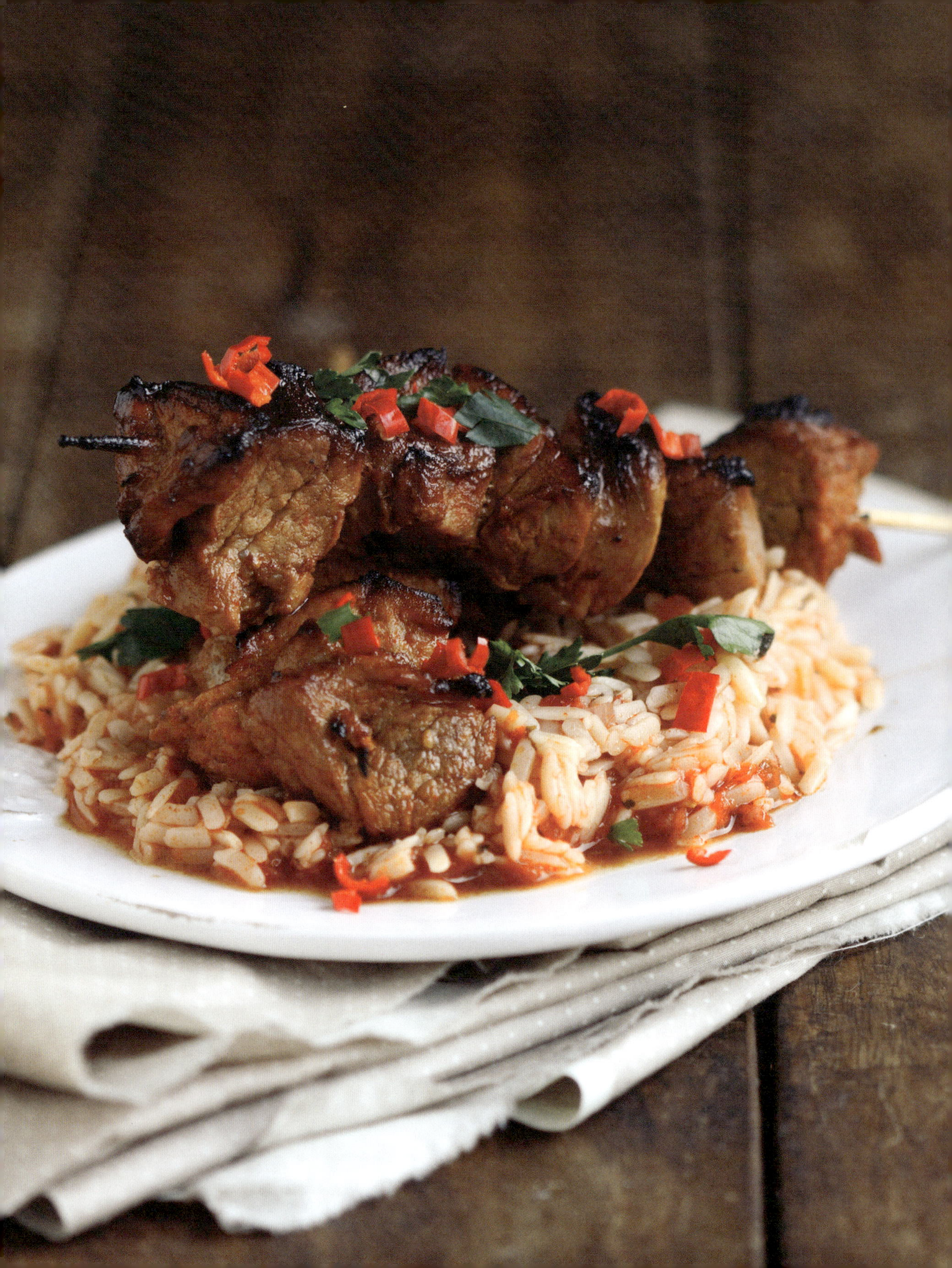

This is a great idea for a fast weeknight meal as the preparation is minimal. If you like you can put the pork in the marinade the night before, but even 10 minutes is enough time. Pork fillet is readily available in most supermarkets lately but I find the ones at my butcher to be of much better quality and also much cheaper. To make this more child-friendly, simply leave the chillies out of the sauce.

PORK KEBABS ON SPICY TOMATO ORZO

Serves 4

2 x 300-400 g pork fillets, cut into rough cubes

50 ml olive oil

200 ml apple juice

1 teaspoon paprika

1 garlic clove, crushed

1 teaspoon salt

2 tablespoons lemon juice

Spicy tomato orzo

1 red onion, finely chopped

olive oil

2 garlic cloves, crushed

1 tin chopped tomatoes

1 tablespoon red chilli, finely chopped (seeds removed if you want it less spicy)

1 teaspoon fresh thyme

1 teaspoon sugar

salt and pepper to taste

300 g orzo or risoni pasta

1. If you are using wooden kebab skewers, soak them in water for at least an hour before you start cooking (or even overnight).
2. Combine the pork fillet cubes with all the marinade ingredients and allow to marinate for at least 10 minutes.
3. In the meantime, get started on the tomato sauce. Sauté the onion in a little olive oil until soft and translucent. Add the garlic, tomatoes, chilli, thyme and sugar and allow to simmer until the sauce has reduced slightly. Season to taste and set aside.
4. Thread the pork cubes onto the soaked skewers (or metal skewers if you have them). Grill or fry the pork, until cooked throughout.
5. Cook the orzo in salted, boiling water until al dente (about 10 minutes) and toss with the tomato sauce.
6. Serve the pork kebabs on the spicy tomato orzo with a side salad.

A Sunday roast with all the trimmings must be one of my absolute favourite meals. It is so synonymous with home, it just calls for a family gathering. A leg of lamb is particularly indulgent and delicious; it's definitely my number one choice of roast. And I love almost anything with it. Smooth butternut flavoured with cinnamon, sautéed green beans, roast potatoes and creamy spinach are all amazing, but over the years I've decided that beans smothered in crème fraîche and honey-roasted carrots are my favourite sides to serve with a roasted leg of lamb.

ROAST LAMB
WITH 3-HOUR POTATOES, CRÈME FRAÎCHE-SMOTHERED GREEN BEANS AND HONEY-ROASTED CARROTS

Serves 8–10

3 kg leg of lamb (to make carving easier, you could ask the butcher to debone it for you, which will also cut down on the roasting time)

3 tablespoons olive oil

1 tablespoon salt

½ tablespoon pepper or roasting rub

4 sprigs fresh rosemary

handful fresh thyme

2 onions, quartered

1 garlic bulb, halved

1 cup lamb stock

3-hour potatoes

1 large potato per person, peeled and chopped into large chunks

2 teaspoons salt

Honey-roasted carrots

1–1½ kg carrots, peeled and cut into thirds

3 tablespoons olive oil

3 tablespoons honey

1 teaspoon salt

Crème fraîche-smothered green beans

700 g green beans, trimmed and halved

2 garlic cloves, finely sliced

2 heaped tablespoons crème fraîche

salt and pepper to taste

Gravy

juices from roasting tray

1–2 cups lamb stock

2 tablespoons flour mixed with 2 tablespoons water

salt and pepper to taste

1. Pre-heat the oven to 180 °C.
2. Pour the oil over the leg of lamb and with your hands and rub it all over. Season the lamb with the salt and roasting rub or spice.
3. Place the herbs, onion and garlic in a large roasting tray and put the leg of lamb on top. Pour in the lamb stock.
4. Place the peeled and chopped potatoes around the lamb and season with the salt.
5. Cover the roasting tray with foil and place in the oven.
6. Allow 45 minutes per 500 g lamb. If you want your lamb to be pink when carving, work on about 30–35 minutes per 500 g.
7. 45 minutes before the lamb and potatoes should come out of the oven, remove the foil to allow the lamb to brown.
8. Combine the carrots with the oil, honey and salt in a large bowl and tip into a roasting tray. Place into the oven and allow to roast for 30–35 minutes alongside the lamb and potatoes.
9. To prepare the green beans, steam the trimmed and halved beans for 10 minutes.
10. When they have steamed, sauté with the garlic for 5 minutes before adding the crème fraîche. Season to taste.
11. When the lamb is cooked to your liking, remove it from the oven and cover with foil. Allow to rest for 15–20 minutes while you make the gravy.
12. Simply pour the juices from the roasting pan into a small saucepan. You need about 2 cups of liquid so make up the rest of the liquid with lamb stock if there isn't enough in the roasting tray.
13. Allow to come to the boil and add 2 tablespoons flour mixed with 2 tablespoons water. Allow to simmer and thicken for 10 minutes. Season to taste.
14. Serve the carved lamb with the potatoes, green beans, carrots and gravy.

People often complain that they buy big bottles of spices and then only use them for one recipe, and I always feel sad when I hear that. It is because of spices and herbs that I am a good cook today. When I was growing up we didn't have very extravagant ingredients in our freezer or pantry but we always had a lot of spices and dried herbs. I was always very adventurous and would add any spice to a dish without thinking twice about it. Through a lot of trial and error I developed a very good palate and I realised what works and what doesn't.

With these beautiful Bollywood lamb chops, spices play a big roll. If you don't have all the ones listed in the ingredients, you can use a good-quality garam masala. The cucumber and red onion salad adds just the right amount of tang to complement the chops, while at the same time acting as a cooling agent for the fiery chillies.

BOLLYWOOD LAMB CHOPS WITH CUCUMBER SALAD

Serves 4

8 lamb chops

1 onion, finely chopped

2 garlic cloves, crushed

2 teaspoons ground cumin

2 tablespoons ground coriander

2 teaspoons smoked paprika

½ teaspoon each nutmeg and ground cloves

2 teaspoons turmeric

1–2 teaspoons chilli powder

olive oil

Cucumber salad

1 large cucumber, peeled, seeds removed

1 large red onion, peeled

5 tablespoons white vinegar

1 teaspoon sugar

½ teaspoon salt

black pepper to taste

1. Fry the onion and garlic in a little olive oil until soft and translucent and then add the spices. Allow to fry for a minute then transfer to a food processor.
2. Blend with just enough olive oil to make a thick paste.
3. Rub the paste onto the lamb chops and allow to rest for 2–3 minutes while you get the griddle pan heated and you make the cucumber salad.
4. Slice the cucumber and onion thinly and add to a medium bowl.
5. Dissolve the sugar in the vinegar and add the salt and pepper. Pour over the cucumber and onion and allow to marinate for 10–15 minutes before serving.
6. In a hot griddle pan, cook your lamb chops for 3–4 minutes per side and allow to rest for 5 minutes before serving with the cucumber salad.

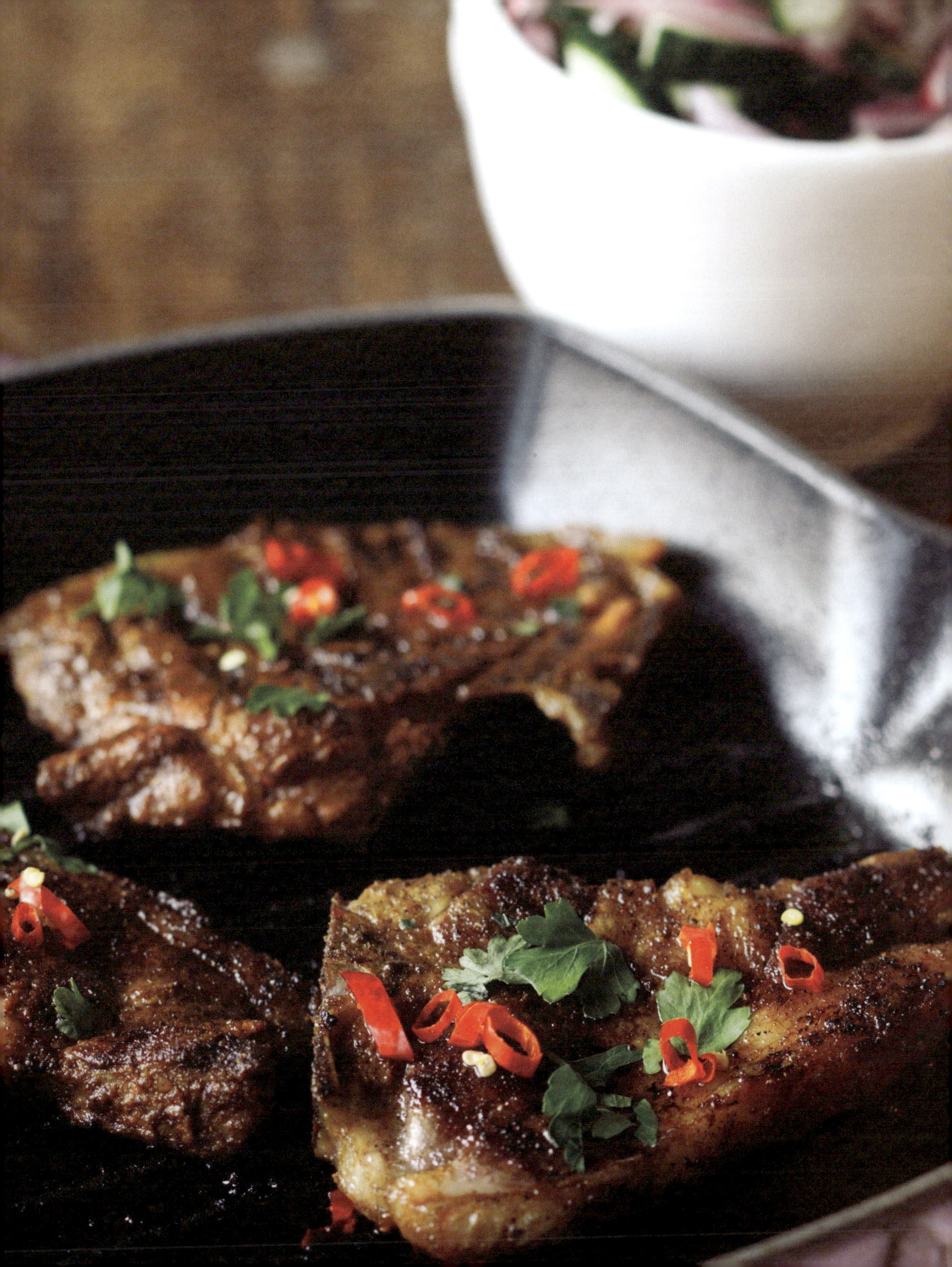

I love any food I can eat out of a bowl with just a fork. I find it instantly comforting, so when I need a little TLC I go for anything saucy, served with rice, pasta or mashed potatoes.

Beef stroganoff is one of my ultimate comfort food recipes. It's insanely simple to make, really delicious and slightly indulgent when you use beef fillet and mixed mushrooms.

I normally just buy the tubs of mixed mushrooms (sometimes labelled exotic mushrooms) from a supermarket but if you are lucky enough to get your hands on fresh, wild mushrooms, use them.

BEEF STROGANOFF WITH MIXED MUSHROOMS

Serves 4

- 1 onion, finely chopped
- 3 garlic cloves, finely sliced
- 300 g mixed mushrooms, wiped clean and sliced if they are large
- 500 g beef fillet, sliced into strips
- 2 teaspoons paprika
- 200 ml cream
- juice of ½ lemon
- handful fresh parsley, finely chopped
- salt and pepper to taste
- steamed rice, to serve
- crème fraîche or sour cream, to serve

1. In a large saucepan, fry the onion until soft and translucent and add the garlic. Fry for another minute.
2. Add the mushrooms and allow to fry for 5 minutes until they have softened. Remove from the pan and set aside.
3. In the same saucepan, fry the beef strips until browned all over. Put back the mushroom mixture and add the paprika, cream and lemon juice.
4. Allow to simmer for 5 minutes uncovered, until the sauce has thickened slightly and the beef is cooked.
5. Add the chopped parsley and season to taste.
6. Serve over steamed rice with a dollop of crème fraîche or sour cream.

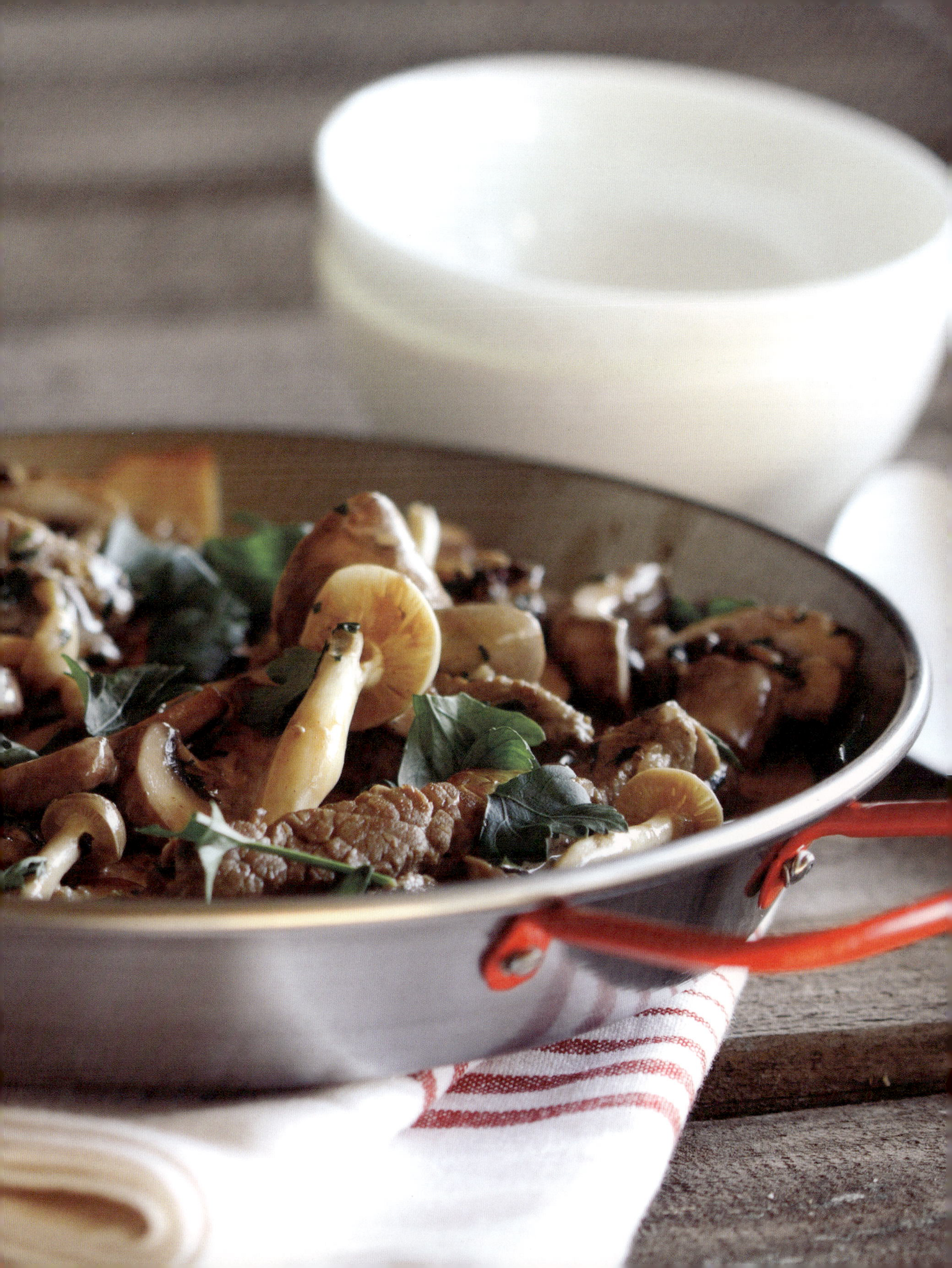

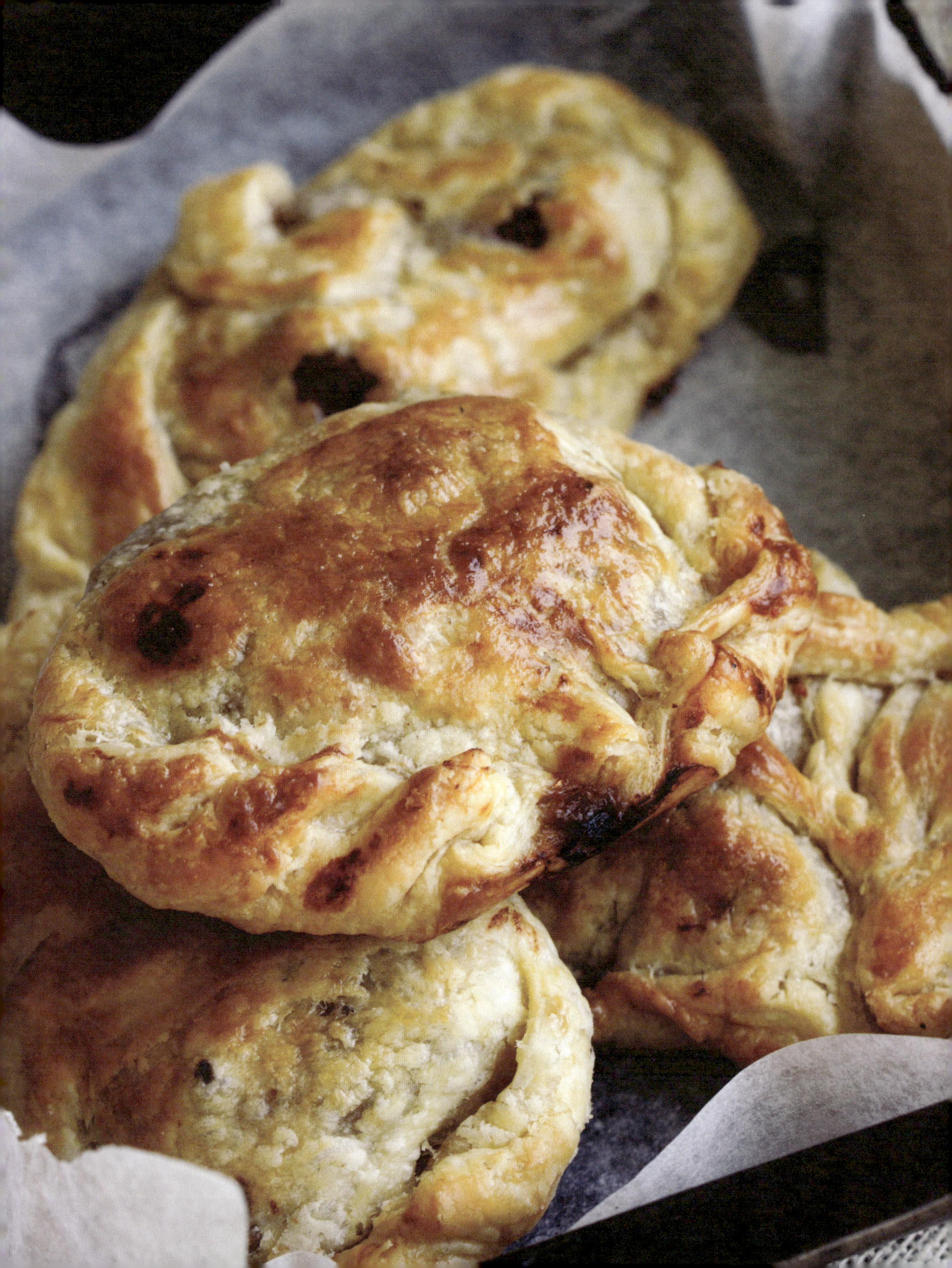

When you take flaky, buttery pastry and wrap it around an aromatic and spicy lamb curry, you achieve perfection in my books. This is such a great recipe for leftover curry but I love it so much that I'm willing to make the curry from scratch just to be able to stuff it into puff pastry.

LAMB CURRY EMPANADAS

Makes 6–8 empanadas

Curry

1 kg braising or stewing lamb, deboned
¾ cup flour seasoned with 1 teaspoon salt
2 onions, sliced
8 garlic cloves, crushed
5 cm piece of ginger, minced
2½ teaspoons garam masala
2 teaspoons ground coriander
2 teaspoons ground cumin
2 teaspoons turmeric
2 teaspoons fresh chilli (I leave the seeds in because I like it hot but if you prefer it milder either remove the seeds or use less chilli)
2 bay leaves
5 cardamom pods
2 cups lamb stock
1 tin chopped tomatoes

Empanadas

2 rolls ready-made puff pastry, defrosted
2 eggs, beaten

1. Dust the lamb with the flour.
2. In a large saucepan, brown the lamb in batches in some oil.
3. Remove all the meat from the pot and fry the onions, garlic and ginger until softened and lightly golden. Add the spices and fry until the mixture looks dry.
4. Add the bay leaves and cardamom pods and put the lamb back in.
5. Pour in the stock and the chopped tomatoes and stir to combine everything.
6. Allow to simmer (covered) for approximately 2 hours or until the lamb is really tender.
7. To make the empanadas, pre-heat the oven to 200 °C and line a roasting tray with baking paper.
8. Roll the pastry out slightly and cut out medium-sized ovals (approximately 10 cm in length).
9. Place a few tablespoons of the curry in the centre of the pastry and brush the edges with beaten egg. Fold the pastry over and crimp the edges. Brush with more egg and place on the tray. Continue until all the pastry has been used.
10. Place the tray in the oven and allow to bake for 15–20 minutes until the pastry is golden brown and cooked.
11. Serve immediately.

A few years ago I would've turned my nose up at this burger and told you that I don't eat fruit with meat. I actually didn't like anything sweet near anything savoury. But my palate has matured a bit since then and I appreciate the effect sweet and savoury flavours have on each other. I'm still not a big fan of fruit with meat (and don't bring stewed fruit anywhere near me) but pork and apples is just one of those classic, delicious combinations.

With these burgers the apple is used as a subtle flavouring more than a partner to the pork and its sweetness is just noticeable. I like to serve them with caramelised onions (I sometimes add some thinly sliced apples), sliced Camembert and fresh rocket.

PORK AND APPLE BURGERS

Serves 4

1 kg pork mince
2 apples, peeled and grated
1 red onion, grated
½ cup fresh parsley, chopped
2 cups fresh breadcrumbs
1 teaspoon salt
1 cup grated pecorino

To assemble

4 large bread rolls, sliced and toasted
100 g Camembert, sliced
caramelised onions
fresh rocket

1. In a large bowl, combine all the ingredients for the pork patties.
2. Mix well and to taste for seasoning, fry a teaspoon of the mixture in a frying pan to test. Adjust seasoning accordingly.
3. Shape the mixture into 4 patties and refrigerate for 20 minutes. (If you cover them with cling wrap, you can leave them overnight.)
4. Fry the patties in a large, heavy-based frying pan until golden on both sides and cooked through. Alternatively you can bake them on a baking sheet for 10–15 minutes.
5. Serve the patties on the toasted bread rolls with rocket, caramelised onions and slices of Camembert.

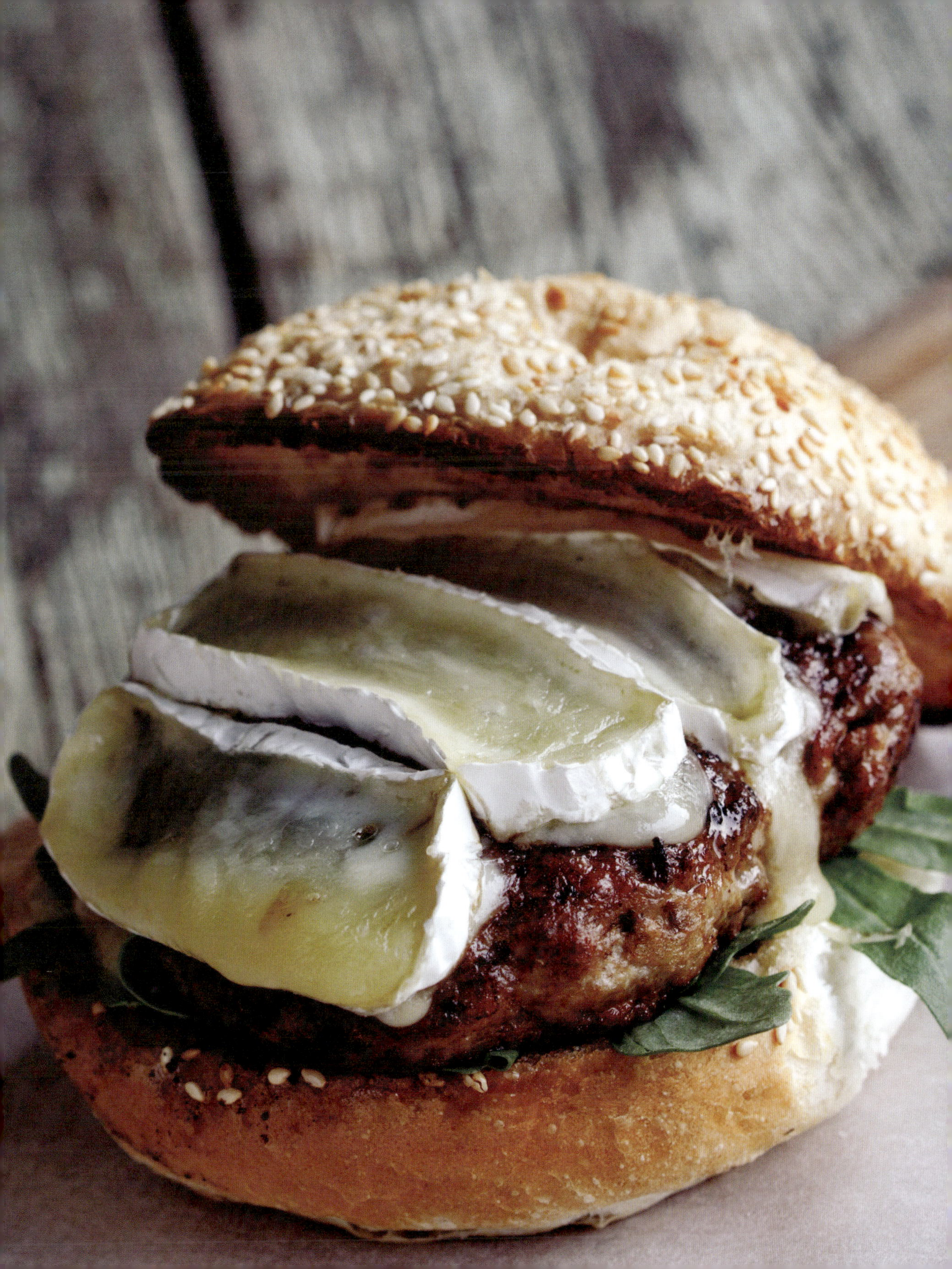

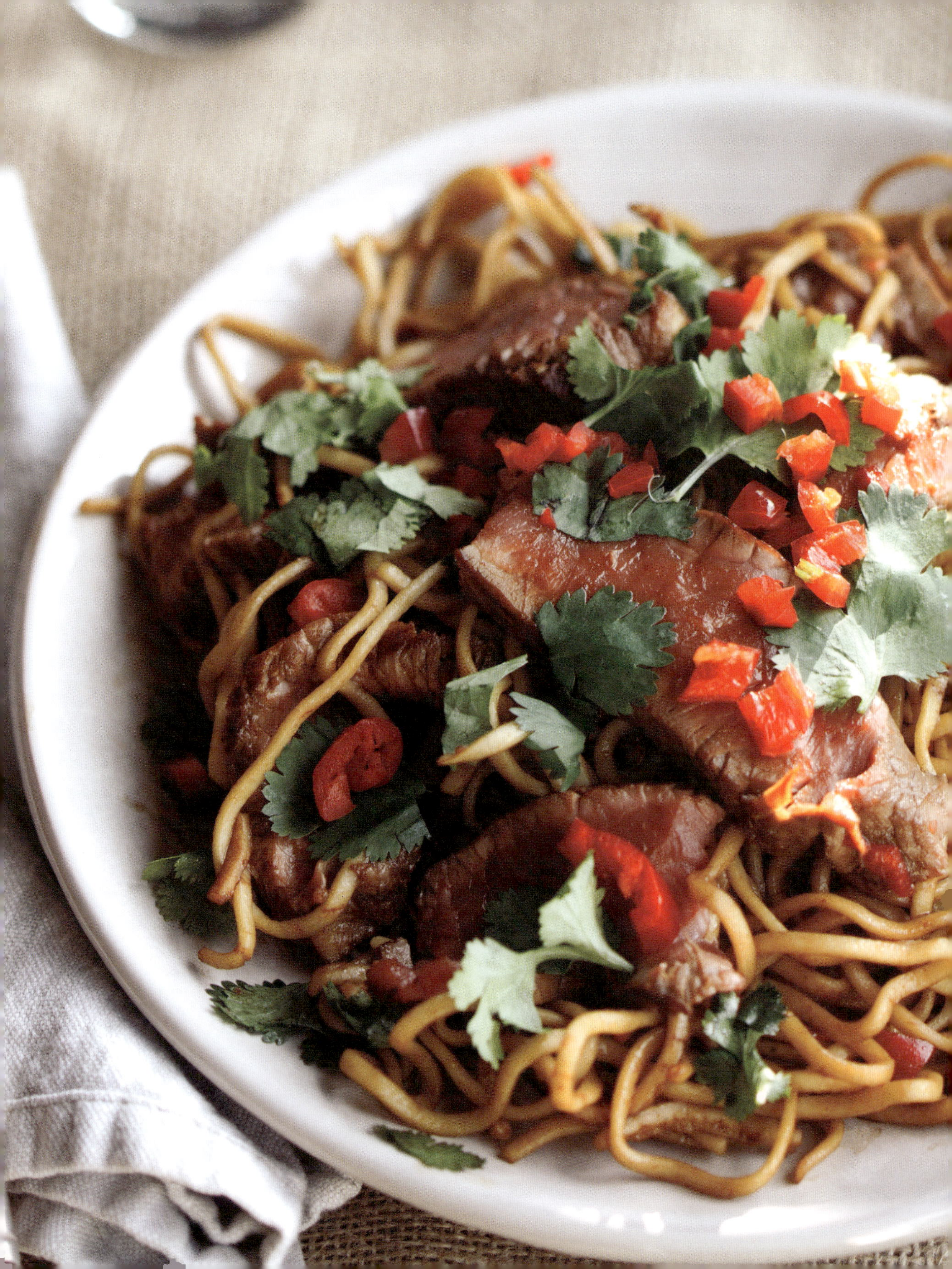

This is my go-to meal during scorching hot summer months when standing in the kitchen for longer than it takes to fill a glass with ice is just unbearable. I think what I love about it most is that the steak takes just a couple of minutes (if you like it rare to medium-rare like I do). If you can't find egg noodles (they should be available at most supermarkets), you can use the instant kind.

The dressing is light, fresh and zesty with just the right amount of chilli to add that necessary tingle. I enjoy this most sitting on the patio with the kids splashing in the pool and a big glass of Chenin in my hand.

THAI BEEF AND NOODLE SALAD

Serves 4

2 large rump steaks
2 tablespoons soy sauce

Noodle salad

300–400 g egg noodles
1 cup crushed salted peanuts

Dressing

1 onion, very finely chopped
2 garlic cloves, minced
2 cm piece of fresh ginger, minced or grated
1 red chilli, finely chopped (use as much as you can handle)
2 tablespoons honey
3 tablespoons soy sauce
3 tablespoons fish sauce
2 tablespoons canola oil

1. Place a griddle pan over high heat and allow to get hot. Fill a large pot with water and allow it to come to the boil for the noodles.
2. Brush the steaks with the soy sauce and grill to your liking. I like my steak to be rare to medium-rare so I only cook it for approximately 3–5 minutes (depending on thickness) per side.
3. Remove the steaks from the pan and allow to rest while you make the noodle salad.
4. Cook the noodles according to the package instructions, drain and put aside.
5. To make the dressing, combine all the dressing ingredients, except for the oil, in a food processor (or pestle and mortar) and pulse until everything is finely chopped.
6. Whilst the processor is running, drizzle in the oil and mix for another minute.
7. Toss the cooked noodles with the dressing and the crushed peanuts.
8. Slice the steaks and serve on top of the noodle salad. Serve with extra chopped chillies and fresh coriander.

The mellow sweetness and mild spiciness of korma make it a comforting and satisfying dish to make in winter. I also like the fact that it can be made over a few days (in fact I recommend this, as it improves the flavour) so you don't feel run off your feet chopping, marinating and cooking a curry. Keep things simple – steamed basmati rice and crispy, fried poppadoms are all you need to round off this stunning curry.

LAMB KORMA

Serves 4–6

Marinade

1½ cups cashew nuts
1 large onion, finely chopped
2 garlic cloves, crushed
2 teaspoons ginger, grated (about a 3 cm piece of fresh ginger)
2 teaspoons sugar
4 cups plain yoghurt
a little lamb stock or water if necessary for thinning out
1 teaspoon salt

Curry

1 kg lamb cubes, boneless (I use deboned leg of lamb)
2 onions, thinly sliced
canola oil
1 cinnamon stick
1 bay leaf
2 bruised cardamom pods
2 teaspoons turmeric
1 tablespoon garam masala (I use a mild one)
1 tablespoon ground coriander
2 teaspoons ground cumin
1–2 cups strong lamb stock or water
1 cup cream
salt to taste

1. To make the marinade, start by roasting the cashews for 5–10 minutes at 200 °C until they are golden brown. Keep an eye on them as they burn easily (you can also toast them in a frying pan).
2. Fry the onion, garlic and ginger until soft and translucent and add the sugar.
3. Place the onion mixture and roasted cashews in a food processor and process until you have a rough paste. Add some of the yoghurt and a little lamb stock or water to thin it out if necessary. You want the nuts to be finely chopped.
4. Mix the paste with the rest of the yoghurt and the salt and cover the lamb with the marinade.
5. Allow to marinate for at least an hour but up to a day, covered and refrigerated.
6. When you are ready to cook the lamb korma, fry the sliced onion in some canola oil with the cinnamon stick, bay leaf and cardamom pods until the onion is soft and translucent and the aromas have started escaping from the spices.
7. Add the ground spices and fry for another minute.
8. Add the lamb with the marinade and mix to combine everything.
9. At this point the curry might look a bit thick so to thin it out I like to use strong lamb stock, but you could also use water.
10. Turn the heat down, cover and allow to simmer for 1–2 hours until the lamb is meltingly tender and the sauce has thickened slightly. (Give it a stir every now and then as the nuts in the marinade can catch and burn easily.) Add the cream and season to taste.

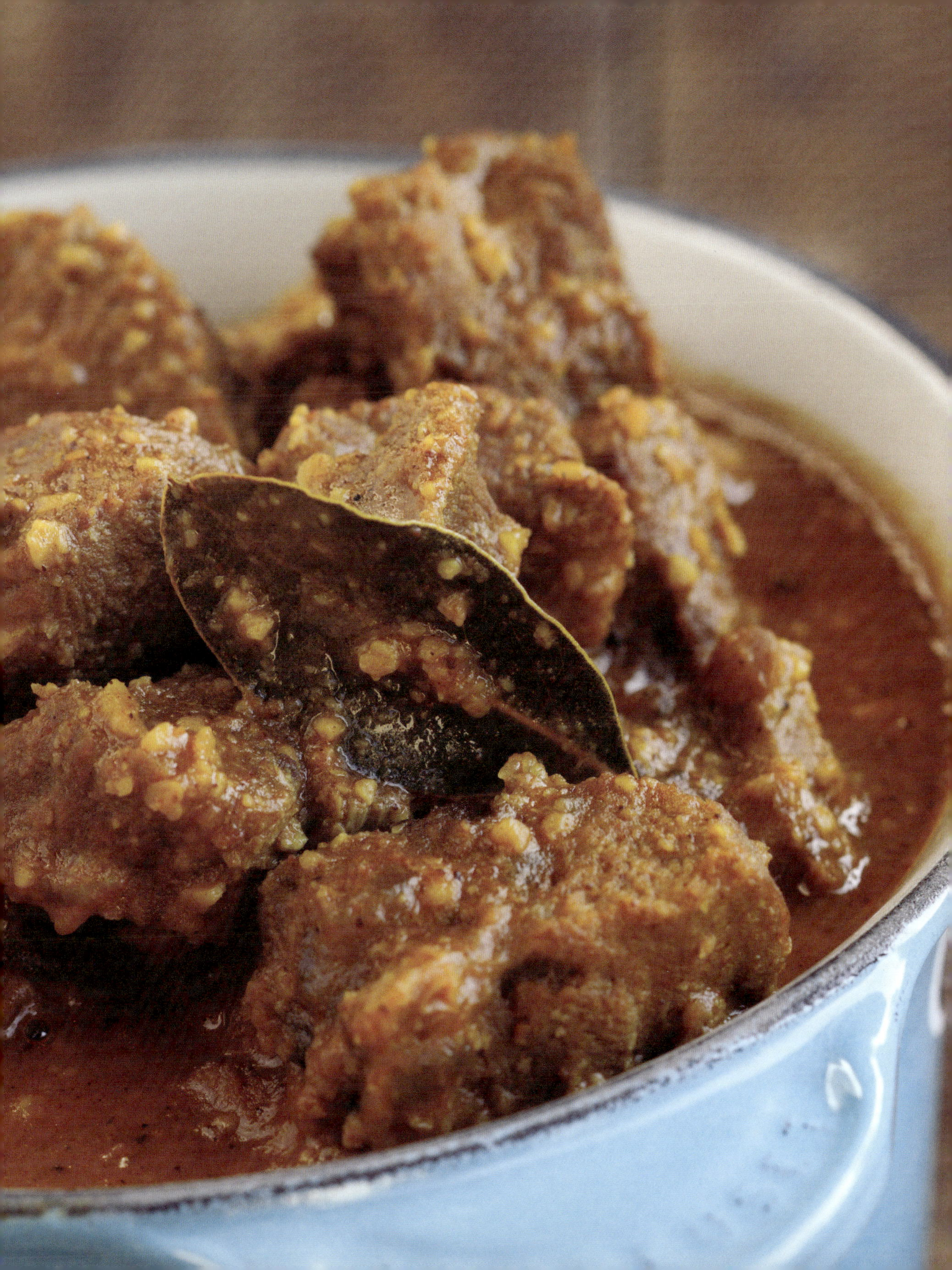

PORK CHOPS WITH MUSTARD SAUCE

Serves 4

Pork chops

4 pork chops, rind removed

2 tablespoons olive oil

juice of ½ lemon

salt and pepper to taste

Mustard sauce

½ onion

2 garlic cloves, crushed

2 teaspoons wholegrain mustard

2 teaspoons Dijon mustard

1 cup cream

juice of ½ lemon

salt and pepper to taste

1. Drizzle the olive oil and lemon juice over the pork chops and season with salt and pepper.
2. Fry the pork chops in a hot pan until golden brown and cooked through.
3. Meanwhile, chop the onion and then the garlic separately in the food processor until very finely minced.
4. Fry the onion in olive oil until soft and translucent. Add the garlic and fry for another 30 seconds.
5. Add the mustard and allow to fry for another 30 seconds before adding the cream and lemon juice.
6. Allow the sauce to simmer and reduce for 5-10 minutes.
7. Season to taste and serve over the cooked pork chops.
8. Serve with mashed potato and steamed greens.

Oxtail is such a proudly South African ingredient, I'm always shocked when I hear of people who don't eat it. This recipe is really simple but the slow braising in aromatic liquid brings out the delicious flavour of the meat and leaves it soft and tender. This is great served with steamed rice or buttery mash.

SLOW BRAISED OXTAIL

Serves 6–8

2 kg oxtail, sliced

few tablespoons olive oil for browning

2 large onions, finely chopped

5 stalks celery, finely chopped

4 large carrots, peeled and finely chopped

5 garlic cloves, crushed

1 cup red wine

2 large tomatoes, chopped (or use tinned)

1 litre beef stock

3 bay leaves

5 fresh thyme sprigs

handful fresh parsley, finely chopped

salt and pepper to taste

1. In a large, heavy-based pot, brown the oxtail in batches in olive oil.
2. Remove and set aside, add some more oil to the pot and fry the onions, celery and carrots until golden and just starting to soften.
3. Add the garlic and sauté for another minute.
4. Add the red wine and allow to reduce for 5 minutes.
5. Add the tomatoes and put the oxtail back in the pot.
6. Pour in the beef stock and add the bay leaves and fresh thyme.
7. Reduce the heat and simmer gently for 3–4 hours (if it gets too dry, add a bit more water or beef stock)
8. When the meat is tender, add the fresh parsley and season to taste.

Serving a simple pork steak with sweet and tangy balsamic onions takes an everyday ingredient and turns it into something special.

I like to serve these pork steaks with garlicky, crushed baby potatoes and steamed green beans for a simple and delicious meal.

PORK STEAKS WITH BALSAMIC ONIONS

Serves 4

½ cup olive oil

½ cup soy sauce

juice of 1 lemon

1 teaspoon salt

4 pork steaks

Balsamic onions

3 red onions, thinly sliced

2 tablespoons olive oil

2 tablespoons balsamic vinegar

2 teaspoons sugar

juice of ½ lemon

pinch of salt

1. Combine the olive oil, soy sauce, lemon juice and salt and marinate the pork steaks for 10–20 minutes while you get going on the onions.
2. Fry the onions in 2 tablespoons olive oil for 10–15 minutes over gentle heat, uncovered, until they are soft and just starting to turn golden.
3. Add the balsamic vinegar, sugar, lemon juice and salt and allow to cook for another 5–10 minutes until they are sticky and caramelised.
4. Cook the pork steaks in a hot pan for 4–5 minutes per side, depending on thickness. Make sure that the steaks are cooked all the way through but still juicy and moist.
5. Serve the steaks with the balsamic onions.

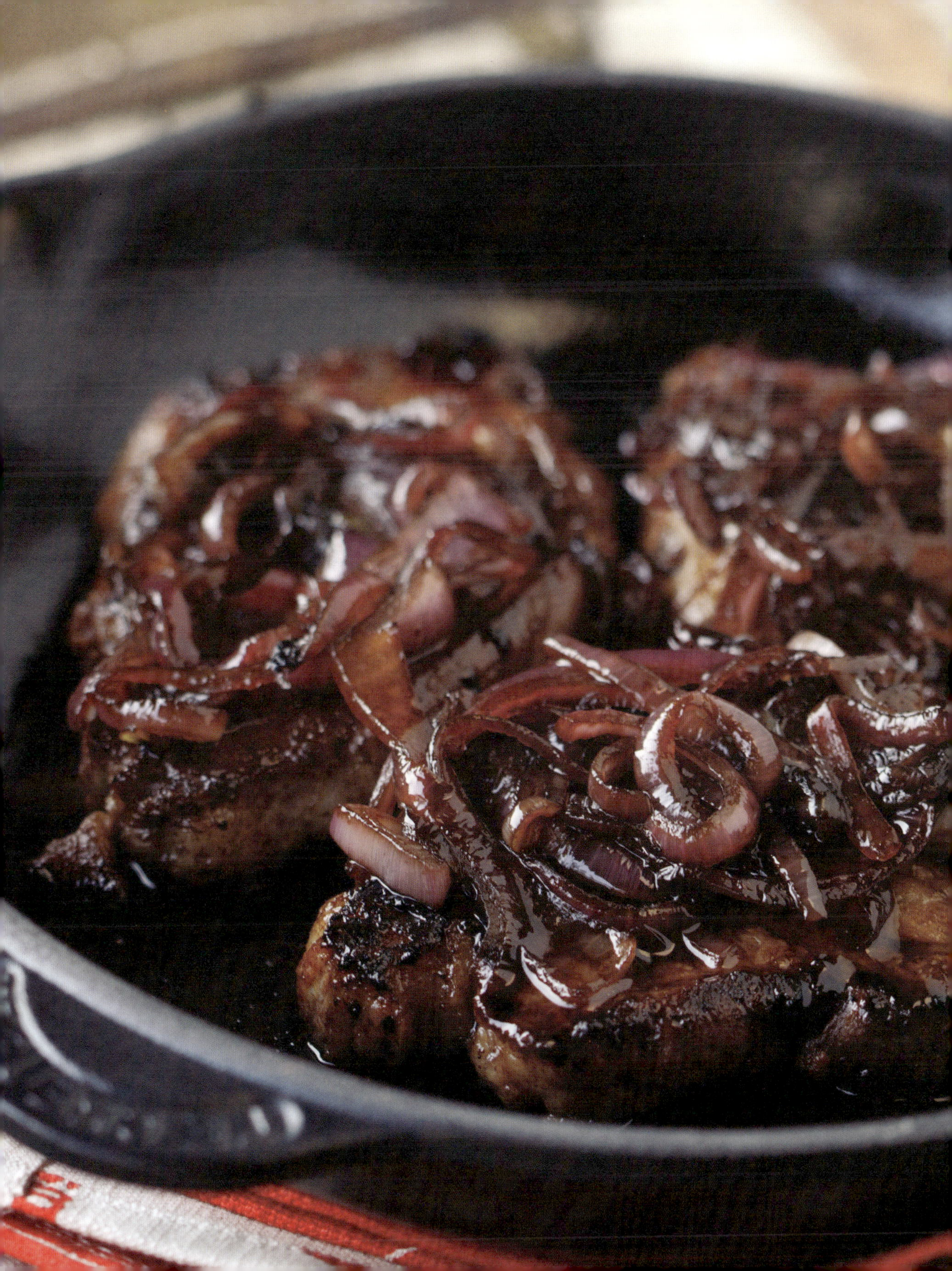

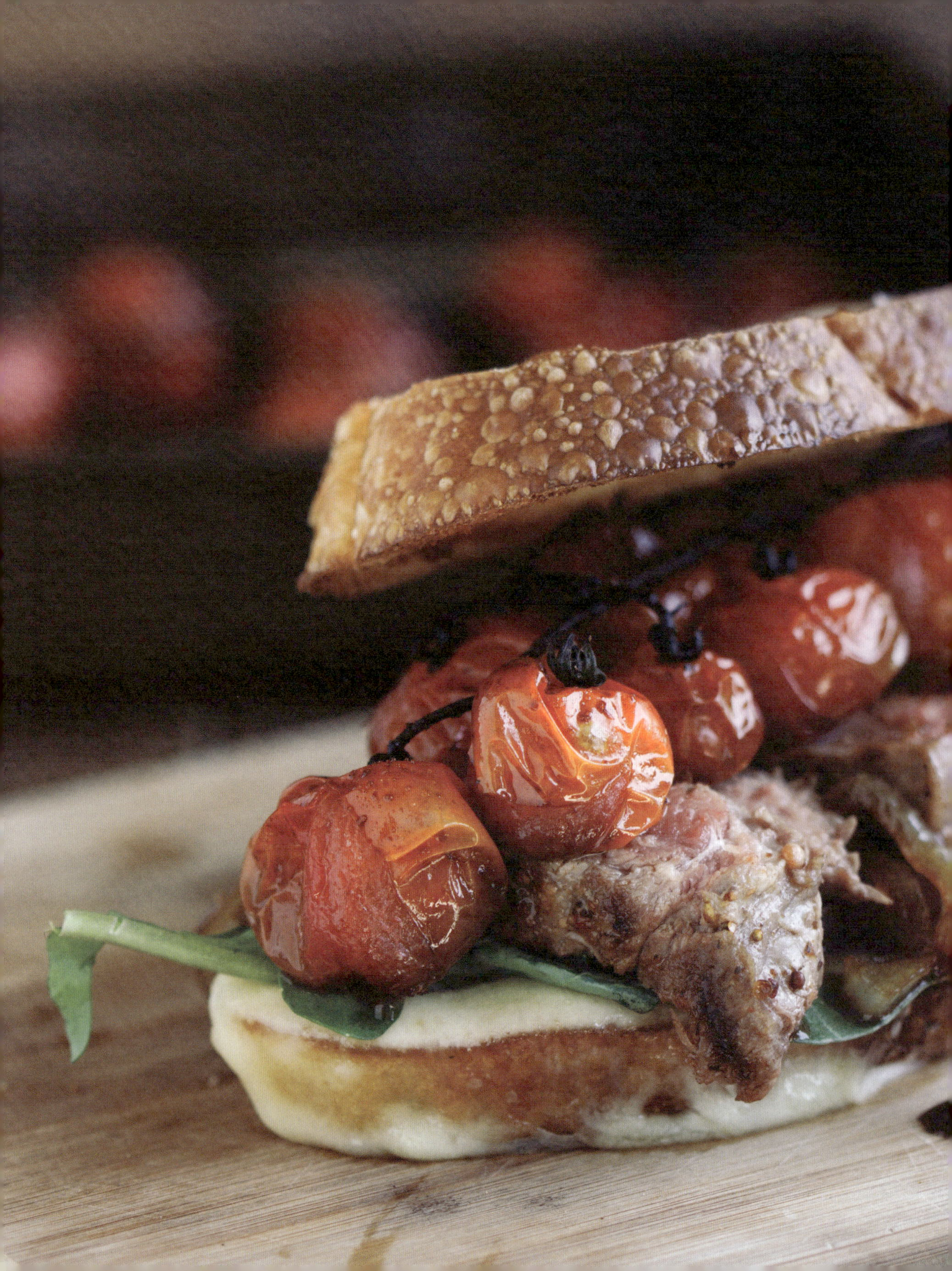

I've been making steak sandwiches for years now and have made them with every type of bread imaginable, all types of cheese, as well as assorted vegetables, sauces and condiments. Through trial and error I've come up with my absolute favourite combination but, as always, if you feel like adding an ingredient or leaving one out, feel free to do so.

MY ULTIMATE STEAK SANDWICH

Serves 2, generously

Roasted tomatoes

2 large tomatoes, sliced thickly or
    2 cups cherry tomatoes, halved
2 tablespoons olive oil
1 tablespoon balsamic vinegar
1 teaspoon salt

Caramelised onions

2 onions, thinly sliced
2 teaspoons sugar
1 tablespoon balsamic vinegar
pinch of salt

Steaks

2 x 200 g rump steaks
2 tablespoons olive oil
steak seasoning or salt

To assemble

4 slices sourdough bread
100 g mozzarella, sliced
hot English mustard
fresh rocket

1. Pre-heat the oven to 220 °C.
2. Place the tomatoes in a roasting tray and drizzle with olive oil and balsamic vinegar and season with salt.
3. Place in the oven and allow to roast for 15–20 minutes. Remove from the oven and set aside. Switch on the grill of your oven to toast the bread later.
4. In a frying pan, fry the onions until soft and translucent. Add the sugar and balsamic vinegar and allow to cook for 5–10 minutes until the onions are caramelised. Set aside.
5. Drizzle the steaks with olive oil and season with either steak seasoning or salt. Fry or grill in a hot pan until cooked to your preference. I only cook the steaks for 2–3 minutes per side so they are still quite rare.
6. Remove from the pan and allow to rest for 5–10 minutes.
7. Before you start assembling the sandwich, drizzle the sourdough bread with olive oil and place under the hot grill until toasted on both sides.
8. Place the sliced mozzarella on two of the slices and place back under the grill until melted and golden.
9. Spread some hot English mustard on the slices of bread without mozzarella.
10. To assemble the sandwich, place some fresh rocket on the slice of bread with melted mozzarella, followed by the sliced steak, roasted tomatoes and caramelised onions. Top with the other slice of bread and serve.

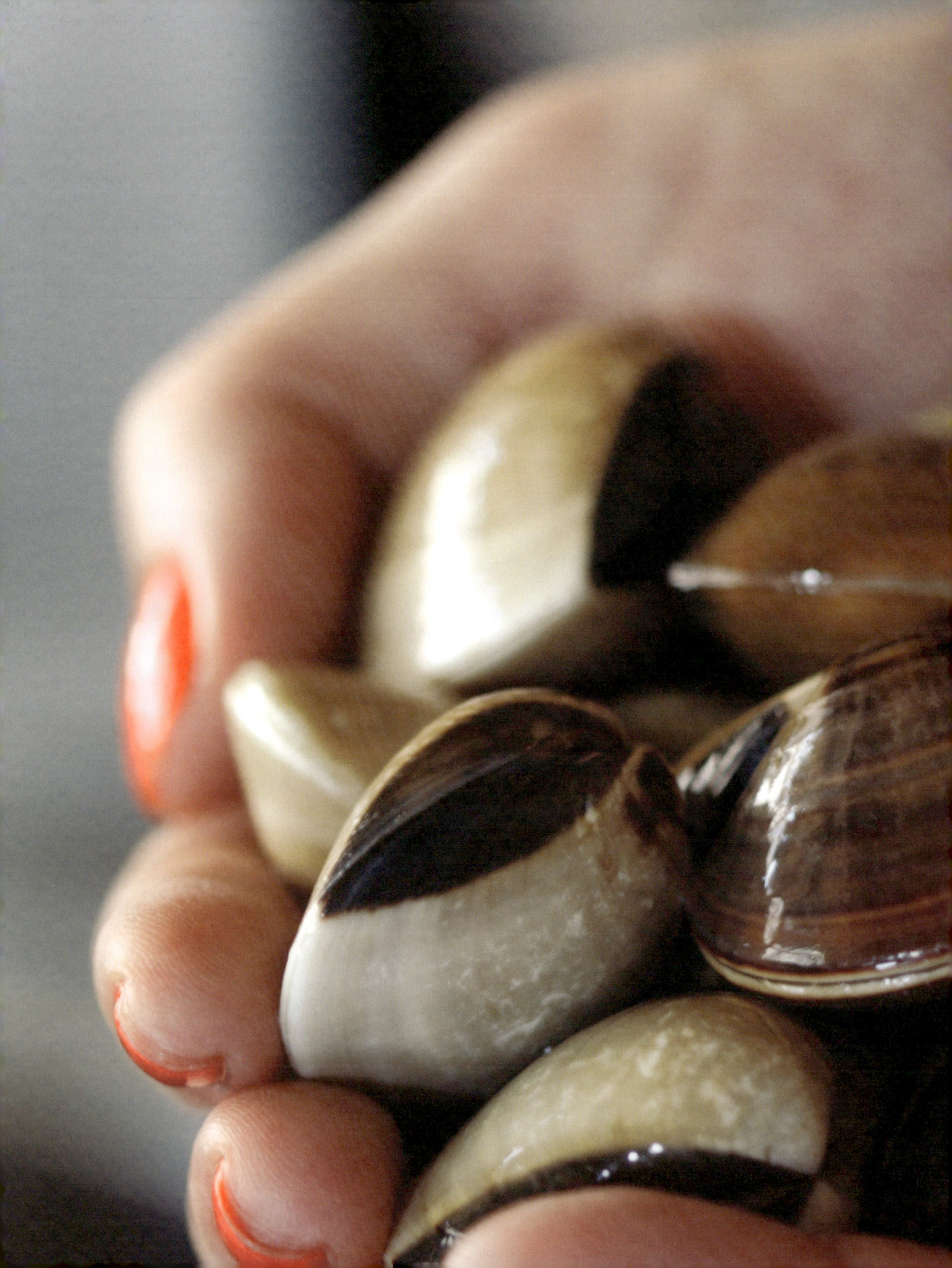

SEAFOOD

This is really a simpler version of paella without the chicken, chorizo or saffron. I came up with it for the simple reason that I didn't have those ingredients at the time and I wanted to create a dish I could serve to my pescatarian friends.

As with most of my recipes, the seafood used here can be replaced with anything you fancy. I've chosen prawns, calamari and mussels as those are three of my favourites, but firm white fish, scallops or clams can all be added or substituted. If you are using fresh mussels, steam them in white wine first to allow them to open and to ensure there's no grittiness left in them. If you are using half-shell, frozen mussels, simply add them to the rice when you add the prawns and calamari.

Baking this in the oven allows you some freedom to enjoy a glass of wine with your guests or to relax after work while it cooks. I like to serve this with a simple green salad and some extra lemon butter.

BAKED SEAFOOD RICE

Serves 4–6

50 g butter

1 tablespoon olive oil

2 red onions, finely chopped

4 garlic cloves, thinly sliced

1 teaspoon smoked paprika

500 g Arborio rice

50 g tomato paste

1½ litres chicken, vegetable or fish stock

500 g fresh mussels, debearded and cleaned

500 g prawns, deveined

500 g calamari tubes, cleaned and sliced into rings

juice of 1 lemon

salt and pepper to taste

1. In a large, ovenproof frying pan, melt the butter with a tablespoon of olive oil.
2. Fry the onion and garlic until soft and translucent.
3. Add the smoked paprika and Arborio rice and stir to combine all the ingredients.
4. Dissolve the tomato paste in the stock and reserve 1 cup of the stock for later use. Pour the rest of the stock into the rice, stir and cover with a lid or foil.
5. Place in the oven and allow to bake for 25–30 minutes until the rice is almost cooked but still has some bite to it.
6. At this stage the rice might be quite dry, in which case add the reserved stock and lemon juice. You can also season to taste at this point.
7. Add the seafood to the rice. Lightly mix everything so that the seafood doesn't just sit on top.
8. Cover with a lid once more and place back in the oven for 10–15 minutes until the seafood is cooked.
9. Serve with lemon butter and a green salad.

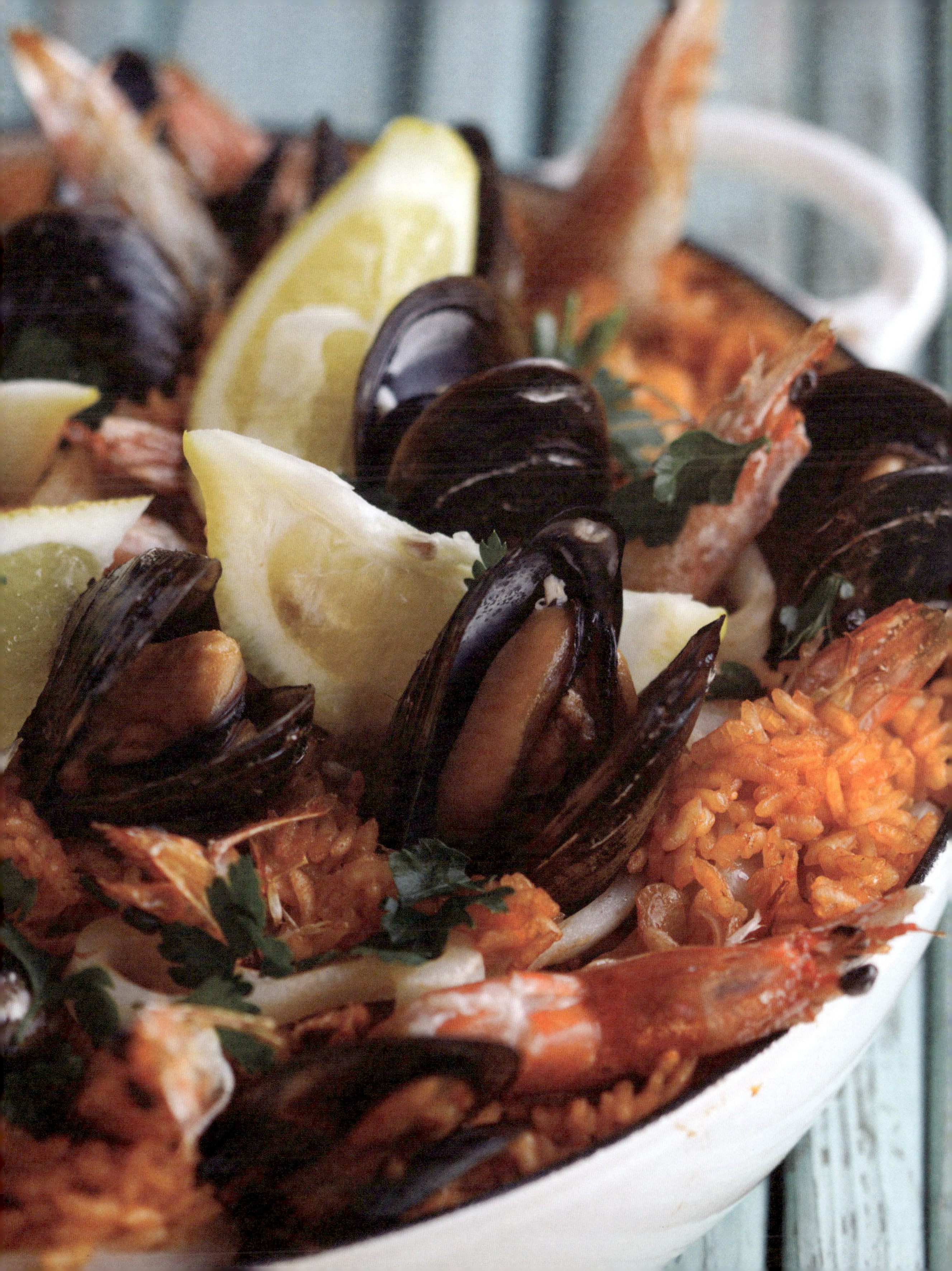

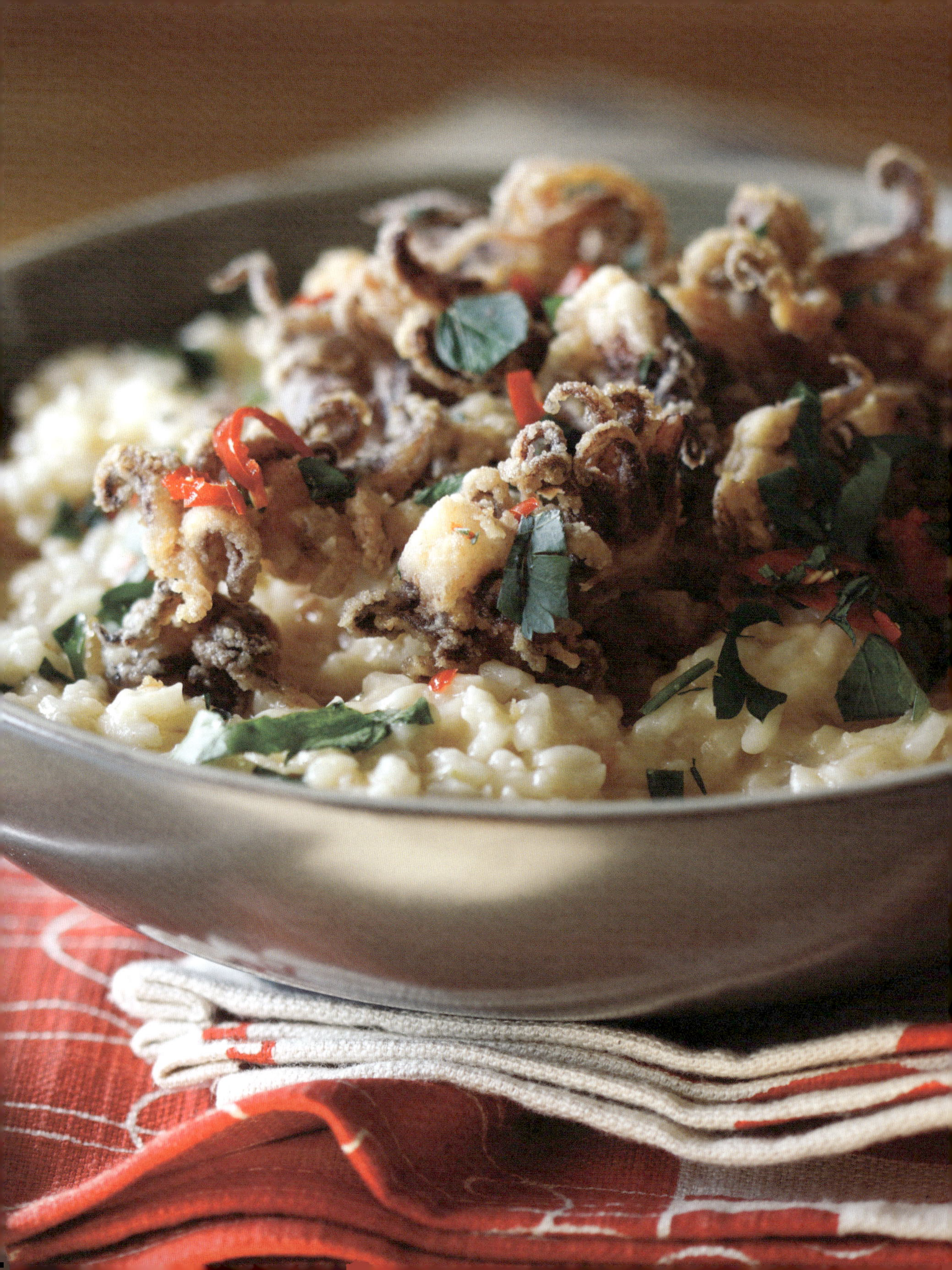

This is one of my favourite risotto recipes. I love the way the creamy and spicy risotto is complemented by the lemony, crispy calamari. The spiciness of this risotto really depends on your own taste. If you want it to be milder, simply remove the seeds from the chillies before chopping them up.

Making a risotto is a laborious process because you can't leave the pot unattended and you have to add the hot stock ladle by ladle, but it is well worth the effort.

SPICY RISOTTO WITH CRISPY CALAMARI

Serves 4

2 litres chicken stock
2-3 tablespoons olive oil
1 large onion, finely diced
4 garlic cloves, crushed
1-2 chillies, finely chopped
2 teaspoons paprika
500 g Arborio rice
200 ml white wine
juice of 1 lemon
100 g pecorino, grated

Crispy calamari

400 g calamari rings/ squid, cleaned
2 tablespoons cornflour
2 tablespoons cake flour
1 teaspoon salt
oil for deep frying

1. Have your prepared hot stock ready, either simmering in a separate pot, or in a jug or bowl.
2. In a large pot or pan, heat the olive oil and fry the onion until translucent. Add the garlic, chilli and paprika and fry for another minute or two.
3. Add the rice and stir, coating the rice with the spicy oil. Add the wine and allow to reduce.
4. Now add the stock ladle by ladle, stirring in between additions and allowing the rice to absorb the stock. The rice shouldn't be completely dry before you add more; it should always be moist. Take care not to stir too much as you don't want it to go stodgy, but you want to prevent the rice from sticking too much on the bottom.
5. When the rice is cooked to your liking (approximately 25-30 minutes), add the lemon juice and pecorino and stir.
6. Season to taste.
7. To make the crispy calamari, heat the oil in a medium pot.
8. Combine the calamari with the flours and salt.
9. Shake off the excess flour and carefully place the calamari in the hot oil.
10. Allow to fry for 3-5 minutes until the calamari is crisp and golden.
11. Serve the risotto with the crispy calamari and extra chopped chilli if desired.

I love making this chowder on those colder days when only a hearty bowl of food can put a smile on my face. This really is a meal in itself but if you like you can serve it with lots of crusty, toasted bread with lashings of butter.

CORN AND CLAM CHOWDER

Serves 6

- 2 tablespoons butter
- 2 onions, peeled and finely chopped
- 4 large carrots, peeled and finely chopped
- 2 celery sticks, finely chopped
- 6 bacon slices, chopped
- 4 garlic cloves, finely sliced
- 4 large potatoes, peeled and cubed
- 1 tablespoon fresh thyme
- 1 bay leaf
- 1 litre full-cream milk
- 2 cups chicken or vegetable stock
- 2 cups fresh corn kernels
- 2 cups clam meat
- handful fresh parsley, finely chopped
- salt and pepper to taste
- fresh lemon wedges, to serve
- chopped parsley, to serve

1. In a large pot, melt the butter and fry the onion, carrot and celery with the bacon until the vegetables are soft and fragrant (approximately 10 minutes).
2. Add the garlic and the potatoes and sauté for another 10 minutes before adding the thyme, bay leaf, milk and stock.
3. Allow to come to the boil and then reduce the heat. Allow to simmer for 10 minutes until the potatoes are cooked but still holding their shape.
4. Add the corn and clam meat and simmer for 10 minutes.
5. Add the parsley and season to taste.
6. Serve in deep bowls with extra parsley and a squeeze of lemon juice.

Serving fish with garlic butter is hardly groundbreaking, but taking something that everyone knows and loves and adding a twist and some creative presentation can revitalise and refresh it, especially if you have fallen into a boring routine with your cooking.

For these skewers, I suggest you use a firm white fish (such as hake). Have the fishmonger skin and bone it for you. You can then just chop it into large chunks and thread the pieces onto skewers. Remember to soak the bamboo skewers in water for a few hours before cooking to prevent them from burning.

GRILLED FISH SKEWERS WITH GARLIC BUTTER

Makes 4–6 skewers

500 g firm white fish, cut into large chunks
3 tablespoons olive oil
juice of 1 lemon
salt and pepper to taste

Garlic butter

250 g butter
5 garlic cloves, crushed
juice of 1 lemon
handful fresh parsley, finely chopped

1. To make the skewers, thread the chopped fish onto soaked bamboo skewers and drizzle with the olive oil and lemon juice. Season with salt and pepper.
2. You can bake these in the oven (200 °C) or fry them in a large pan. Either way they will take 10–12 minutes to cook.
3. In the meantime, melt the butter in a small saucepan and add the garlic, lemon juice and fresh parsley. When the butter has melted, switch off the heat and allow the flavours to infuse for 5 minutes before serving with the cooked fish skewers.

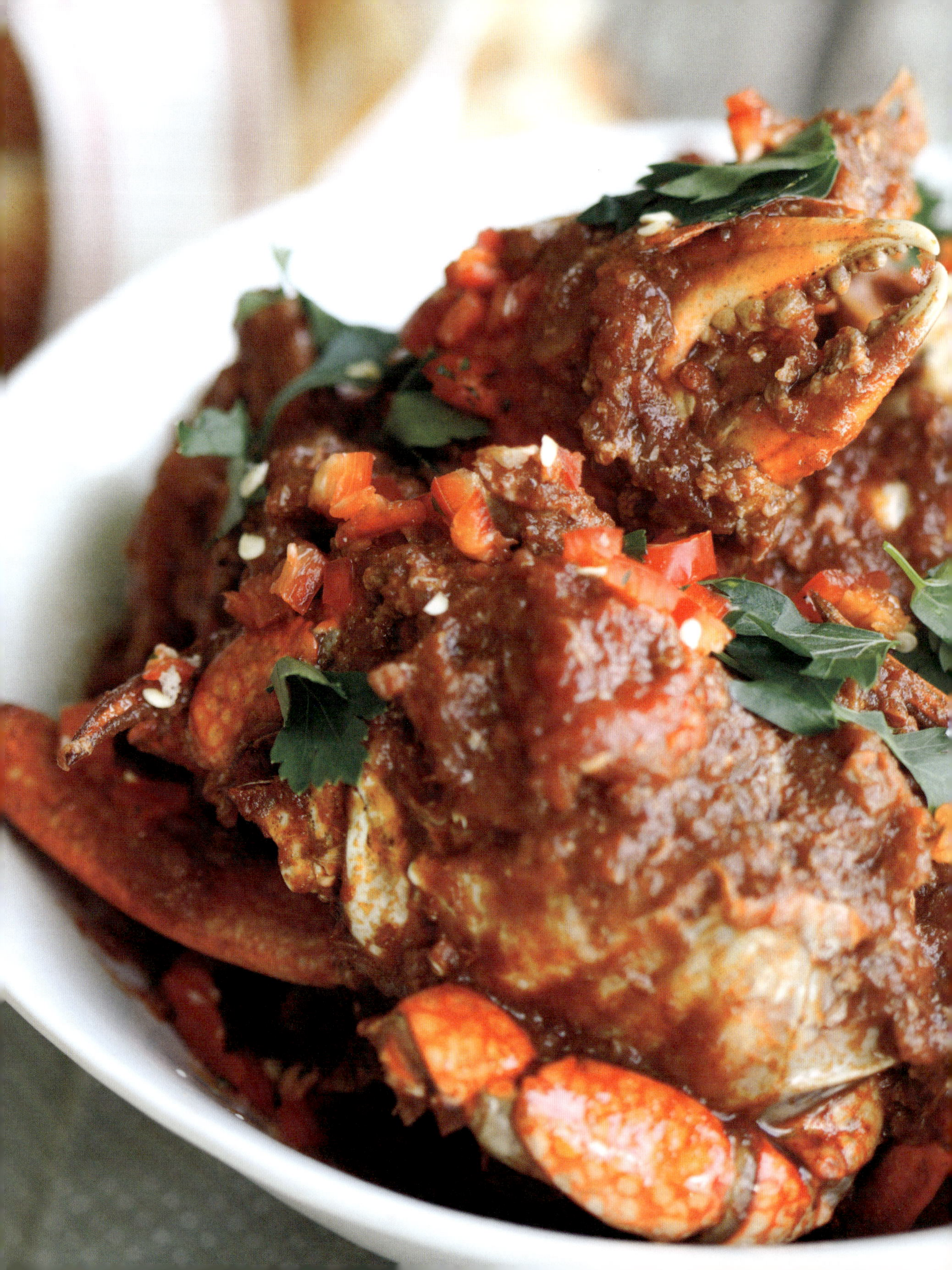

This curry is not for quick eating. Picking the meat out of the claws can take up to an hour, but don't let this put you off! This is the perfect thing to serve to friends you want to catch up with. Add a few bottles of ice-cold beer and lots of finger bowls and I guarantee your friends will sing your praises.

CRAB CURRY

Serves 4–6

- 100 g butter
- 2 tablespoons canola oil
- 2 red onions, finely diced
- 5 garlic cloves, crushed
- 1 heaped teaspoon crushed ginger
- ½ teaspoon turmeric
- 1 heaped teaspoon coriander
- 1 heaped teaspoon cumin
- 2 teaspoons paprika
- 3 teaspoons hot garam masala
- 2 x 400 g tins chopped tomatoes
- 2 cups water or fish stock
- 1 teaspoon salt
- 1 tablespoon sugar
- 2 kg crab pieces
- fresh chopped chillies, to serve
- steamed jasmine rice, to serve

1. In a large pot, melt the butter and the oil together and fry the onion until soft and translucent. Add the garlic, ginger and spices and fry for another minute until the mixture is fragrant.
2. Add the tinned chopped tomatoes and water or fish stock.
3. Add the salt and sugar and allow the sauce to simmer for 10 minutes.
4. Add the crab pieces and stir, coating the pieces with the sauce.
5. Allow to cook until the crab has turned bright red and the meat inside is cooked (about 15 minutes).
6. Serve with chopped chillies and steamed jasmine rice.

Seafood

When it comes to seafood, prawns are my favourite. I grew up in a seafood-loving family and prawn braais were for celebrating or simply bringing us all together (because no one misses a prawn braai!). So I was delighted to discover my future in-laws felt exactly the same about the delicious prawn and I secretly wish for prawn braais every single time we're invited for lunch.

The family way of cooking prawns involves a huge frying pan set over an open flame, tons of butter and lots of flavourings like garlic, lemon and chilli. There is absolutely nothing wrong with this way of doing things and it's my favourite way of cooking and eating prawns, but sometimes it's necessary to simplify things a bit (especially when the weather's bad and you can't cook the prawns outside). By seasoning and flavouring the prawns and popping them into the oven, you get juicy, succulent prawns but with half of the trouble and a little less fat too.

To serve the prawns I suggest some steamed basmati rice and a good peri-peri sauce. Most fishmongers sell really good bottled peri-peri sauces but nothing beats making your own and with this incredibly easy way of doing it, you really have no excuse not to try it at least once.

OVEN-ROASTED PRAWNS WITH PERI-PERI SAUCE

Serves 2–4 (depending on appetites, but be warned, these are addictive and it's not often that you have leftovers)

Peri-peri sauce

- 4 large onions, peeled and quartered
- 4 garlic cloves, peeled
- 3–5 chillies, chopped (depending on how spicy you want the sauce)
- ½ cup red wine vinegar
- 2 teaspoons sugar
- 2 teaspoons salt

Prawns

- 1 kg prawns, deveined
- 6 garlic cloves, crushed
- juice of 2 lemons
- 1 tablespoon seafood spice or seasoning salt
- 100 g butter, cubed

1. To make the peri-peri sauce, combine all the ingredients in a blender and blend until smooth.
2. Transfer the sauce to a saucepan and allow to simmer for 15–20 minutes until it's reduced and thick. Adjust the seasoning and serve with the prawns.
3. To make the prawns, pre-heat the oven to 200 °C.
4. Place the prawns, garlic, lemon juice and seafood spice in a bowl and gently toss to combine.
5. Place the prawns into a large baking dish or roasting pan and dot the cubed butter on top.
6. Place in the oven and allow to roast for 7–10 minutes before turning the prawns over and roasting for a further 10 minutes until the prawns are cooked.
7. Serve the cooked prawns with the peri-peri sauce and steamed rice.

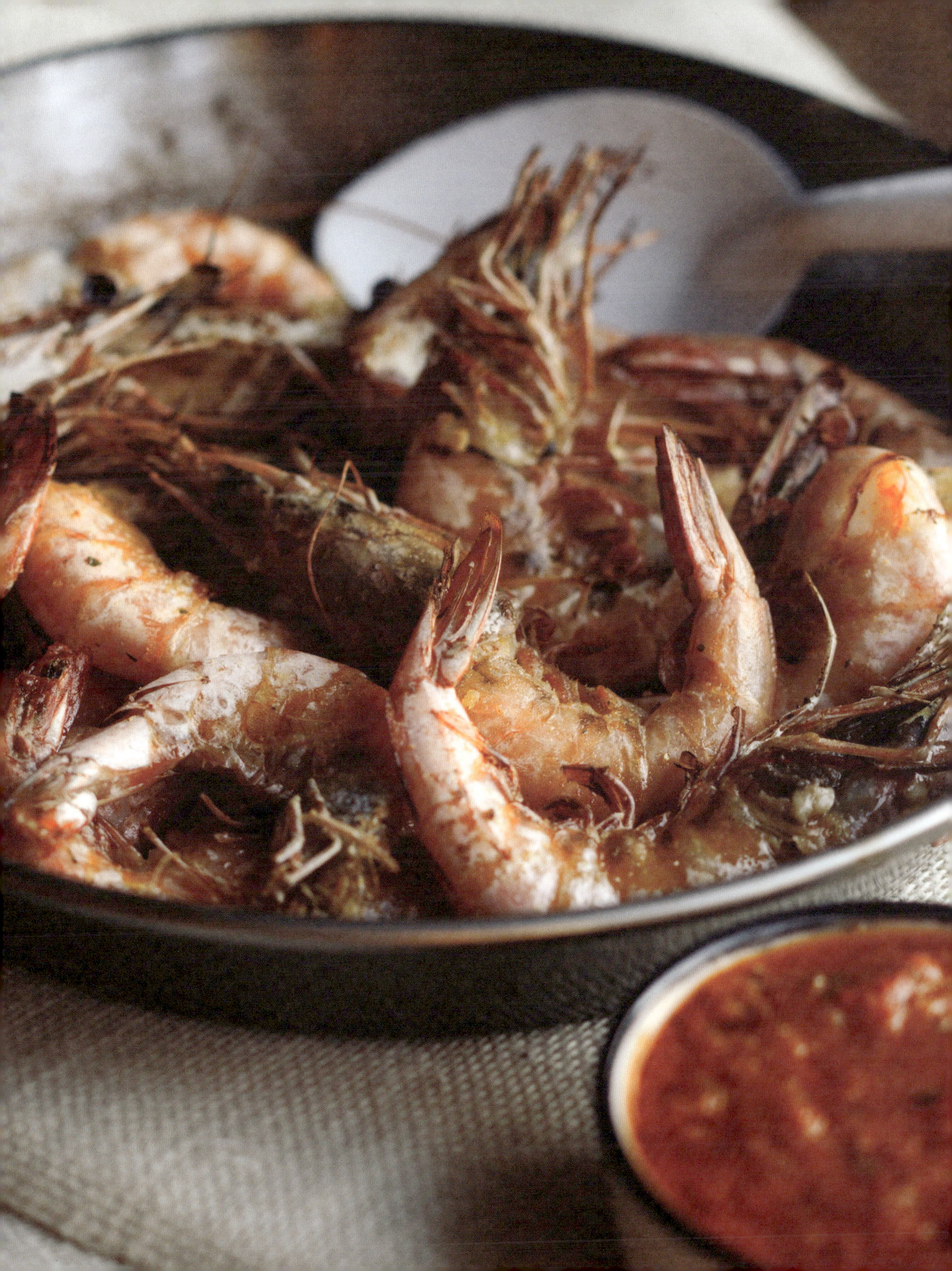

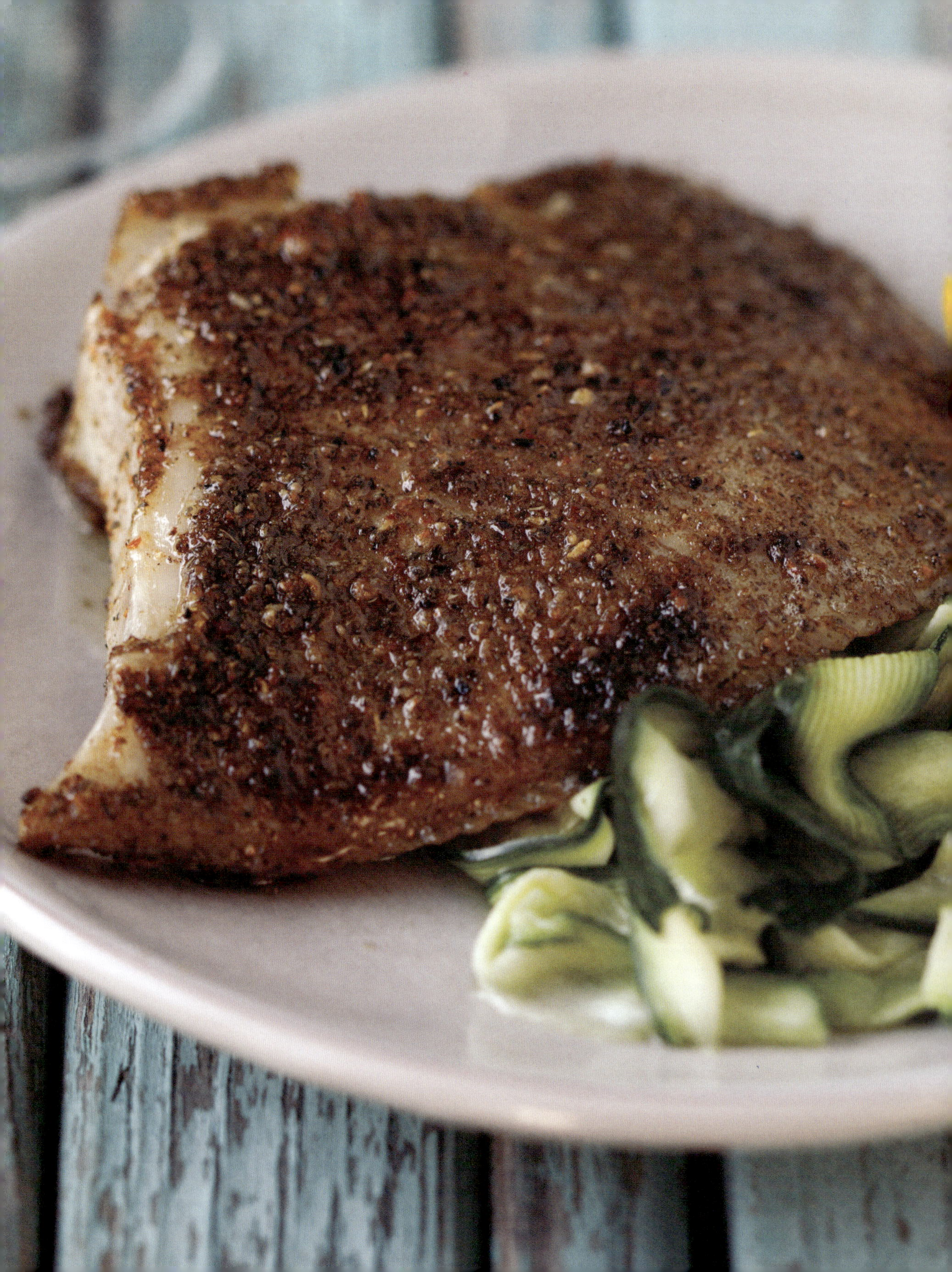

For me, a piece of fish is most delicious cooked with the ingredients that complement it best – butter, lemon, garlic and a bit of seasoning. It's a guaranteed way of ensuring success and it couldn't be easier.

I recommend serving the slightly spicy fish with the simplest courgette salad you will ever make but if you want a more substantial meal, you can add some roasted potato wedges or creamy mash.

CAJUN ROAST FISH WITH COURGETTE SALAD

Serves 4

4 portions white fish (I use skate wings)
50 g melted butter
juice of 1 lemon
2 garlic cloves, crushed
2–4 teaspoons Cajun spice
salt to taste

Courgette salad

300 g courgettes, washed and thinly sliced (I use a vegetable peeler to get really thin slices)
juice of 2 lemons
2 tablespoons olive oil
salt and pepper to taste

1. Pre-heat the oven to 220 °C.
2. Combine the melted butter, lemon juice and garlic and brush over the fish. Sprinkle over the Cajun spice and season to taste. (Be sure to taste your Cajun seasoning before adding salt and pepper as some pre-made spice mixes can be very salty.)
3. Place the fish in the oven and roast for 10–15 minutes until the spice has formed a crust and the fish is cooked through.
4. To make the salad, combine the ingredients and toss together.
5. Serve the fish with the salad and extra lemon wedges.

Seafood

When I make this risotto, I feel instantly better. The green peas (which look like polka dots according to my daughter) and the rosy pink of the prawns remind me of spring, and like the smell of jasmine and blue skies – they cheer me up every time. As with all risottos, the use of a good-quality stock is very important and here you have two choices. You could use vegetable stock (either concentrate or home-made) or you could do what I normally do and boil the prawn shells and heads in about 1½ litres of weak vegetable stock for 20 minutes until the stock is a pretty coral-pink colour and the taste of prawns is gently infused into the stock.

PRAWN AND PEA RISOTTO

Serves 4 (or 6 as a starter)

- 1–1½ litres vegetable stock or prawn and vegetable stock
- ½ red onion, finely chopped
- 2 garlic cloves, crushed
- 2–3 tablespoons butter or olive oil
- 500 g Arborio or Carnaroli rice
- 1 cup frozen peas
- 500 g prawns, cleaned, shells and heads removed
- 100 ml cream
- juice of ½ lemon
- 100 g Parmesan, grated
- salt and pepper to taste

1. Start by preparing your stock and keep it warm while you make the risotto.
2. Fry the onion and garlic in butter or olive oil in a heavy-based pot until soft and fragrant.
3. Add the rice and fry for another minute, coating the rice in the butter or oil.
4. Lower the heat and start adding the stock, ladle by ladle, stirring in between and allowing the rice to absorb the stock. The rice should never be completely dry and be careful not to stir too vigorously as you don't want to break up the rice.
5. After about 20 minutes, add the frozen peas and continue adding the stock little by little as you've been doing.
6. When the risotto is almost done (after about 30 minutes) add the prawns, cream and lemon juice.
7. Allow the prawns and rice to cook thoroughly, then add the Parmesan and season to taste.
8. Serve immediately.

I just love the sweet stickiness of this teriyaki sauce. Whether I serve it with chicken or salmon, it's always a hit with my family. Great served with steamed jasmine rice and bright green sugar snap peas.

TERIYAKI SALMON

Serves 4

½ cup teriyaki sauce

½ cup soy sauce

3 tablespoons sweet chilli sauce

2 tablespoons fish sauce

2 tablespoons soft brown sugar

2 teaspoons ginger, crushed

2 garlic cloves, crushed

juice of 2 lemons

4 x 150–200 g salmon portions, skin on

canola or vegetable oil for frying

1. Combine all the marinade ingredients in a microwave-safe bowl and heat in the microwave oven until the sugar has dissolved (approximately 2–3 minutes in a 750 W oven). Allow to cool for 10 minutes and pour over the salmon.
2. Allow to marinate for 20 minutes.
3. Heat a large frying pan and fry the salmon for 3–5 minutes on the one side and when you turn it over, pour in 2 cups of the marinade. Allow to cook until the marinade has reduced and gone sticky.
4. Serve the salmon with steamed jasmine rice and sugar snap peas.

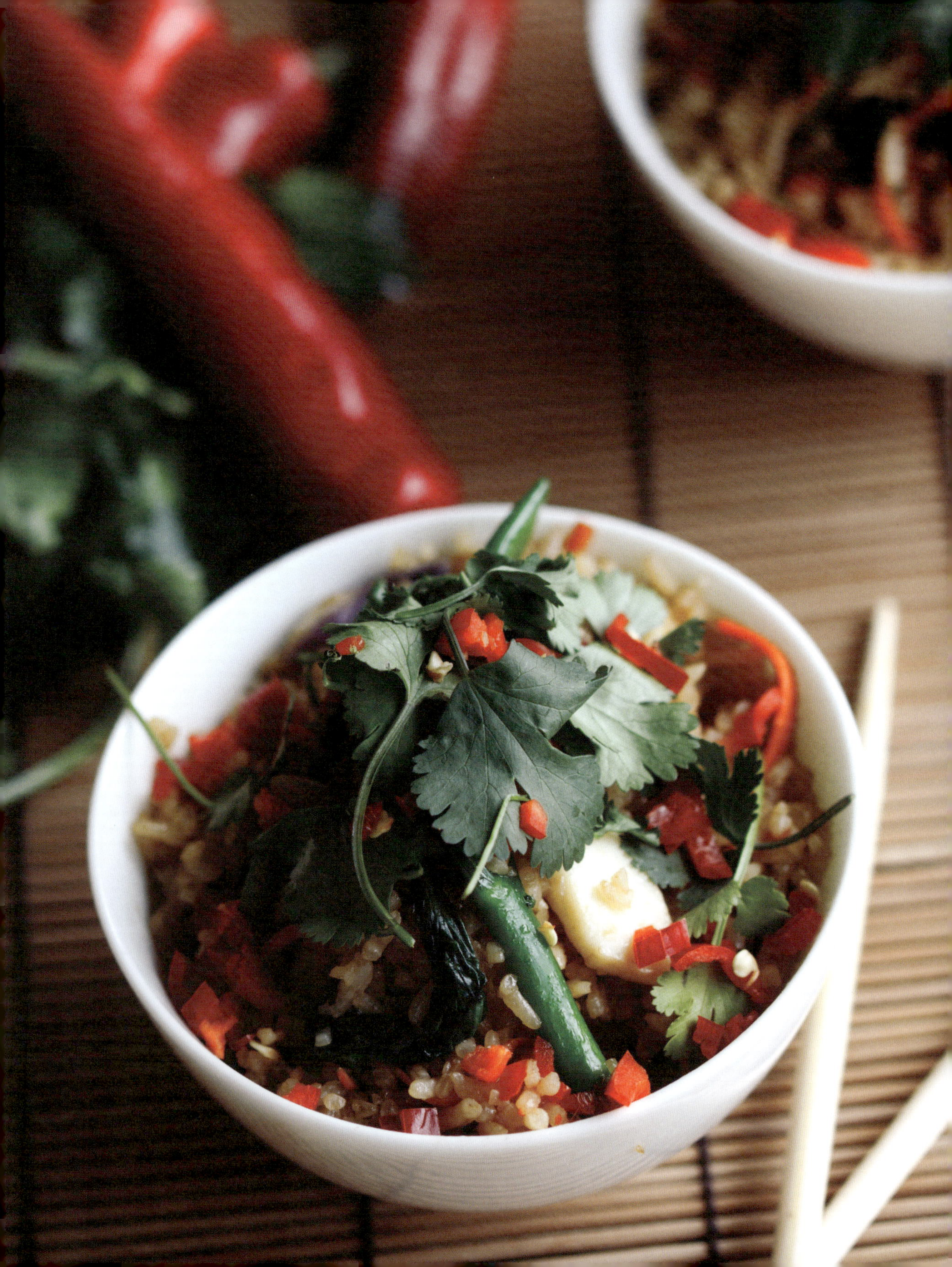

This quick stir-fry can be made even more quickly if you use leftover rice, which is what I often do. And using up any leftover vegetables in your fridge makes it a dish that can be slightly different every time you make it. Using calamari is lovely but really anything goes. You could use chicken, prawns, beef strips, pork, or even leave out the protein altogether and make it a vegetarian stir-fry. Anything goes!

THAI FRIED RICE WITH CALAMARI

Serves 4

1 cup spring onions, finely chopped
2 garlic cloves, crushed
1 teaspoon crushed ginger
2 tablespoons canola oil
600–800 g calamari steaks, sliced into strips
300 g mixed vegetables (I like using sugar snap peas, baby corn, broccoli and fine green beans)
2 tablespoons soy sauce
1 tablespoon fish sauce
¾ cup coconut milk
2 teaspoons honey
4 cups cooked jasmine rice (1 cup per person)
juice of 2 limes
fresh coriander, to serve
chopped chillies, to serve

1. In a wok, fry the spring onions, garlic and ginger in canola oil until fragrant.
2. Add the calamari and vegetables and stir-fry for 5–7 minutes until the calamari is cooked but not rubbery.
3. Add the soy sauce, fish sauce, coconut milk and honey. Allow to simmer for 5 minutes. Pour off some of the sauce and reserve.
4. Add the rice to the wok and stir to combine with the calamari and vegetables.
5. At this stage I like to add the reserved sauce back in. Add a little at a time until the stir-fry is just moist – not soggy and wet.
6. Check to see if the seasoning is correct and adjust with lime juice and soy.
7. Serve with fresh coriander, chopped chillies and lime cheeks or wedges.

'Stoup?' I hear you ask. Yes, stoup is what I call a dish that is just too thick and chunky to be called a soup but contains too much liquid to be called a stew. It's the perfect thing to serve on those chilly spring evenings when you want the comfort that only food in a bowl can bring, yet you yearn for summer days spent on the beach, salty skin and fresh seafood.

I'm not a big fan of pre-packed mixed seafood as I find poor-quality seafood is often used to make up the bulk of the mix. I prefer to choose an assortment of seafood myself from my fishmonger. Mussels, clams, prawns, calamari, squid heads and firm white fish are usually best in a stoup like this.

It would be a sin to serve this with anything other than loads of crusty bread and a few bottles of wine.

SEAFOOD 'STOUP'

Serves 4

- 1 onion, finely chopped
- 3 garlic cloves, crushed
- 1 tablespoon mild garam masala or curry powder
- 1 tin chopped or cherry tomatoes
- 1 tin (50 g) tomato paste
- 1 teaspoon sugar
- 1 litre fish or vegetable stock
- 400 g mixed seafood of your choice, cleaned
- 100 ml cream
- handful fresh parsley, finely chopped
- juice of ½ lemon
- salt and pepper to taste
- crusty bread, to serve

1. In a large saucepan, sauté the onion and garlic until soft and translucent. Add the garam masala or curry powder and fry until the mixture becomes dry.
2. Add the tomatoes, tomato paste and sugar.
3. Pour in the stock and simmer for 10–15 minutes until the sauce has reduced slightly.
4. Add the seafood and cream, and simmer for another 10 minutes until the seafood is cooked.
5. Add the chopped parsley and lemon juice, and season to taste.
6. Serve in bowls with crusty bread.

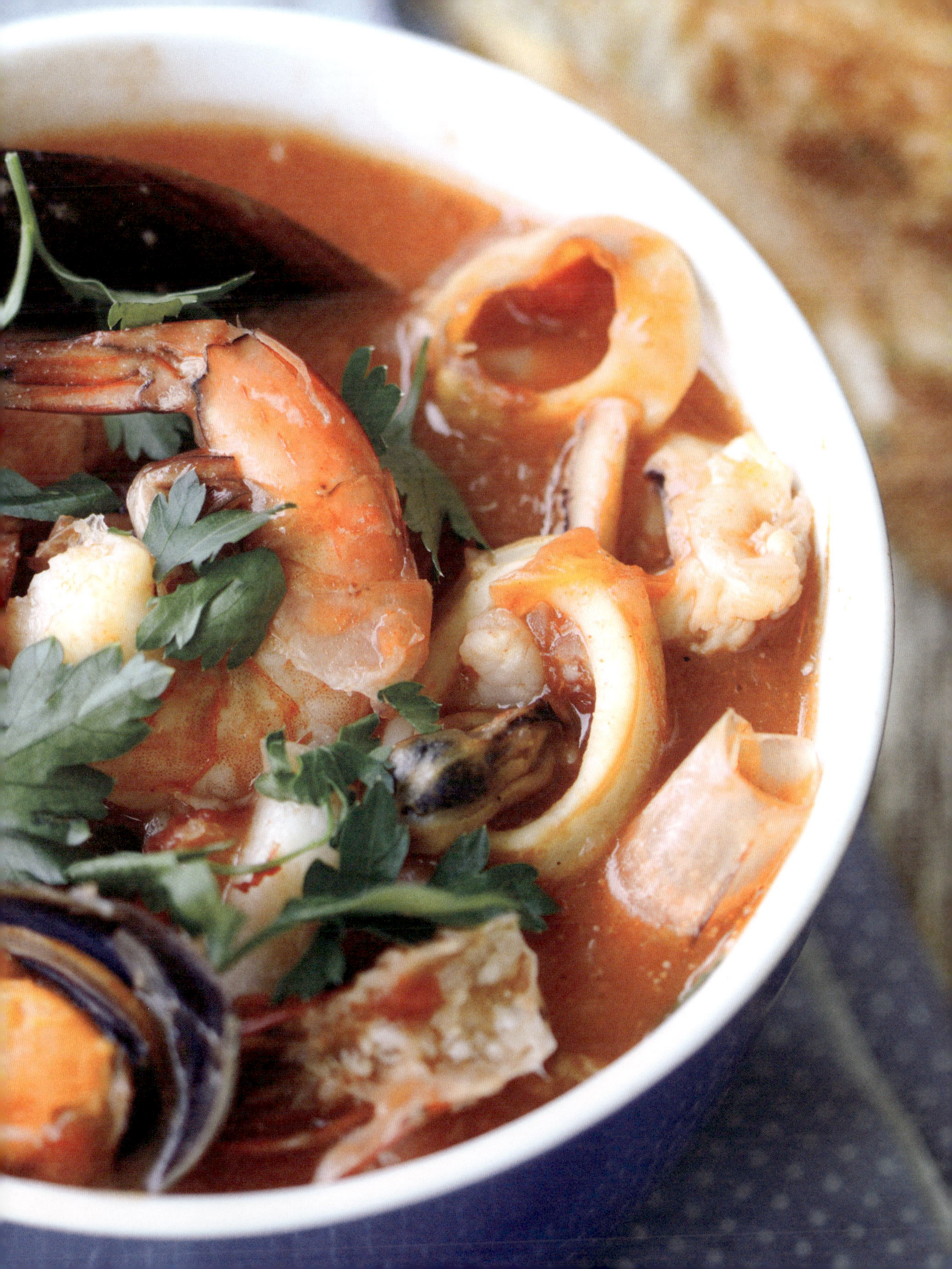

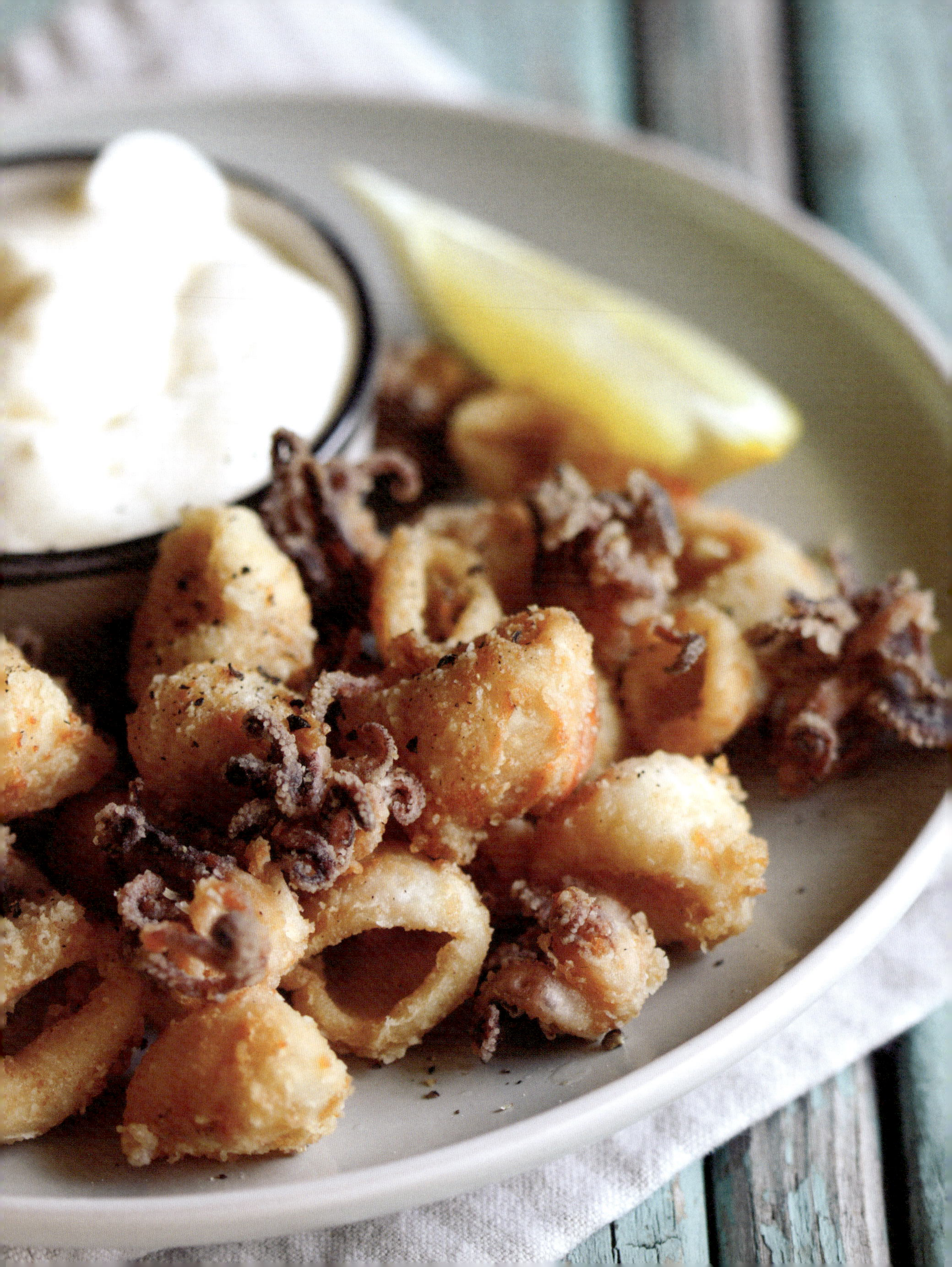

I have always been mad about calamari and as my mother was a Greek food fanatic we often went to Greek restaurants. I'll never forget ordering crispy calamari for the first time and being presented with a plate full of suspicious-looking creatures that resembled spiders way too much for my liking. My mother convinced me to take a bite and I was instantly in love.

To this day crispy calamari or squid is one of my favourite things to eat and making it myself just allows me to have it more often. This recipe is really easy and served with home-made aioli (see page 24 for therecipe, or even a good-quality bought mayo with a garlic clove crushed into it will do) it makes the perfect light lunch or snack to have with drinks.

SALT AND PEPPER SQUID

Serves 4 as a starter

- canola oil for deep frying
- 500 g squid tentacles or calamari tubes, cleaned and sliced
- 1 cup cake flour
- ½ cup cornflour
- 1½ teaspoons salt
- 2 teaspoons cracked black pepper
- oil for frying
- aioli, to serve
- fresh lemon wedges, to serve

1. Heat enough oil to deep-fry the squid.
2. While the oil is heating up, coat the squid/ calamari in the flours, salt and pepper. Make sure every piece is completely coated in the mixture.
3. When the oil is hot, fry the squid in two batches until crisp and golden (approximately 5–7 minutes). Remove from the oil and allow to dry on kitchen paper.
4. Serve with aioli and fresh lemon.

Sometimes I feel quite embarrassed at the simplicity of some of my recipes, but I guess that's the charm of my food. If I spend more than an hour in the kitchen, it better be well worth it and there are very few dishes to which I will commit that much time. The older I get, the more I realise that it's not about the time I spend faffing in the kitchen that makes my friends and family enjoy my food; it's about the love and passion I put into every pot and pan and the amount of time I spend with the people I love.

These tacos are a prime example of an easy peasy recipe which is just perfect served to friends and family to pick at and assemble themselves. Serve all the components of the tacos in bowls and plates, add a few finger bowls, a couple of bottles of ice-cold beer and you will have very happy guests.

FISH TACOS WITH FRESH CORIANDER AND LIME

Serves 4

Fish

oil for frying

500 g firm white fish, sliced into strips

1 cup flour seasoned with 1 teaspoon salt and 1 teaspoon paprika

2 eggs, beaten

2 cups breadcrumbs seasoned with 1 teaspoon salt and 1 teaspoon paprika

To assemble

4–8 soft tacos

sour cream

fresh avocado, cubed

fresh coriander

chopped chillies

fresh limes, halved

1. Heat the oil in a medium saucepan.
2. Meanwhile, coat the fish strips in the seasoned flour, dip in the beaten egg and then coat in the seasoned breadcrumbs.
3. When the oil is hot, fry the fish strips in batches for 5–7 minutes until they are crisp and golden.
4. Remove each batch as it's done from the oil and drain on kitchen paper while you fry the rest of the fish.
5. To serve, spread some of the sour cream onto each taco, followed by avocado, coriander, chillies, fried fish and a squeeze of lime juice.
6. Eat immediately.

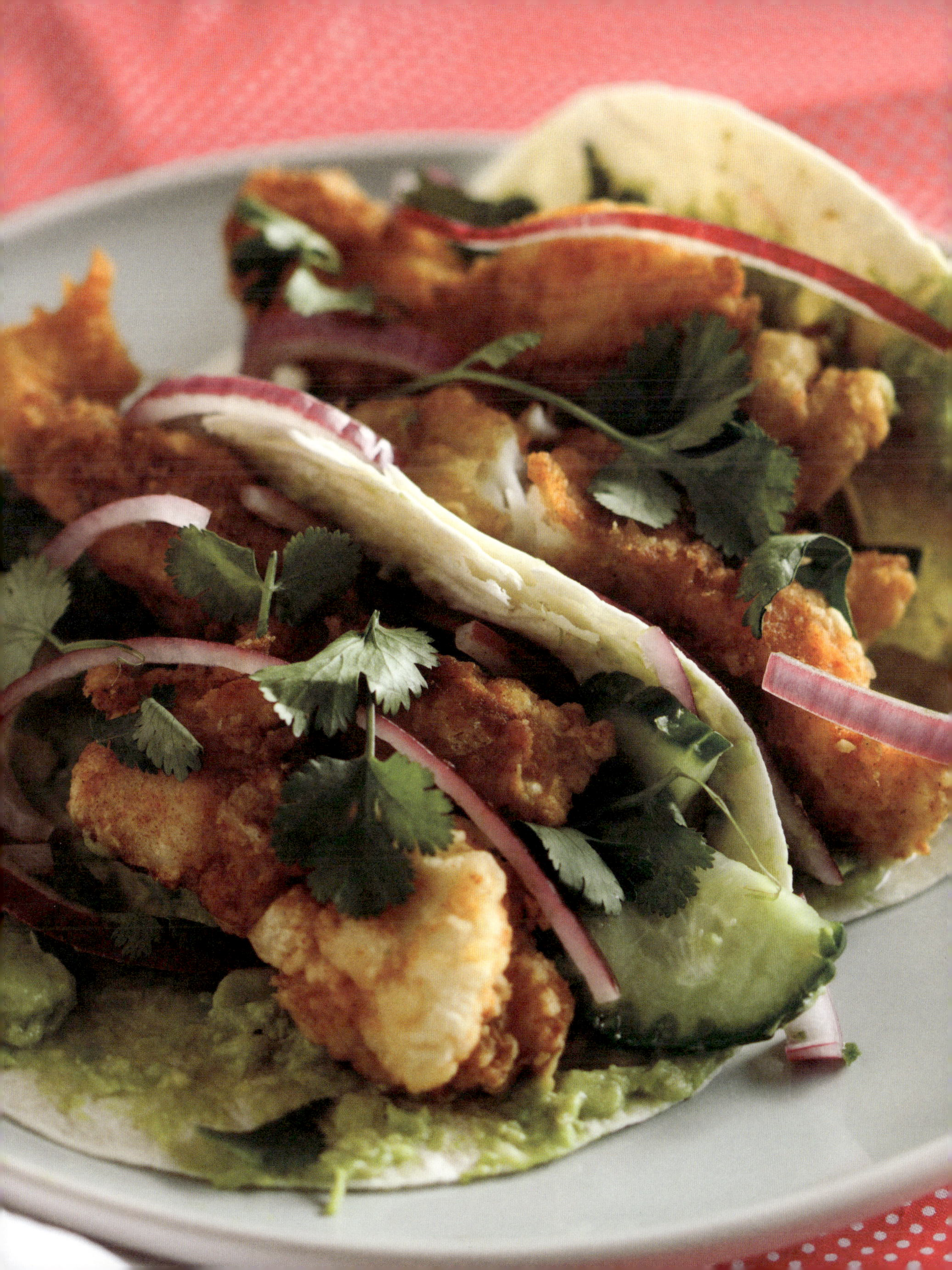

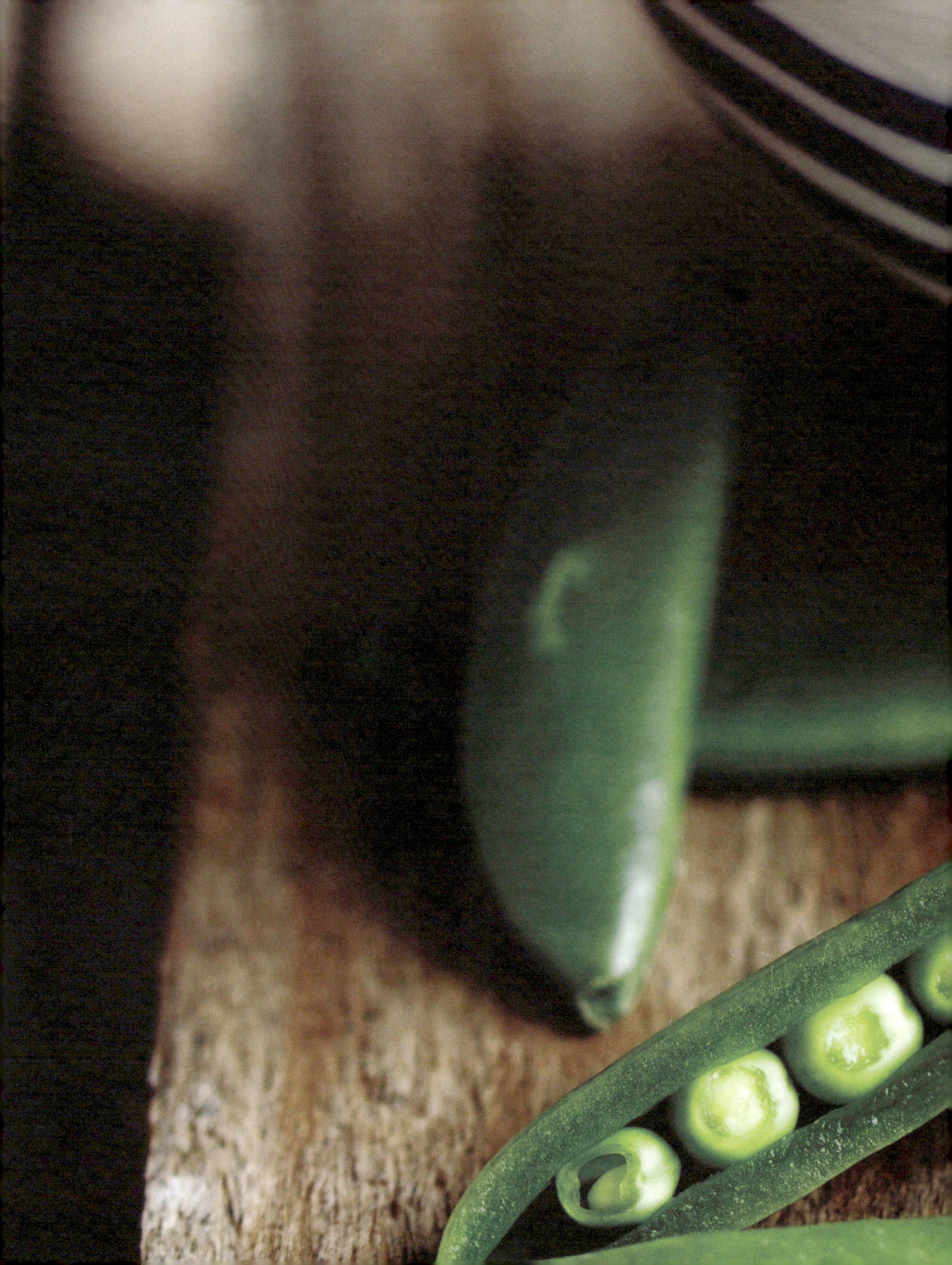

VEGETARIAN

I think it's safe to say that I am a complete and utter risotto addict. I love it in its classic form, or baked or rolled into balls to make arancini (fried rice balls).

This risotto is light and fresh and just perfect for summer eating. I like to use the freshest, ripest tomatoes I can get my hands on but if you can't find bright red, juicy tomatoes, use tinned cherry tomatoes. They are sweet and the reddest of reds.

It's also important to use beautiful bright and bouncy basil, but I have made it before using a dollop or two of basil pesto and it was equally delicious.

TOMATO AND BASIL RISOTTO

Serves 4

- 1–1½ litres vegetable stock
- 2 leeks, washed and finely chopped
- 2 garlic cloves, finely sliced
- 500 g Arborio rice
- 200 ml white wine
- 2 cups chopped ripe tomatoes or 1 tin cherry tomatoes
- 1 small tin (50 g) tomato paste
- 1 teaspoon sugar
- 1 cup fresh basil, roughly chopped
- 100 g pecorino, grated
- salt and pepper to taste

1. Prepare the stock and keep it hot while you start the risotto.
2. In a large pot or pan, heat some oil and fry the leeks until translucent. Add the garlic and fry for another minute or two.
3. Add the rice and stir, coating the rice with the oil. Add the wine, the tomatoes and the sugar, and allow to reduce.
4. Now, add the hot stock ladle by ladle, stirring in between and allowing the rice to absorb it. The rice shouldn't be completely dry before you add more; it should always be moist. Take care not to stir too much as you don't want it to become stodgy.
5. When all the stock has been absorbed, add the grated pecorino (reserving some for serving) and chopped basil, and season to taste.
6. Serve immediately.

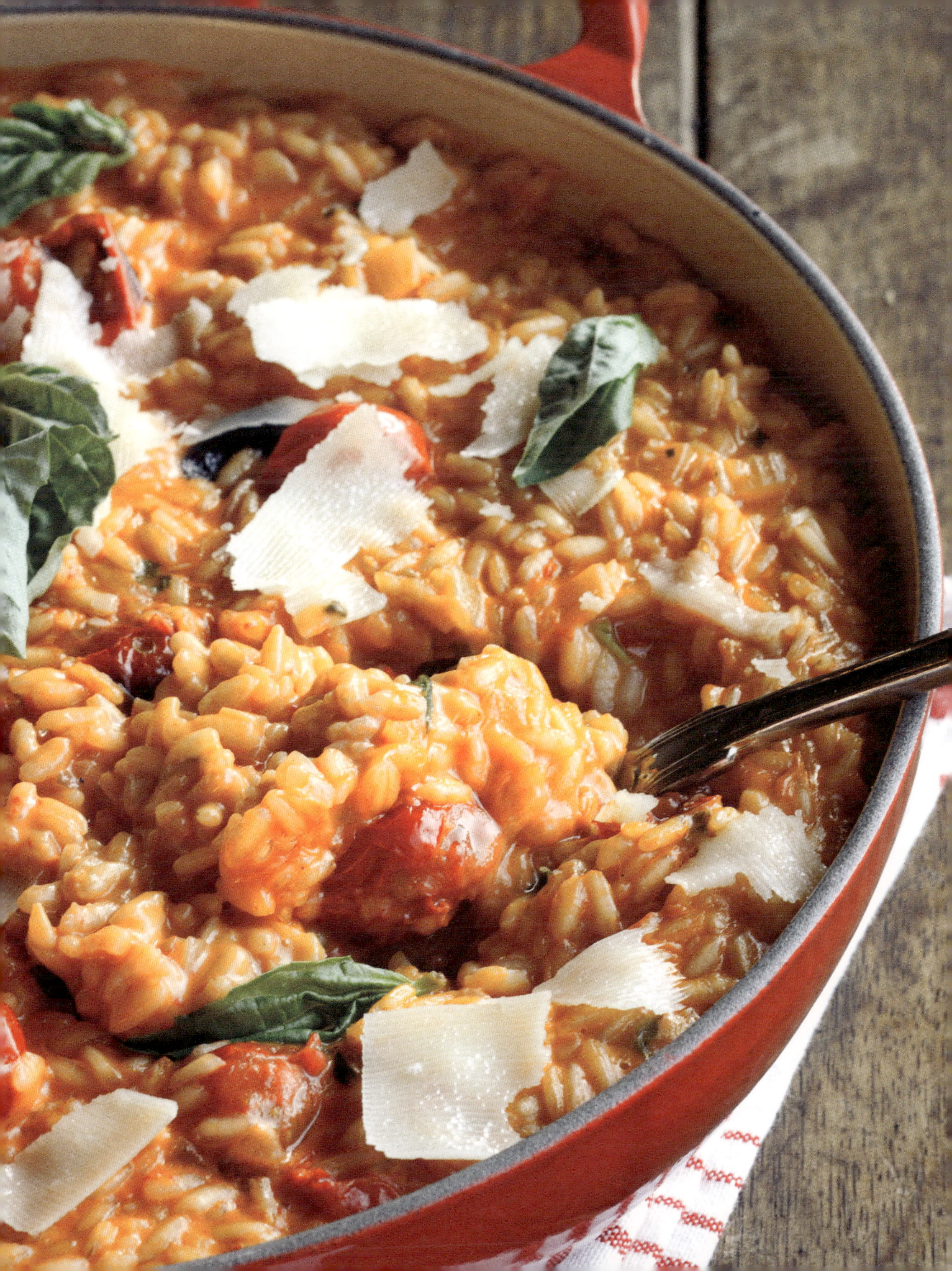

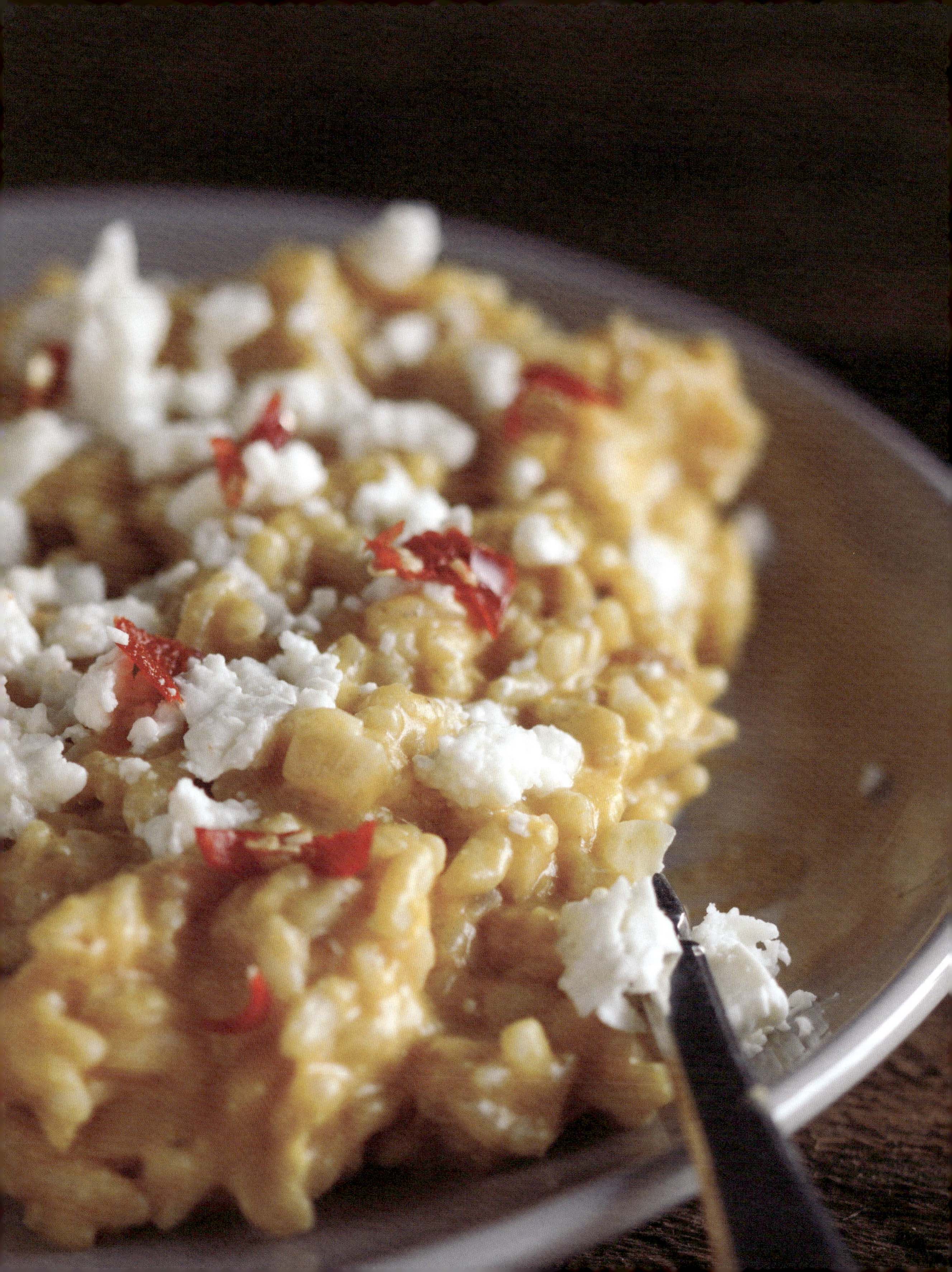

BUTTERNUT RISOTTO WITH FETA AND CHILLI

Serves 4

Butternut purée

500–750 g whole butternut, cut in half and seeds removed
1 tablespoon oil
2 tablespoons honey
2–4 sprigs rosemary
2–4 sprigs thyme
½ teaspoon nutmeg

Risotto

8 cups (2 litres) chicken stock
2 tablespoons olive oil
1 large onion, finely diced
4 garlic cloves, crushed
500 g Arborio rice
200 ml white wine
¾ cup cream
1 cup feta, roughly crumbled
2 red chillies, deseeded and finely chopped
½ cup Parmesan, grated

1. For the butternut purée, pre-heat the oven to 220 °C. Place the butternut skin-side down on a roasting tray. Drizzle with the oil and honey and place a sprig of rosemary and thyme on each half. Cover with foil and roast until soft (approximately 30 minutes).
2. Remove from the oven and purée with ½ teaspoon nutmeg. I prefer to include the skin but the flesh can be scooped before it is processed. Set aside.
3. Prepare your stock and keep it warm while you get going with the risotto.
4. In a large, heavy-based pot or pan, heat some oil and fry the onion until translucent. Add the garlic and fry for another minute or two.
5. Add the rice and stir, coating the rice with the oil. Add the wine and 2 cups of the puréed butternut and allow to reduce.
6. Now add the warm stock ladle by ladle, stirring in between and allowing the rice to absorb the stock. The rice shouldn't be completely dry before you add more; it should always be moist. Take care not to stir too much as you don't want it to go stodgy.
7. When all the stock has been absorbed, add the cream, feta cheese, grated Parmesan and chilli and allow to cook for another 5 minutes. Check for seasoning and serve immediately.

Vegetarian

This makes for a fabulous breakfast, lunch or dinner. It is truly an all-day dish. And on top of that, it's a real crowd-pleaser. I often make it when I have leftover cooked potatoes in the fridge, which makes this frittata a 15-minute dish from start to finish.

Serve it with a zesty watercress salad for lunch or lots of buttered toast for breakfast or supper.

POTATO AND TALEGGIO FRITTATA

Serves 2–4

1 onion, finely chopped
1 garlic clove, crushed
2 cups cooked baby potatoes, halved
½ teaspoon paprika
1 teaspoon salt
6 eggs, beaten
50 ml cream
100 g taleggio, cut into cubes

1. Pre-heat the oven to 220 °C.
2. In an ovenproof pan, fry the onion until soft and translucent. Add the garlic and fry for another minute.
3. Add the potato and fry for 2 minutes. Add the paprika and salt and stir.
4. To the beaten eggs, add the cream and pour over the potato mixture. Scatter the taleggio over the egg mixture.
5. Allow to cook for 5 minutes on the stove then pop it into the oven for 5 minutes to finish the cooking.
6. Serve at room temperature, with toast or a watercress salad.

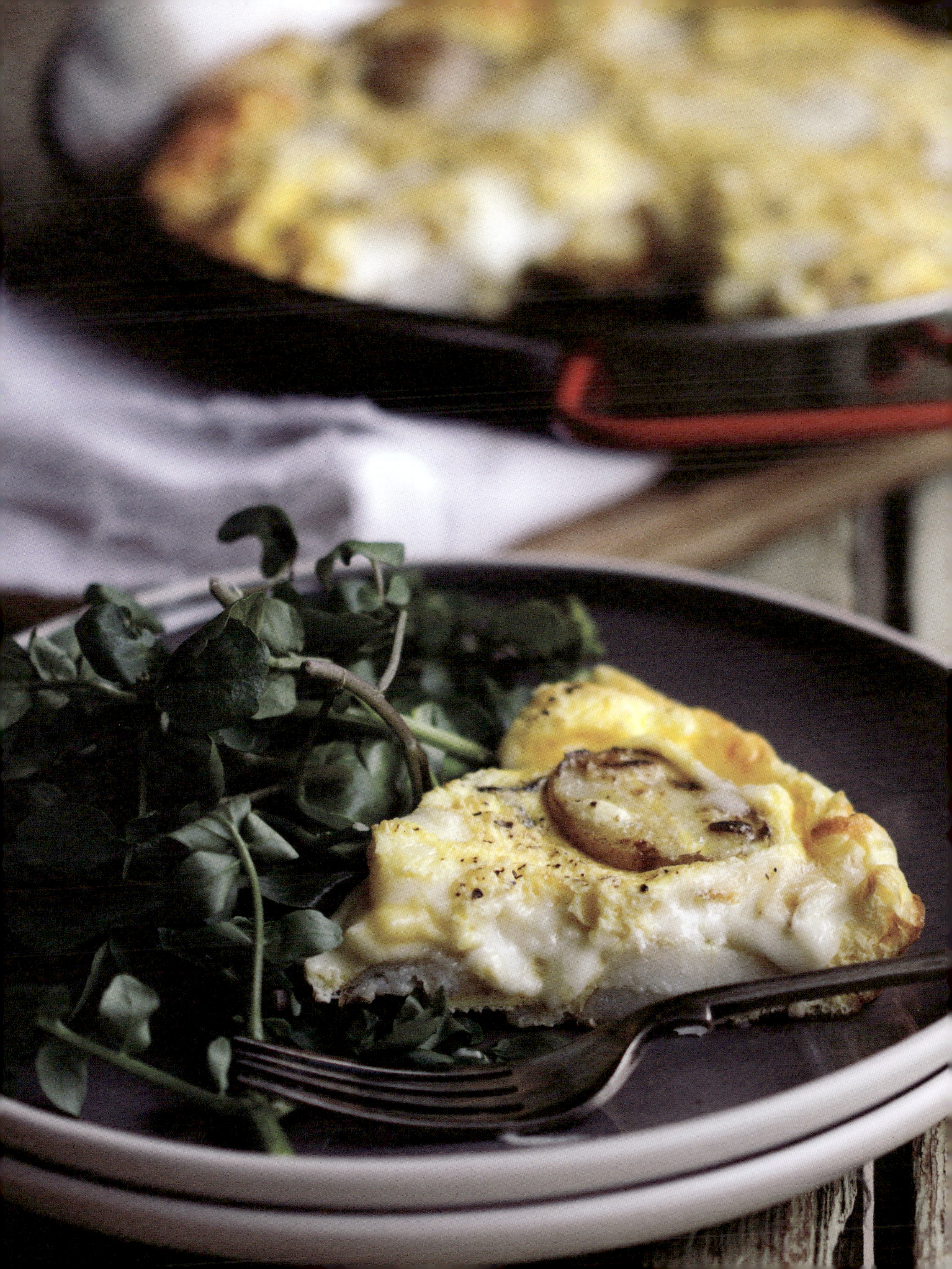

This must be one of my all-time favourite side dishes. I love serving it as part of a vegetarian feast with other vegetable dishes, salads and breads.

CREAMY BAKED BUTTERNUT

Serves 4

1 large butternut, seeds removed and chopped into large chunks
2 tablespoons olive oil
½ teaspoon salt
½ teaspoon pepper
100 ml vegetable stock
150 ml cream

1. Pre-heat the oven to 200 °C.
2. Drizzle the olive oil over the butternut chunks and season with salt and pepper.
3. Place the butternut in a roasting tray and pour over the stock and cream.
4. Cover with foil and place in the oven.
5. Allow to roast for 15–20 minutes until the butternut is cooked.
6. Remove the foil and allow to roast for another 10 minutes until the edges of the butternut start to brown.
7. Remove from the oven and serve.

In general, I am not a huge fan of mushrooms. They are great when teamed with cream, garlic and lemon but on their own I find them bland and boring most of the time. That's why I like to jazz them up.

I like serving these mushrooms as a side dish to almost anything, but they are also great as a vegetarian main served with a goat's cheese and roasted tomato salad. To make this, simply combine 2 cups of cherry tomatoes with a drizzle of oil, balsamic vinegar, 2 teaspoons of sugar and a pinch of salt, and roast for 20 minutes at 220 °C until the tomato skins are blistered and they have softened. Serve the roasted tomatoes with slices of goat's cheese on a bed of rocket and watercress. Dress with a drizzling of lemon juice and olive oil.

STUFFED MUSHROOMS

Serves 4

- 8 large brown mushrooms
- 2 cups fresh breadcrumbs
- 1 cup grated mozzarella
- 1 cup ricotta
- ½ cup fresh parsley, chopped
- 2 garlic cloves, crushed
- juice of ½ lemon
- salt and pepper to taste

1. Pre-heat the oven to 220 °C.
2. Place the mushrooms on a greased baking sheet.
3. Combine all the other ingredients and mix well. Press handfuls of the mixture onto the mushrooms.
4. Place the mushrooms in the oven and bake for 10–15 minutes until they are cooked and the stuffing is golden brown and crisp.
5. Serve warm with the roasted tomato salad.

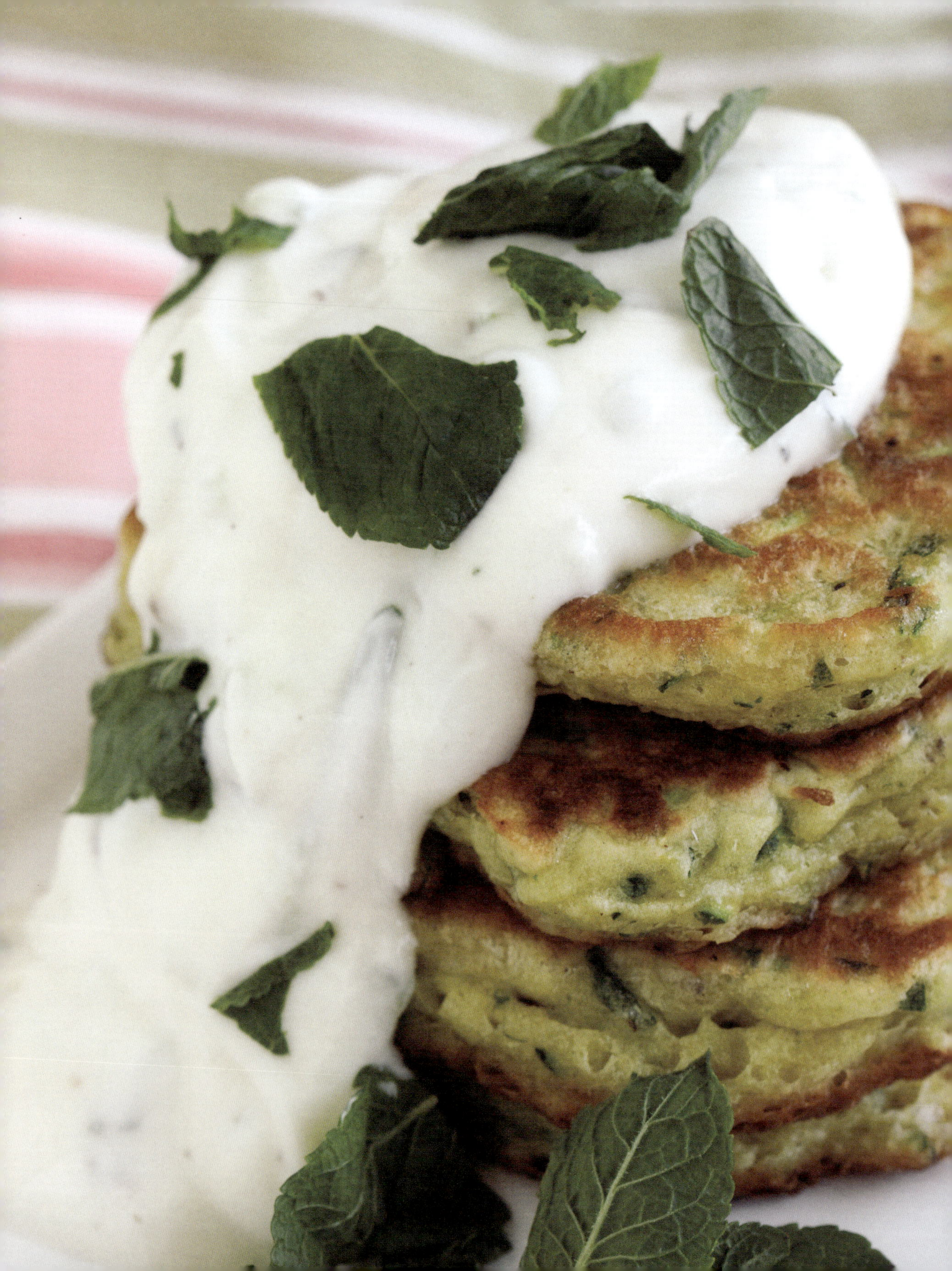

These fritters are the perfect thing for a light lunch or as a side dish with grilled meat, served with thick and creamy tzatziki and some fresh watercress. The fact that it literally takes a few minutes to whip them up, from raw ingredients to fragrant fritters, just adds to the charm. And they're child-friendly too!

COURGETTE FRITTERS WITH TZATZIKI

Makes approximately 10 fritters

400 g medium courgettes

1 cup flour

1 teaspoon baking powder

3 eggs

1 teaspoon salt

1 teaspoon crushed garlic

1 tablespoon lemon juice

fresh watercress, to serve

Add any of the following for variation

1 cup crumbled feta cheese

freshly chopped mint, basil or parsley

thinly sliced spring onion

Tzatziki

3 small Mediterranean cucumbers

2 teaspoons salt

2 cups thick Greek yoghurt

2 garlic cloves, minced

½ cup each dill and mint, finely chopped

salt and pepper to taste

1. Grate the courgettes and place in a mixing bowl.
2. Add the flour, baking powder, eggs, salt, garlic and lemon juice, and mix until you have a thick batter.
3. Heat a large frying pan and fry tablespoons of the batter until crisp and golden on the outside and cooked through in the middle.
4. Serve with tzatziki and fresh watercress.
5. For the tzatziki, grate the cucumbers and combine with the salt. Allow to drain in a muslin cloth-lined sieve for 10–15 minutes. (You could just allow them to drain in the sieve but the cloth allows you to squeeze the excess liquid out more easily.)
6. Combine the Greek yoghurt with the minced garlic and herbs.
7. Squeeze all the excess liquid out of the cucumber and stir into the yoghurt mixture.
8. Season to taste (remember the cucumber has been seasoned already). Serve with the fritters.

Quesadillas are the best thing to make when you're in the mood for something with that 'yum' factor but you have only scraps and leftovers in your fridge and you don't want to be in the kitchen forever. Think of it as a different take on a toasted cheese sandwich.

The combinations of fillings are endless and really anything goes, as long as there's cheese involved to keep everything together. The tortilla will go lovely and crisp, which makes it a good dipping vessel for spicy salsa or creamy guacamole (you can serve just one or both).

The best thing about quesadillas for me is that my kids adore them. I can stuff them with vegetables or just serve them plain with cheese and they will always gobble them up. They're also great as a party snack, with salsa or guacamole, or both.

QUESADILLAS WITH CHEESE, CORN AND KIDNEY BEANS

Serves 2–4

- 4 large tortillas or wraps
- 2 cups grated mature Cheddar
- 1 cup corn kernels
- 1 cup tinned beans, rinsed and drained

Tomato and chilli salsa

- 2 large tomatoes, finely chopped
- 1 red onion, finely chopped
- ½ garlic clove, crushed
- 1 cup fresh parsley, finely chopped
- red chilli, finely chopped (use as much as you can handle)
- juice of ½ lemon
- salt to taste

Guacamole

- 2 avocados
- juice of 1 lemon
- salt and pepper to taste

1. Heat a large frying pan.
2. Place one of the tortillas in the dry pan and sprinkle a quarter of the cheese on top.
3. Add half of the corn and beans and sprinkle another quarter of the cheese over the top. Now place another tortilla on top.
4. Allow the bottom tortilla to go crisp and the cheese to melt.
5. Carefully flip the quesadilla over and allow to cook for another 3–4 minutes on the other side.
6. Remove from the pan and set aside. Repeat with the rest of the tortillas.
7. To make the salsa, simply combine all the ingredients together. (Likewise with the guacamole: blend together the avocado flesh with the lemon juice, salt and pepper until smooth.)
8. Serve the quesadillas warm with the salsa or guacamole.

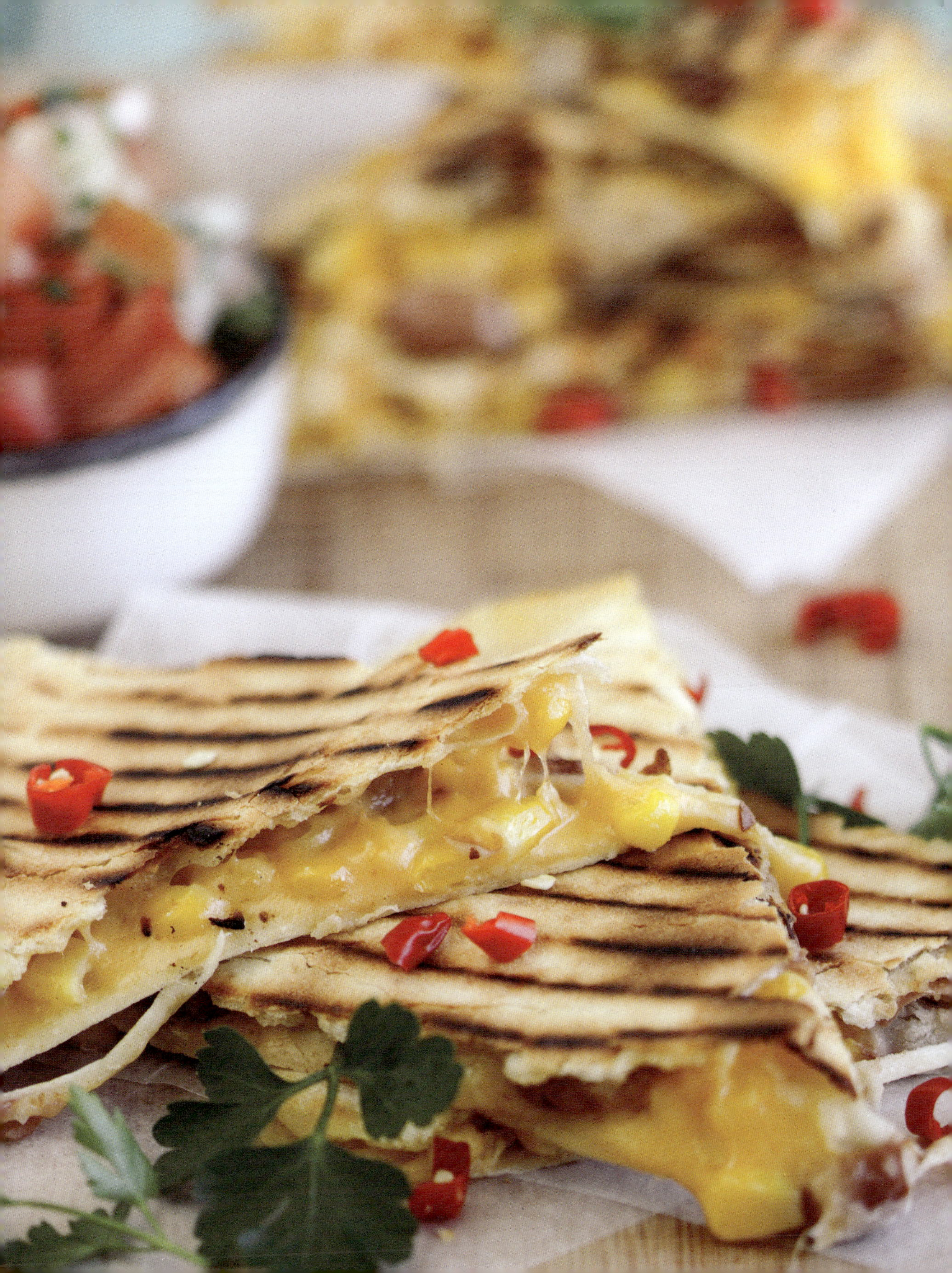

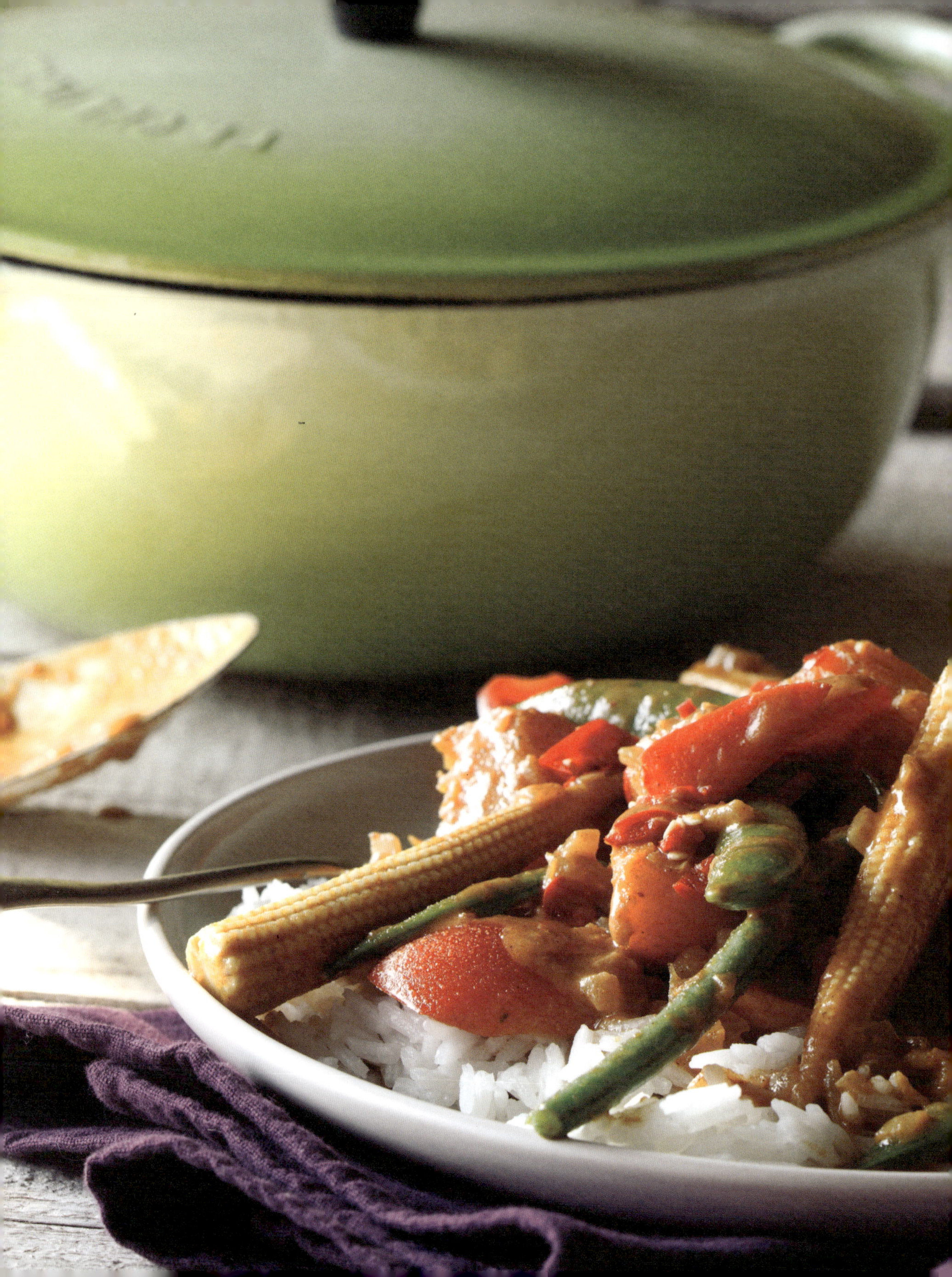

You could serve this curry to your meat-eating friends or family and they wouldn't even know the difference. Hearty vegetables such as butternut and cauliflower bulk up the curry while peppers, sugar snap peas and baby corn add flavour and texture. You could also add any other vegetables you have in the fridge, plus lentils, chickpeas or beans for extra fibre, nutrients and protein.

This is a great weekday alternative as it doesn't need the long cooking time required by lamb or even chicken. If the butternut is chopped into 3–4 cm cubes, it should only take 20–25 minutes for the curry to be ready, from prep to plate. I like to serve it with crispy poppadoms and doughy naan to mop up the juices, but steamed rice would be just as nice.

VEGETABLE AND COCONUT CURRY

Serves 4

- 1 onion, finely chopped
- 2 garlic cloves, crushed
- 2 cm fresh ginger, peeled and grated
- 1 tablespoon garam masala
- 2 teaspoons ground coriander
- 2 teaspoons ground cumin
- 2 teaspoons paprika
- 2 teaspoons turmeric
- 1 tin chopped tomatoes
- 1 teaspoon sugar (optional)
- 250 g butternut, chopped into 3–4 cm cubes
- 250 g cauliflower florets, trimmed and rinsed
- 1 cup vegetable stock
- 100 g sugar snap peas
- 100 g baby corn
- 150 g peppers, deseeded and chopped into bite-sized chunks
- 1 tin coconut milk
- salt to taste
- warm naan bread, to serve
- fried poppadoms, to serve

1. In a large saucepan, fry the onion until soft and translucent. Add the garlic, ginger and spices and allow to fry for another minute.
2. Add the chopped tomatoes and sugar to the spices and allow to cook for 2–3 minutes.
3. Add the butternut and cauliflower and the vegetable stock.
4. Allow to come to a gentle simmer then cover the saucepan and allow to cook for 10 minutes until the butternut and cauliflower are almost tender (a knife should be able to cut through the butternut relatively easily but it shouldn't be able to squash the butternut easily).
5. Add the rest of the vegetables and the coconut milk and allow to simmer for another 10 minutes until all the vegetables are cooked and the sauce has thickened slightly.
6. Season to taste and serve with naan bread and poppadoms.

Vegetarian

I absolutely love a good sandwich – in fact it must rate as one of my top five favourite meals. Using a wide variety of grilled vegetables not only adds depth of flavour but beautiful colour. Grilling the vegetables brings out different characteristics in each of them and the end result is a mouth-wateringly delicious sandwich. The goat's cheese is completely optional, but for me is a must. It adds just the right amount of tang and creaminess to bring all the flavours together.

BAGUETTE WITH GRILLED VEGETABLES AND CHEVIN

There are no quantities given here – the more people you need to feed, the more vegetables you grill and baguettes you halve. Simple.

- thinly sliced vegetables of your choice (I use courgettes, aubergines, red and yellow peppers, and mushrooms)
- olive oil, for grilling
- salt and pepper to taste
- lemon juice (optional)
- fresh baguette, halved
- salted butter, room temperature
- chevin (or other soft goat's cheese)

1. You can char the vegetables either in a very hot griddle pan or under a very hot oven grill. Either way, toss the vegetables in a few glugs of olive oil (they must be moist but not soaking) and season with salt and pepper.
2. Grill until the vegetables are beautifully charred and just softened. Taste and adjust the seasoning if necessary. I like to add a splash of lemon juice at this stage.
3. Spread the butter onto the halved baguette and layer the vegetables onto the bread.
4. Finally add some roughly sliced or crumbled chevin and close with the remaining piece of baguette.
5. Serve immediately.

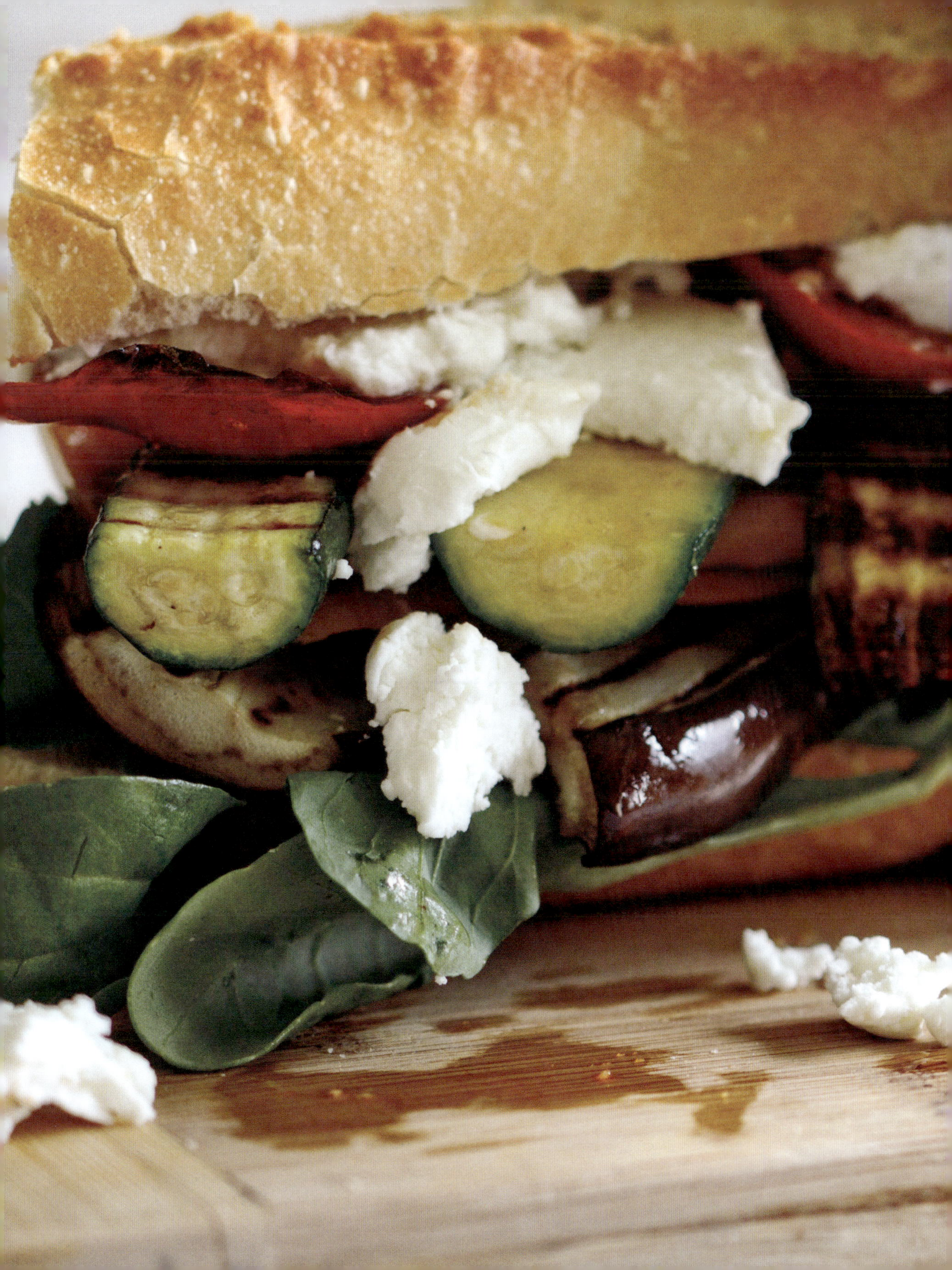

I have a weakness for delicious fillings wrapped in pastry and I'm certain that anyone you serve these to will ask for seconds! If you would prefer to make individual pies completely encased in pastry you'll need two sheets of ready-made puff pastry, but if you're doing them in 'pot-pie' fashion in ramekins, only one sheet will be necessary.

SPINACH AND FETA PIES

Makes 4 pies

1–2 sheets ready-made puff pastry, thawed

1 egg, beaten with 1 tablespoon water, for egg wash

Filling

1 onion, finely chopped

2 garlic cloves, crushed

400 g baby spinach, washed and roughly chopped

pinch of grated nutmeg

juice of ½ lemon

125 ml cream

100 ml milk

3 tablespoons cornflour

salt and pepper to taste

1. Pre-heat the oven to 180 °C and grease 4 ovenproof ramekins or a baking sheet (depending on what type of pie you want to make).
2. Fry the chopped onion and garlic until soft and translucent.
3. Add the baby spinach and nutmeg and allow to wilt down.
4. Add the lemon juice and cream and mix through.
5. Mix the milk and cornflour together and pour into the spinach. Allow to cook for 5–10 minutes until the sauce has thickened. Season to taste.
6. If you are making pot pies, spoon the mixture into the greased ramekins and cover with a round of pastry. Brush the pastry with egg wash and bake for 10–15 minutes until the pastry is golden and crisp.
7. If you are making 'encased pies', cut 4 ovals out of thawed puff pastry. Spoon some of the mixture onto the middle of the pastry, brush the edges with egg wash and fold over the pastry to make a half-moon-shaped pie. Crimp the edges with a fork or your fingers and brush with egg wash. Place onto a greased baking tray and place into the oven. Bake for 15–20 minutes until the pastry is golden and crisp.
8. Serve immediately.

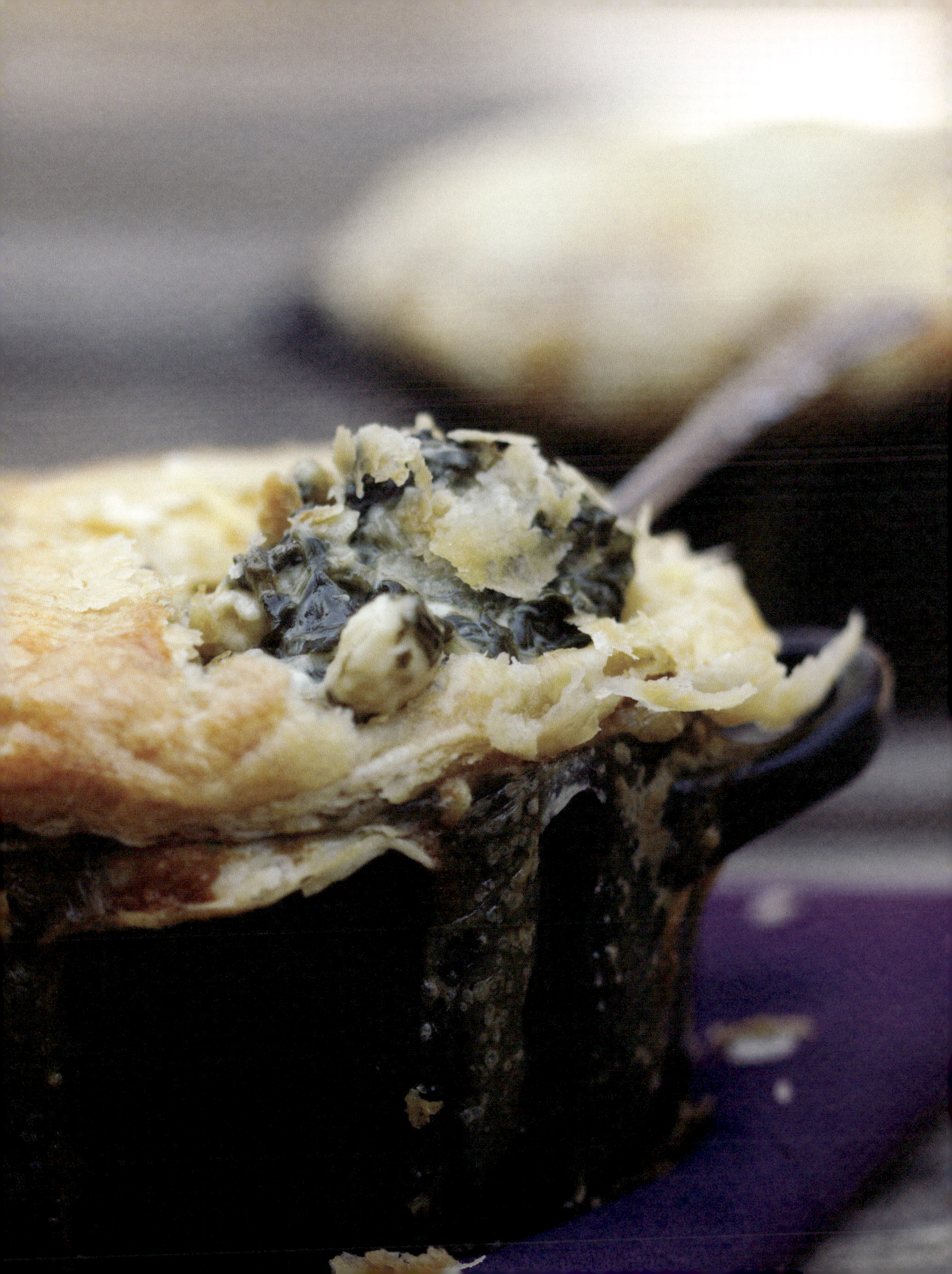

This is one of my favourite side dishes and when served as part of a vegetarian buffet, it's always one of the first dishes to be finished. Even people who don't like aubergine seem to come back for seconds.

AUBERGINE PARMIGIANA

Serves 4–6

Tomato sauce

1 onion, finely chopped

2 garlic cloves, crushed

1 tablespoon fresh oregano, chopped

3 tins chopped or cherry tomatoes

1 small tin (50 g) tomato paste

2 teaspoons sugar

salt and pepper to taste

Aubergines

4 large aubergines

olive oil

2 teaspoons salt

Topping

1 cup mozzarella, grated

1 cup fresh breadcrumbs

1 teaspoon salt

1. Pre-heat the oven to 200 °C.
2. Sauté the onion and garlic in a medium saucepan until soft and translucent.
3. Add the fresh oregano, tomatoes, 1 tin water (using the chopped tomato tin), tomato paste and sugar. Allow to simmer for 10–15 minutes until the sauce has reduced slightly. Season to taste.
4. In the meantime, slice the aubergines and place in a single layer on a roasting tray. Drizzle with olive oil and season with salt and pepper. Place in the oven and roast for 10–15 minutes until cooked.
5. To assemble, pour the tomato sauce into an ovenproof baking dish. Place the roasted aubergines on top of the tomato sauce.
6. Combine the grated mozzarella, breadcrumbs and salt and scatter over the top of the aubergines.
7. Place in the oven and allow to bake for 15 minutes until the topping is golden.
8. Serve immediately.

DESSERTS

I just love using fresh, seasonal fruit to make simple and tasty desserts. This is a more sophisticated version of that timeless old standby, tinned peaches and cream, staying true to those simple flavours. Adding a vanilla bean (or some vanilla paste) to the poaching liquid adds a subtle hint of vanilla, and once the fruit has been chilled it is served with creamy mascarpone – the perfect way to end a meal.

POACHED NECTARINES WITH MASCARPONE

Serves 4

4-6 nectarines, ripe but still firm

¾ cup sugar

4 cups water

1 vanilla bean, split, or 1 teaspoon vanilla paste

mascarpone, to serve

1. If you prefer you can keep the nectarines whole, but I like to cut half of them into wedges and simply halve the rest.
2. Combine the sugar, water and vanilla in a saucepan and allow to come to a boil. Carefully drop the nectarines into the boiling syrup and lower the heat. Allow to simmer for 5-7 minutes until the nectarines are just soft.
3. Remove the nectarines from the syrup and place in a bowl. Allow the syrup to cool to room temperature and pour over the nectarines. Place in the fridge to cool completely.
4. Serve the cooled nectarines with dollops of mascarpone.

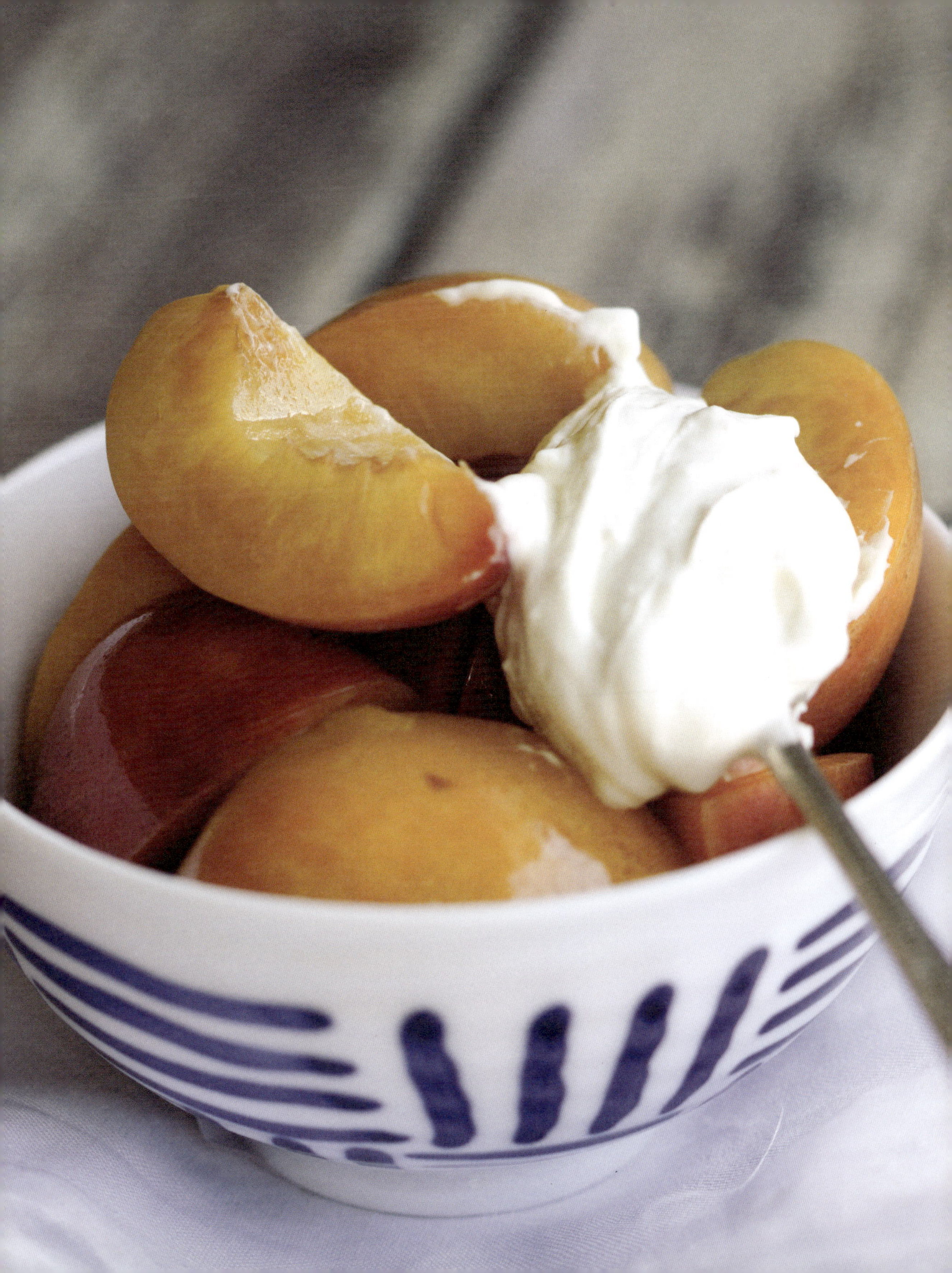

Whenever my gran brought out a tray of these light and fluffy fritters covered in sticky caramel sauce after lunch, I would jump up and down like only a little girl in love with her gran's cooking can. And I am as obsessed with them today as I was then.

Whilst I was writing this book my beloved gran passed away and even though I was heartbroken, the memories I have of her will always put a smile on my face. Like the number of times I begged her to bake cookies. We would roll out the dough, cut the cookies and I would wait patiently while the first batch was in the oven. The moment they were cool enough to touch, I would take the whole tray and go and sit in the corner, scoffing them one by one, leaving my gran to do the rest.

Her memory will forever live on in our minds and hearts, and most tangibly in her recipes. She changed the way our family thought about food and she was definitely the biggest food influence in my life. I will miss her every day but I won't be sad while doing so, because a life like hers should only be celebrated.

MY GRAN'S PUMPKIN FRITTERS IN CARAMEL SAUCE

Makes approximately 24 fritters

Fritters

1 cup pumpkin, cooked

1 cup flour

2 teaspoons baking powder

2 tablespoons caster sugar

1 egg

¼ cup milk

pinch of salt

canola oil, for frying

Caramel sauce

¾ cup sugar

1 cup cream

1 teaspoon vanilla extract

3 tablespoons butter

½ cup golden syrup

1. To make the fritters, combine all the ingredients and mix until you have a smooth batter.
2. Heat the oil in a medium saucepan and fry spoonfuls of the batter until golden brown and cooked throughout.
3. Remove from the oil and drain on kitchen paper.
4. Continue until all the fritters are cooked.
5. To make the caramel sauce, combine all the ingredients in a medium saucepan and cook over a medium heat for 10–15 minutes until the sauce is thick and glossy.
6. Pour the syrup over the fritters and serve.

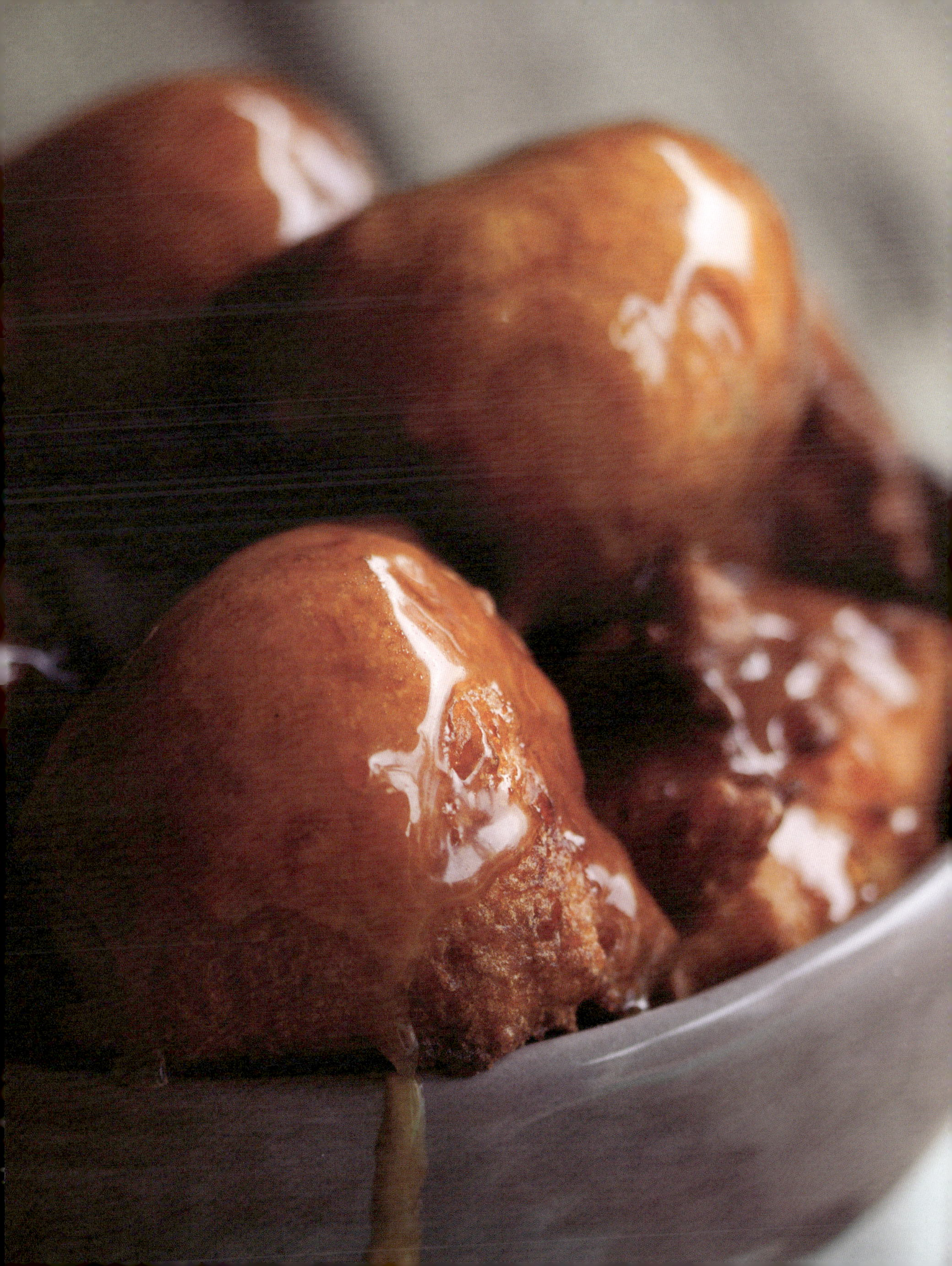

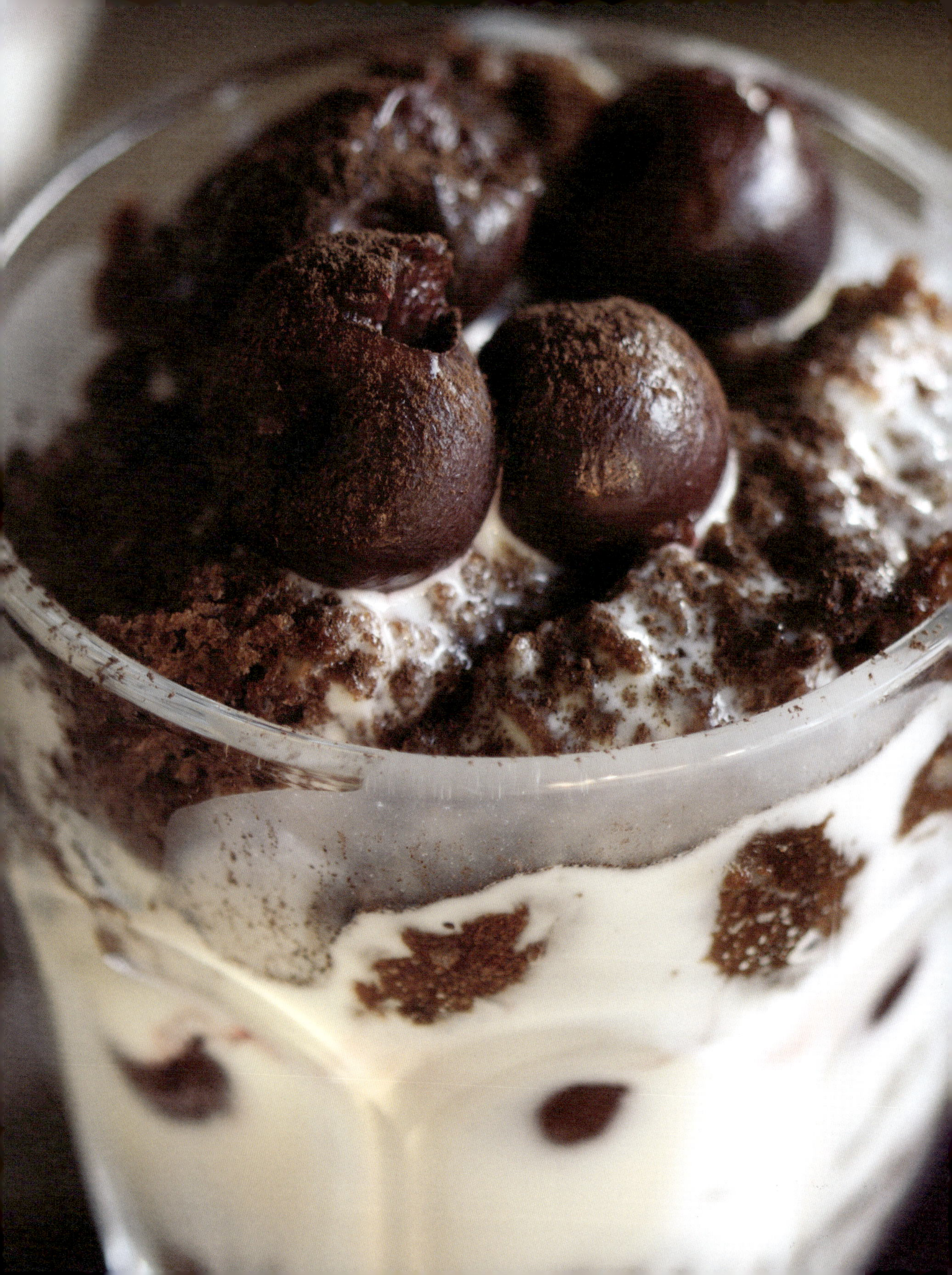

I only make this once a year, on Christmas Eve, when my whole family gets together to open presents and reflect on another year that we have been blessed with. It's incredibly indulgent and just perfect for Christmas.

BLACK FOREST TRIFLE

Serves 10

- 12 chocolate muffins
- 2 tins pitted black cherries
- 500 g cream cheese
- 2 tins condensed milk
- juice of 1 lemon
- ½ cup brandy
- 2 cups cream
- chocolate malt balls (optional)
- icing sugar, sifted

1. Slice the muffins in half.
2. Drain the cherries but keep the juice and mix it with the brandy.
3. Mix the cream cheese and condensed milk and add the lemon juice.
4. Place a layer of muffins in the bottom of a deep bowl (or individual glasses or bowls).
5. Spoon some of the cherry juice and brandy mix over the muffins followed by a few spoons of the cream cheese.
6. Add a few cherries and repeat until all the ingredients are finished.
7. Whip the cream until soft peaks form.
8. Dollop onto the trifle.
9. Decorate with the chocolate malt balls or extra cherries and dust with icing sugar.

I've never come across a South African who doesn't love Peppermint Crisp tart. There's something so endearing and charming about this incredibly sweet dessert. I wanted to pay homage to this national classic but also wanted to add a bit of a twist, so I decided to combine two of my favourites, Peppermint Crisp tart and Eton mess. The end result is not only delicious but incredibly easy. Using shop-bought meringues (which I prefer in this instance) allows you to assemble this dish at the table. Nothing could be simpler, and I promise you, your friends and family will love it!

PEPPERMINT CRISP MESS

Serves 6–8, depending on portion size

2 cups cream

1 tin Caramel Treat

100 g meringues, roughly crumbled, plus more for serving

150 g Peppermint Crisp, crushed

1. Reserve 3 tablespoons of the cream and whip the rest into stiff peaks.
2. Combine the reserved cream with the Caramel Treat. Mix until the caramel is smooth.
3. In small glass bowls or glasses, layer the caramel cream with the crushed Peppermint Crisp and roughly crumbled meringues.
4. Serve with extra meringue and Peppermint Crisp crushed over the top.

Malva pudding needs no introduction for any South African. We all know that there are few desserts that go as well with a proper Sunday lunch. It's sweet, rich and decadent and served with ice-cold custard, it is perfection. This is my aunt Elnette's recipe and I'd just like to thank her for being so generous with her recipes and for always being such an inspiration to me!

MALVA PUDDING

Serves 6–8

- 2 tablespoons unsalted butter
- 1 cup sugar
- 2 tablespoons smooth apricot jam
- 2 teaspoons white spirit vinegar
- 2 cups flour
- 2 cups milk
- 2 eggs
- 2 teaspoons bicarbonate of soda (baking soda)
- pinch of salt

Syrup

- 1 cup sugar
- ½ cup boiling water
- ¾ cup unsalted butter
- 1 teaspoon vanilla extract

1. Pre-heat your oven to 180 °C and grease a 20 cm square pie or baking dish.
2. In a large saucepan, melt the butter, sugar, apricot jam and vinegar together until the sugar has dissolved and the mixture is smooth. Remove from the heat and allow to cool for 5 minutes. Meanwhile sift the flour.
3. Alternating, add the flour and milk until the mixture is smooth and thick.
4. Add the eggs one by one, beating well after each addition.
5. Add the baking soda and salt and beat well.
6. Pour the mixture into your prepared baking dish and bake for 30–45 minutes until the pudding is dark and baked through (a skewer inserted should come out clean).
7. In a small saucepan, heat the syrup ingredients and cook until the sugar has dissolved.
8. Pour the syrup over the cooked pudding and allow to stand for 10 minutes before serving with custard.

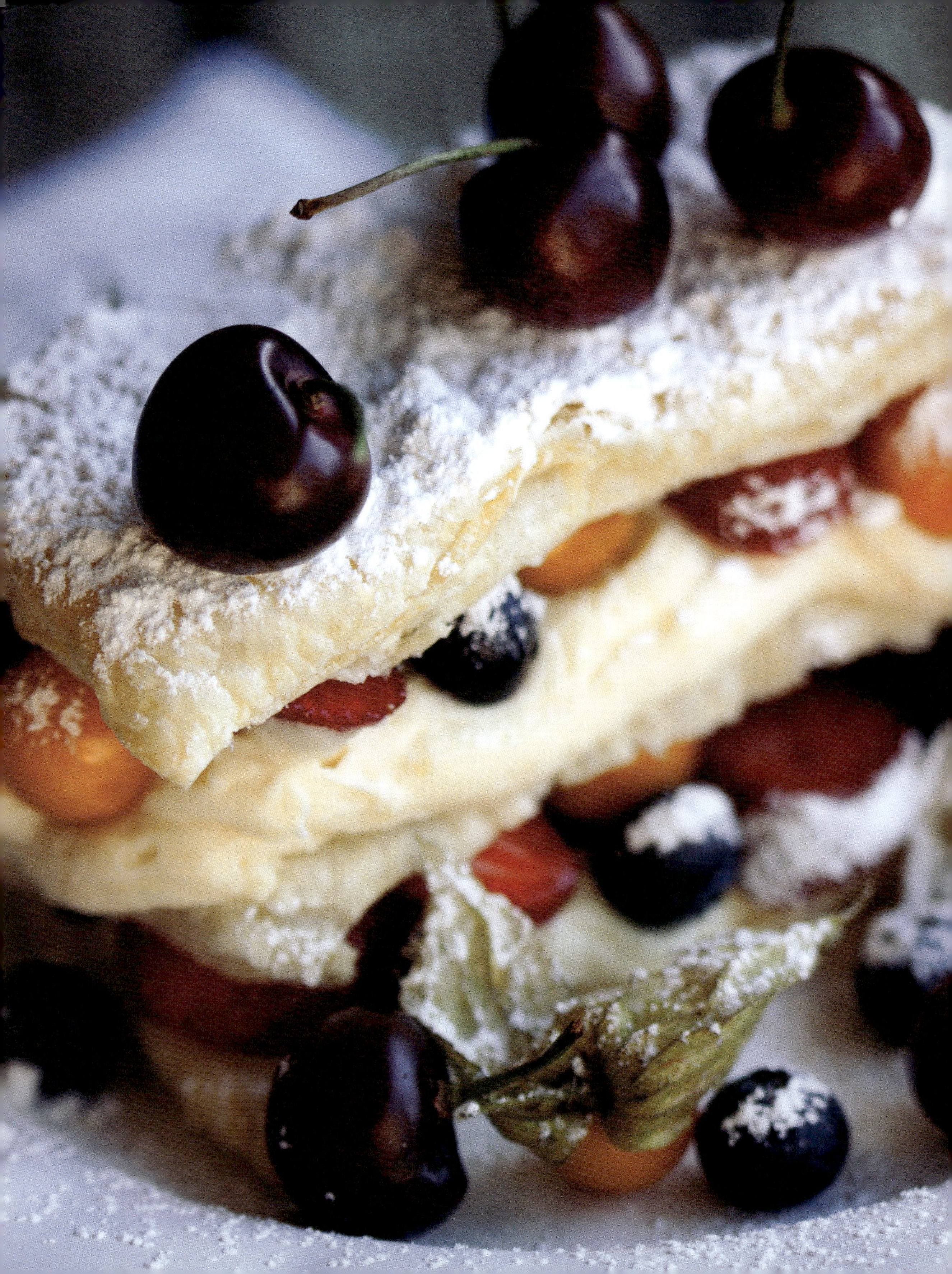

MILLEFEUILLE WITH WHITE CHOCOLATE CREAM AND BERRIES

Serves 4

White chocolate cream

300 ml full cream milk

1 teaspoon vanilla extract

3 egg yolks

50 g caster sugar

2 tablespoons flour (approximately 30 g)

2 tablespoons cornflour (approximately 30 g)

pinch of salt

100 g white chocolate, finely chopped

Pastry layers

1 roll ready-made puff pastry, thawed

3 tablespoons caster sugar

To assemble

fresh berries of your choice

icing sugar

1. To make the white chocolate cream, heat the milk and vanilla in a medium saucepan until just before boiling point (this is called scalding).
2. In the meantime, mix together the egg yolks, sugar, flours and pinch of salt until the mixture is smooth and thick.
3. When the milk mixture is hot, pour it slowly into the egg yolk mixture whilst continuously mixing (I do this in my free-standing mixer to make it easier).
4. When all the milk has been incorporated, transfer the runny mixture back to the saucepan and over a gentle heat, allow it to cook and thicken, whisking continuously.
5. When the mixture is thick and there is no flouriness when you taste it, remove it from the heat and beat in the chopped white chocolate. Stir until the chocolate is melted and then pass the mixture through a sieve just in case there are any lumps.
6. Place in a bowl and put a piece of cling film directly onto the surface of the cream to prevent a skin from forming. Place in the fridge and allow to cool.
7. To make the pastry layers, start by pre-heating the oven to 180 °C and line a baking sheet with baking paper.
8. Roll the puff pastry out on a floured surface and cut into 8–12 rectangles (5 x 10 cm) (depending on whether you want 2 or 3 layers). Place the rectangles onto the prepared baking sheet and sprinkle with the caster sugar.
9. Place in the oven and bake for 10 minutes until the pastry is golden brown and puffed up.
10. Remove from the oven and allow to cool completely.
11. To assemble the millefeuille, layer the pastry rectangles with the white chocolate cream and fresh berries.

Even though I've included this recipe under Desserts, this is actually one of my favourite breakfasts. It's indulgent and a bit sinful and some mornings that's all I need.

The flapjacks take a few minutes to whip up and the fact that all you have to do is open a tub of mascarpone and scatter over a few blueberries makes it all the more worthwhile! You could place some of the blueberries onto each flapjack while it's cooking so they sink into the batter, but I prefer them fresh, scattered over the top.

FLAPJACKS WITH MASCARPONE AND BLUEBERRIES

Serves 2

- 1 cup flour
- 1 teaspoon baking powder
- pinch of salt
- 50 g sugar
- 1 large egg
- 50 ml oil
- 1 cup milk
- mascarpone sweetened with caster sugar, to serve
- fresh blueberries, to serve

1. In a large bowl, sift together the flour, baking powder and salt. Mix in the sugar.
2. Beat the egg lightly and mix with the oil and milk. Pour into the dry ingredients and mix well.
3. Place spoonfuls of the batter in a hot pan and flip once bubbles start appearing on the surface.
4. Serve immediately with the sweetened mascarpone and fresh blueberries.

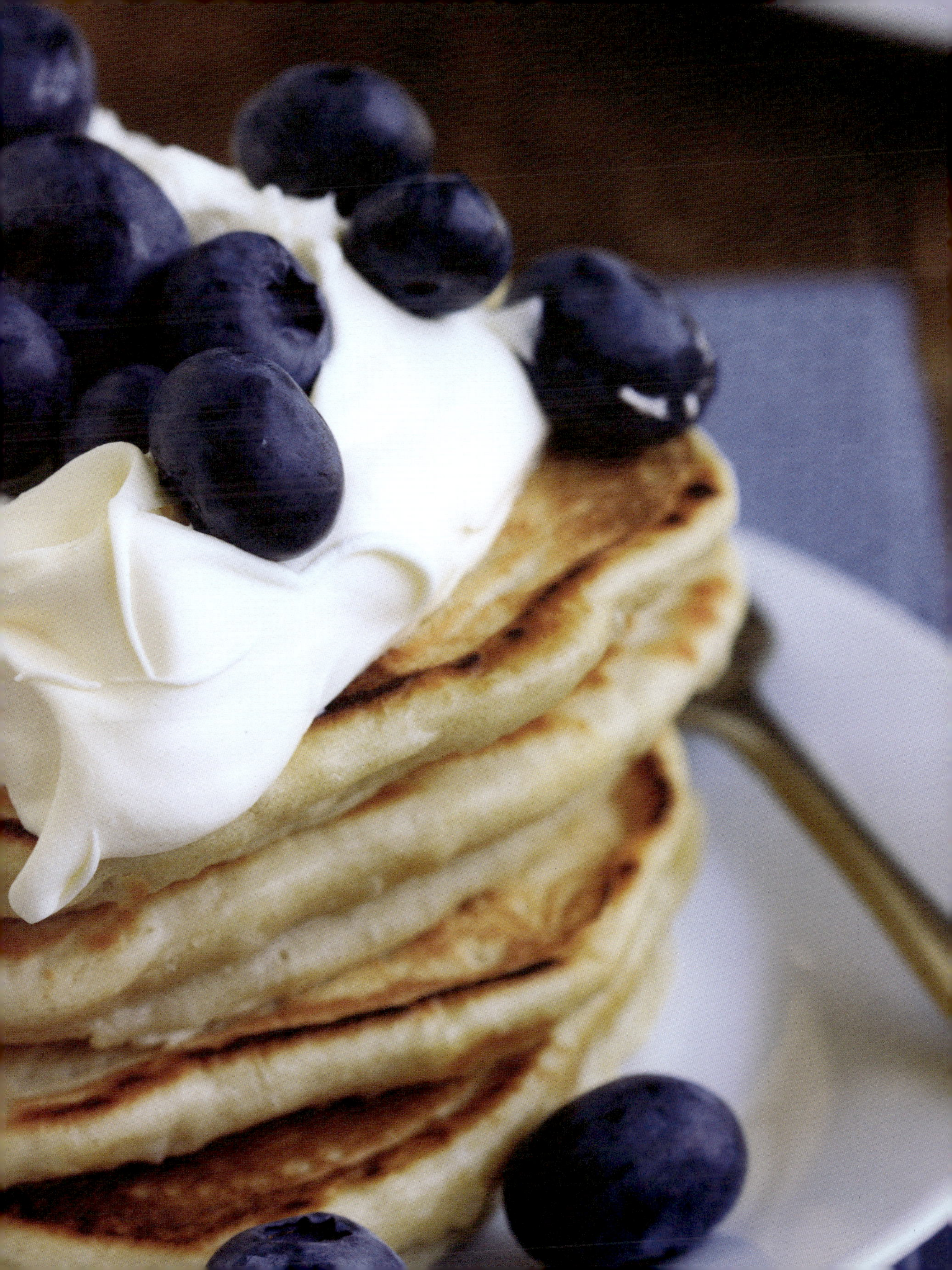

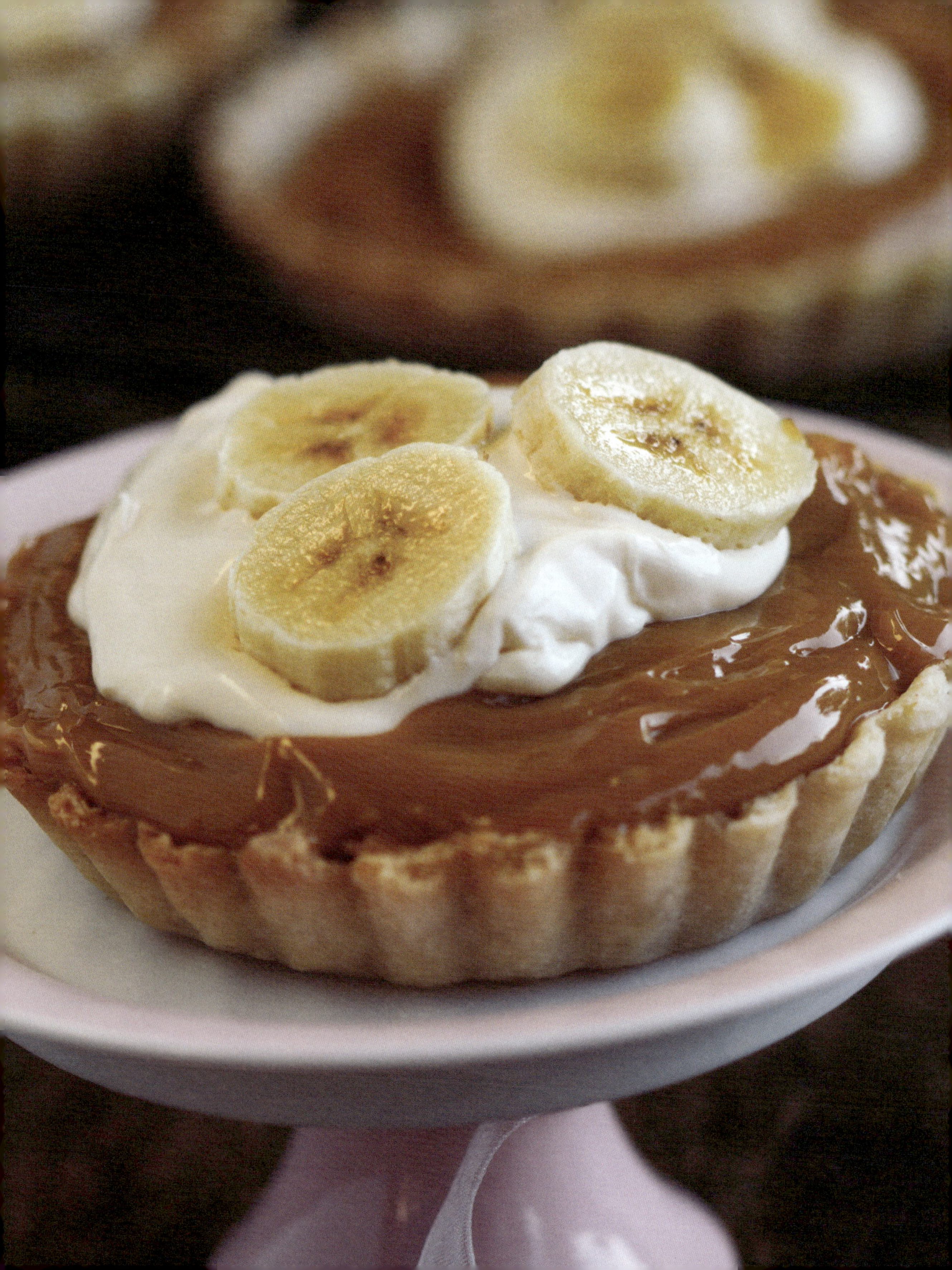

I will never forget the first time I tasted banana with caramel (dulce de leche) when I was about 15. A coffee shop franchise that opened in our local mall served enormous banana-caramel crêpes filled with sticky and sweet caramel, topped with slices of fresh banana and finished off with even more caramel. I have not lost my infatuation with the combination 10 years down the line.

These little tarts are incredibly easy to put together and for the base (crust) you have two options: you can take the lazy route (as I do) and use ready-made shortcrust pastry, or you could crush tennis biscuits (or any similar cookie of your choice), mix it with melted butter, then press it into tart cases and refrigerate for 30 minutes before continuing with the rest of the recipe.

BANANA CARAMEL TARTLETTES

Makes 6 tarts

- 1 roll ready-made shortcrust pastry, defrosted (or crushed biscuits mixed with melted butter)
- 3–4 large bananas, thinly sliced
- 1 tin Caramel Treat (dulce de leche)
- 1 tablespoon lemon juice
- double cream, to serve
- sliced bananas, to serve

1. Pre-heat the oven to 180 °C and grease 6 small tart cases.
2. If you are using pastry, roll the pastry out to fit into the tart tins. Press the pastry into the cases, allowing a bit of 'overhang' in case the pastry shrinks.
3. Place a square of baking paper on top of the pastry and fill with dried beans/ rice/ lentils and bake for 10 minutes (this is known as blind-baking.) Remove and discard the baking paper and beans and bake for another 5–10 minutes until the pastry cases are golden brown and cooked through.
4. Remove from the oven and allow to cool completely.
5. When the pastry has cooled, place a layer of sliced bananas at the bottom of each case.
6. Mix the Caramel Treat with the lemon juice and spoon over the bananas.
7. Place in the refrigerator and allow to set for 1–2 hours.
8. To serve, place a dollop of cream on top of the caramel and add some sliced bananas.

The idea of making chocolate truffles may leave you feeling hopelessly anxious, but you must believe me when I tell you how easy these little nuggets of deliciousness really are. So all I'll do is leave you with the recipe and hope that you'll give it a go!

CHOCOLATE TRUFFLES

Makes approximately 25 truffles

400 g dark chocolate

1 cup cream

60 ml butter, softened and cubed

15 ml liqueur of your choice,
eg Amarula, Frangelico, brandy (optional)

sifted cocoa powder, to roll in

1. Melt the chocolate and cream in a double boiler.
2. Allow to cool slightly before beating in the butter.
3. Make sure that the butter is completely incorporated into the chocolate mixture. At this stage you can add the liqueur of your choice.
4. Cover the bowl with cling film and refrigerate for 3-4 hours until firm enough to roll into balls (depending on your fridge this might take longer).
5. Roll teaspoons of the mixture into balls and place on a baking sheet lined with baking paper.
6. Refrigerate for another 30 minutes before rolling in the cocoa powder.
7. Refrigerate until you're ready to serve them.

Pavlova is one of my favourite desserts because it is so easily transformed between the seasons. My favourite way of serving it is with lots of fresh berries or fresh granadilla, but during the colder months when fresh fruits are limited to citrus, apples and pears, I feel the need to get a bit more creative.

I like to get all the components ready a few hours before I need to serve the pavlovas (except for the chocolate cream) so that the assembly can done quickly and painlessly.

MINI PAVLOVAS WITH ROASTED PEARS AND CHOCOLATE CREAM

Serves 6

Pavlova

4 egg whites

pinch of salt

200 g caster sugar

1 teaspoon cream of tartar

Roasted pears

4 large pears, peeled and cored, and sliced into wedges

juice of 1 lemon

1 tablespoon canola oil

2 tablespoons white sugar

Chocolate cream

200 ml cream

100 g dark chocolate, melted

1. To make the pavlovas, pre-heat the oven to 120 °C and line a baking tray with baking paper.
2. Beat the egg whites with a pinch of salt until foamy. With the mixer running, slowly add the caster sugar until the egg whites have formed stiff and glossy peaks. Sift in the cream of tartar and mix through.
3. Pipe or spoon the meringue mixture onto the baking paper. I like to make pavlovas about 5 cm wide in size.
4. Bake for 1 hour until the meringues are crisp on the outside but still chewy on the inside.
5. Remove from the oven and allow to cool completely before storing in an airtight container.
6. To make the pears, pre-heat the oven to 200 °C.
7. Place the sliced pears, with the other ingredients, on a roasting tray.
8. Put the pears in the oven and roast for 20 minutes until they start to caramelise and they are soft.
9. Remove from the oven and allow to cool.
10. For the chocolate cream, whip the cream until stiff peaks form. With the mixer still running, slowly pour in the melted chocolate. Beat until the mixture is cool and thick.
11. To serve, top the pavlovas with the chocolate cream and roasted pears.

Desserts

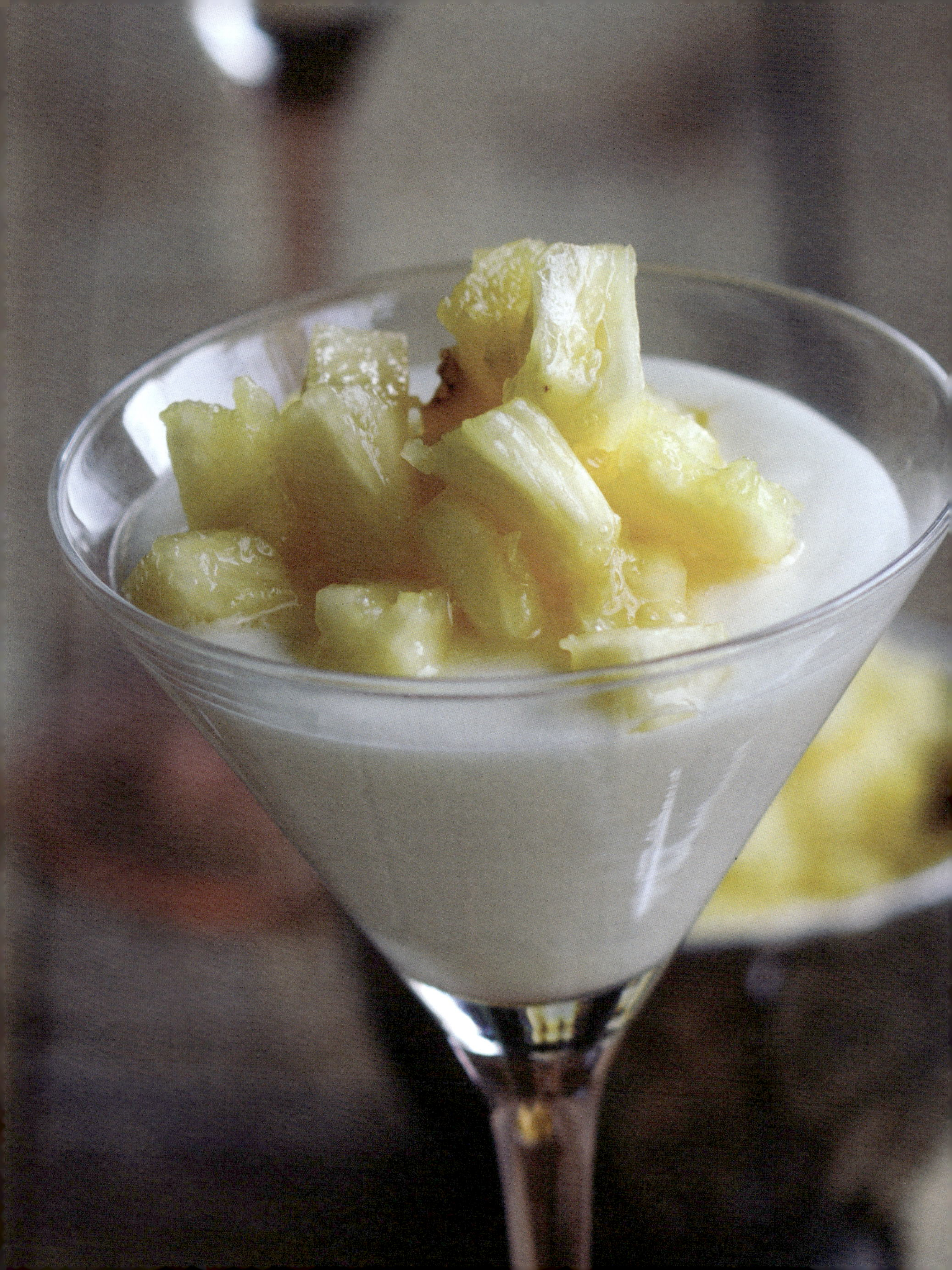

The first time I ate this white chocolate mousse, I thought it must be like eating a cloud. By using both whipped egg whites and whipped cream, you are left with a light and fluffy mousse that is ever so subtly flavoured with white chocolate.

I like to serve a tangy, fresh fruit with this and finely chopped pineapple is just perfect to cut through the creaminess of the mousse. You could also use fresh granadilla if you prefer.

WHITE CHOCOLATE MOUSSE WITH FRESH PINEAPPLE

Serves 4-6

½ cup water
½ cup sugar
3 extra-large egg whites
100 g white chocolate
1 cup cream
fresh pineapple, finely chopped, to serve

1. Combine the water and sugar in a small saucepan and allow to boil for 8-10 minutes until it becomes slightly syrupy ('soft ball stage' – in other words dropping a bit of the mixture in a glass of cold water should result in a soft ball).
2. While the syrup is boiling, melt the white chocolate and allow to cool slightly.
3. Beat the egg whites until soft peaks start to form.
4. With the mixer running, slowly pour in the hot syrup in a thin stream.
5. Pour in the melted white chocolate and beat the mixture until the bowl feels cool again. A lot of the air will have been lost from the egg whites but don't be concerned.
6. Whip the cream until stiff peaks start forming and fold into the cooled egg white mixture.
7. Distribute the mousse between 4-6 glasses or ramekins and place in the fridge to set for 4-6 hours (or overnight).
8. Serve cold with fresh, chopped pineapple.

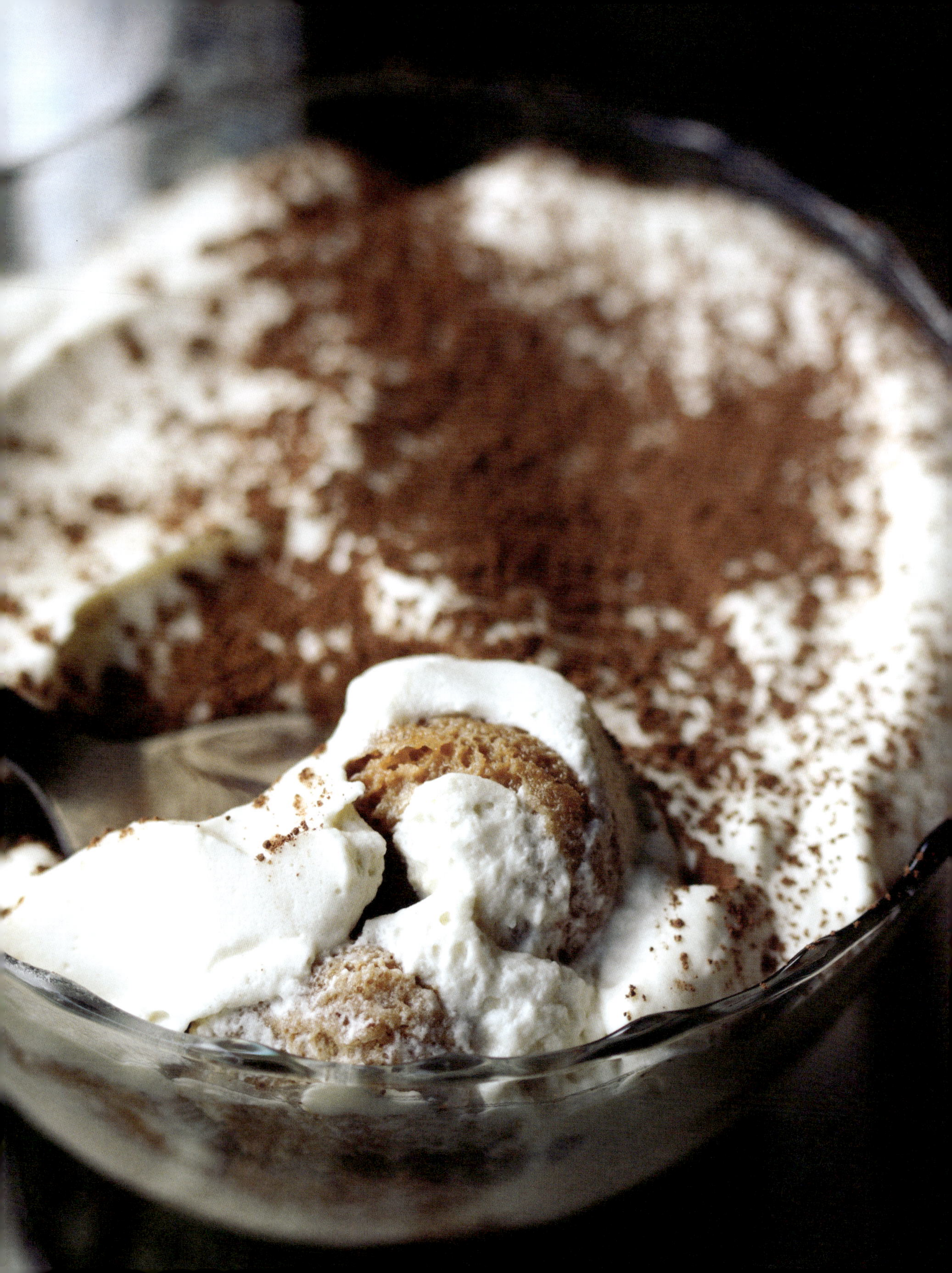

People who used to entertain in the nineties will have a sense of déjà vu at the sight of tiramisu – it was the dessert of the decade according to some. I remember my mom making it on numerous occasions and it was always a hit, but then my mom's tiramisu was amazing.

One thing that can be slightly off-putting about tiramisu is when the biscuits become watery from being left to soak for too long, so this is to be avoided. I also like to inject as much flavour as possible into the espresso used for soaking so I add both Tia Maria and Amarula liqueur.

This recipe serves a small army of people, but even if I just have a few people over for dinner I still make this quantity because there is nothing as delicious as leftover tiramisu!

TIRAMISU

Serves 8–10

6 egg yolks
150 g caster sugar
½ cup espresso, cooled
1 teaspoon vanilla extract
3 cups cream
½ cup Amarula
½ cup Tia Maria
about 800 g finger biscuits
cocoa powder, for dusting

1. To make the cream layer, beat the egg yolks with the sugar until thick and creamy (about 10 minutes).
2. With the mixer running, add the cooled espresso and vanilla extract and beat until well mixed.
3. In a separate bowl, whip the cream until stiff peaks form.
4. With the mixer running, add the whipped cream to the egg yolk mixture and beat until thick and creamy and well incorporated.
5. Place the espresso, Amarula and Tia Maria in a shallow dish suitable for dunking the finger biscuits into.
6. Coat the biscuits in the espresso mixture. It's important that you don't let them soak in the liquid; they should just be covered or they will start breaking apart and become soggy.
7. Place the biscuits at the bottom of a large rectangular dish or in individual glasses.
8. Cover the biscuits with the cream mixture. (If you want to you can create layers with the biscuits and cream mixture.)
9. Add a dusting of cocoa powder over the top of the cream mixture and place in the fridge to set for 2–3 hours (or overnight).

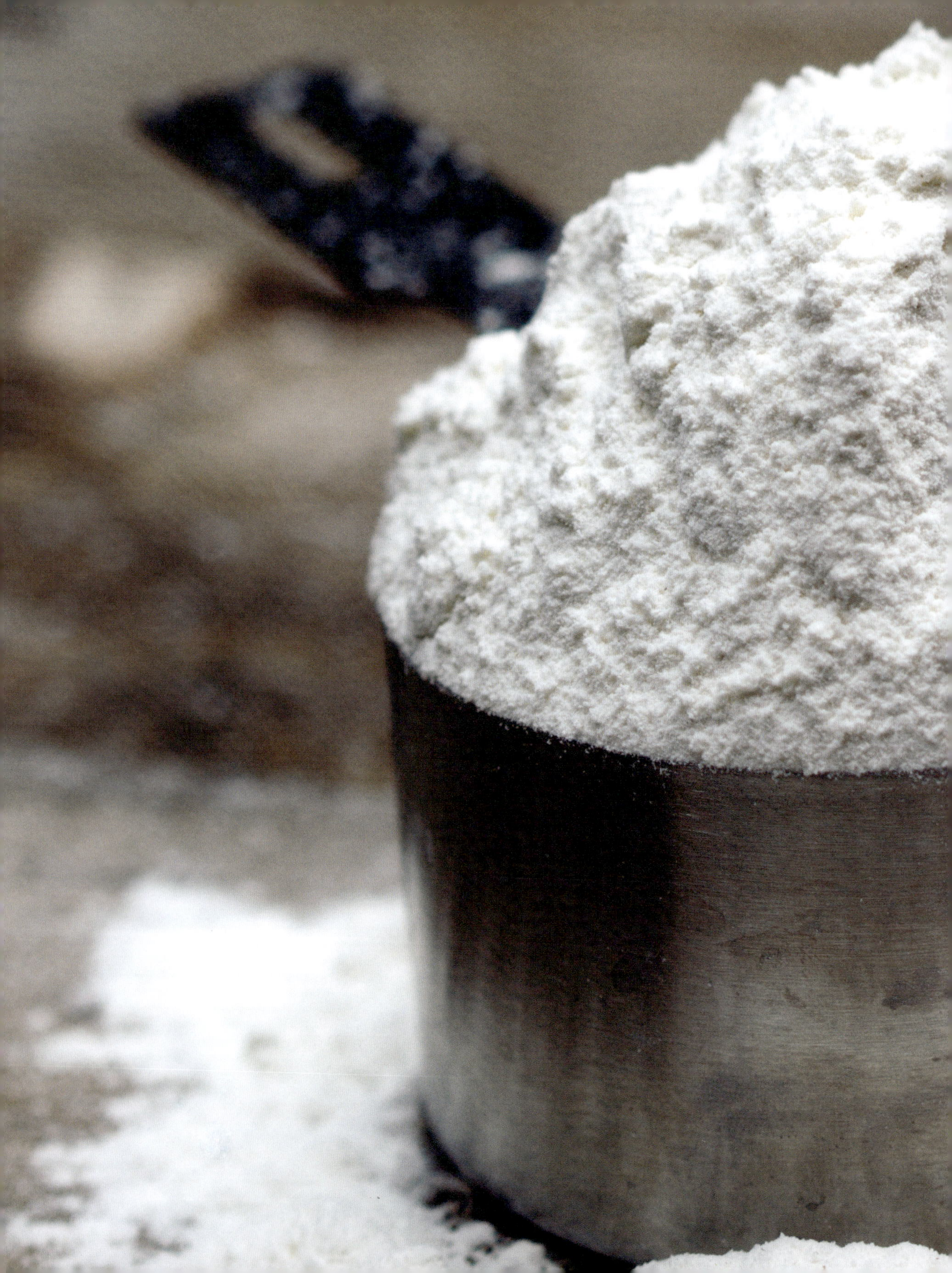

BAKING

Cupcakes have gained almost cult-like popularity over the last few years, which probably leaves me with very little to say to convince you to get stuck into a cupcake (or three). Believe me, a platter filled with these little darlings won't last very long.

STRAWBERRY AND CREAM CUPCAKES

Makes 12 cupcakes

Strawberry purée (makes approximately 100 ml)

250 g fresh strawberries

3 tablespoons icing sugar

Cupcake mixture

200 g cake flour

150 g caster sugar

125 g butter, room temperature

½ cup milk

2 large eggs

2 teaspoons baking powder

Butter cream icing

100 g unsalted butter, room temperature

400 g icing sugar, sifted

1 teaspoon vanilla extract

2–4 tablespoons milk

fresh strawberries, for decorating

1. Pre-heat the oven to 180 °C and grease and line a 12-hole muffin or cupcake tray with cupcake liners.
2. First make the purée by blending the strawberries with the icing sugar.
3. Place the rest of the cupcake ingredients in a large mixing bowl together with the purée and beat for 2 minutes until the mixture is smooth and thick.
4. Divide the batter between the cupcake liners and place in the oven.
5. Bake for 20–25 minutes until a skewer inserted comes out clean.
6. Remove from the oven and allow to cool completely before icing and decorating the cupcakes.
7. To make the butter cream, beat the butter and icing sugar until pale and fluffy. Add the vanilla extract and, if necessary, thin out slightly with milk.
8. Pipe or spread the butter cream onto the cupcakes and decorate with fresh strawberries.

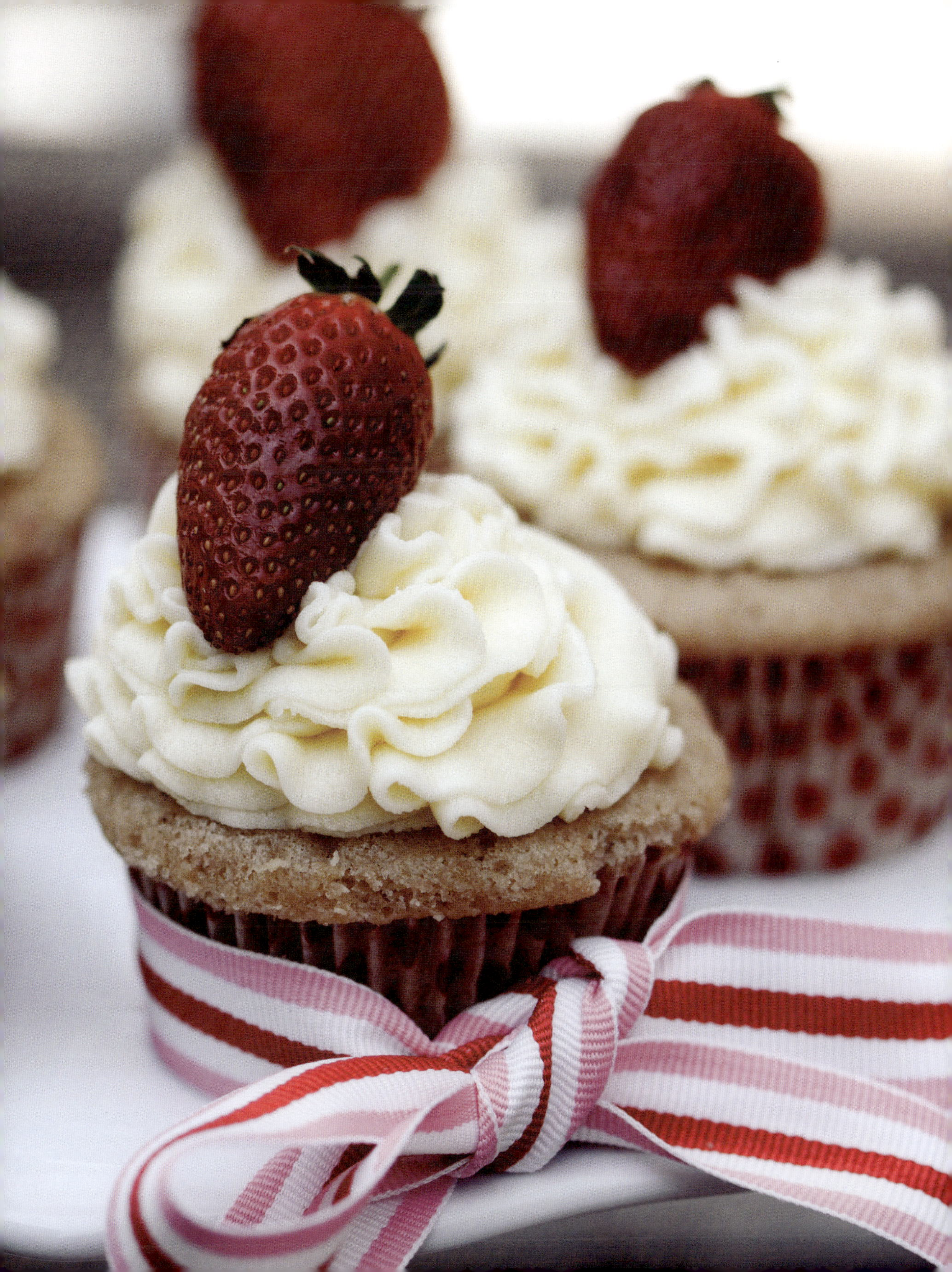

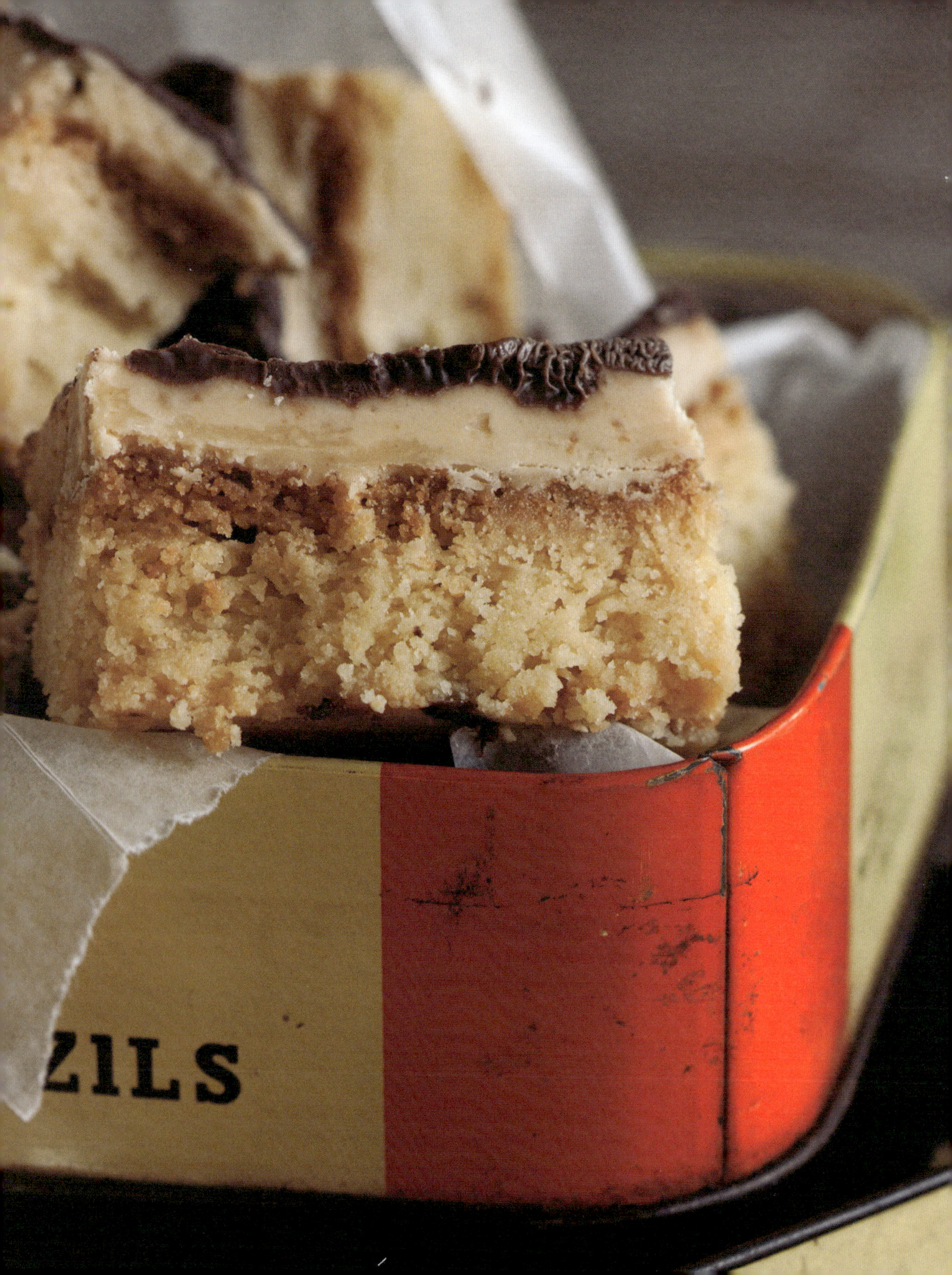
ZILS

Not much has to be said about millionaire's shortbread. Buttery shortbread, sweet and sticky caramel and dark chocolate? Yes please!

MILLIONAIRE'S SHORTBREAD

Shortbread

450 g butter, room temperature

450 g flour

200 g caster sugar

2 tablespoons cornflour

1 teaspoon vanilla extract

Caramel filling and chocolate layer

1 can condensed milk

100 g butter

200 g dark chocolate

1. Pre-heat the oven to 160 °C and grease and line (with baking paper) a 25 cm square or rectangular baking tin.
2. In a bowl, beat the butter until pale before adding all the other shortbread ingredients. Work this mixture into a soft and pliable dough.
3. Press the dough into the prepared pan and prick the surface with a fork.
4. Bake the shortbread for 25–30 minutes until golden brown and firm.
5. Remove from the oven and allow to cool slightly.
6. For the filling, combine the condensed milk and butter in a small saucepan and allow to bubble and cook over a medium heat until the mixture thickens and turns into a golden brown caramel. Stir regularly as the mixture will catch and burn easily.
7. When the caramel is cooked (it will be quite tacky), pour it over the shortbread and spread with a wet spatula.
8. Allow the caramel to set slightly.
9. Melt the dark chocolate and pour over the caramel. Smooth the top and place in a cool spot to set.
10. When the chocolate and caramel have set (at least 3 hours), remove from the tin and cut into bite-sized pieces.
11. The millionaire's shortbread will last for 1 week in a sealed container.

For me, the perfect cookie is crisp and golden on the outside but still slightly chewy in the middle. There is no reason to mess with an old favourite, but when I couldn't find choc-chips recently, I decided to chop up a bar of chocolate myself and the end result was a real winner. I love how chocolate-packed these cookies are and it's also much cheaper than buying the equivalent weight in choc-chips. Remember to serve them with an ice-cold glass of milk!

CHOC-CHUNK COOKIES

Makes approximately 30 cookies

- 250 g butter
- 200 g light-brown sugar
- 100 g caster sugar
- 2 eggs
- 1 teaspoon vanilla extract
- 350 g cake flour
- 1 teaspoon bicarbonate of soda (baking soda)
- 2 ml salt
- 500 g chopped dark chocolate

1. Pre-heat the oven to 180 °C and line a baking tray with baking paper.
2. Beat together the butter and sugars until pale and fluffy.
3. Add the eggs, one at a time, beating well after each addition.
4. Add the vanilla extract and mix through.
5. Sift in the cake flour, bicarbonate of soda and salt and mix well.
6. Lastly, fold in the chocolate chunks.
7. Place spoonfuls (I use approximately 2 tablespoons worth of dough per cookie) of the mixture on the baking tray, spaced about 5 cm apart.
8. Place the cookies in the oven and bake for 10 minutes until golden brown.
9. Remove from the oven and transfer to a wire rack and allow to cool.
10. The cookies will last for just more than a week if kept in a sealed container.

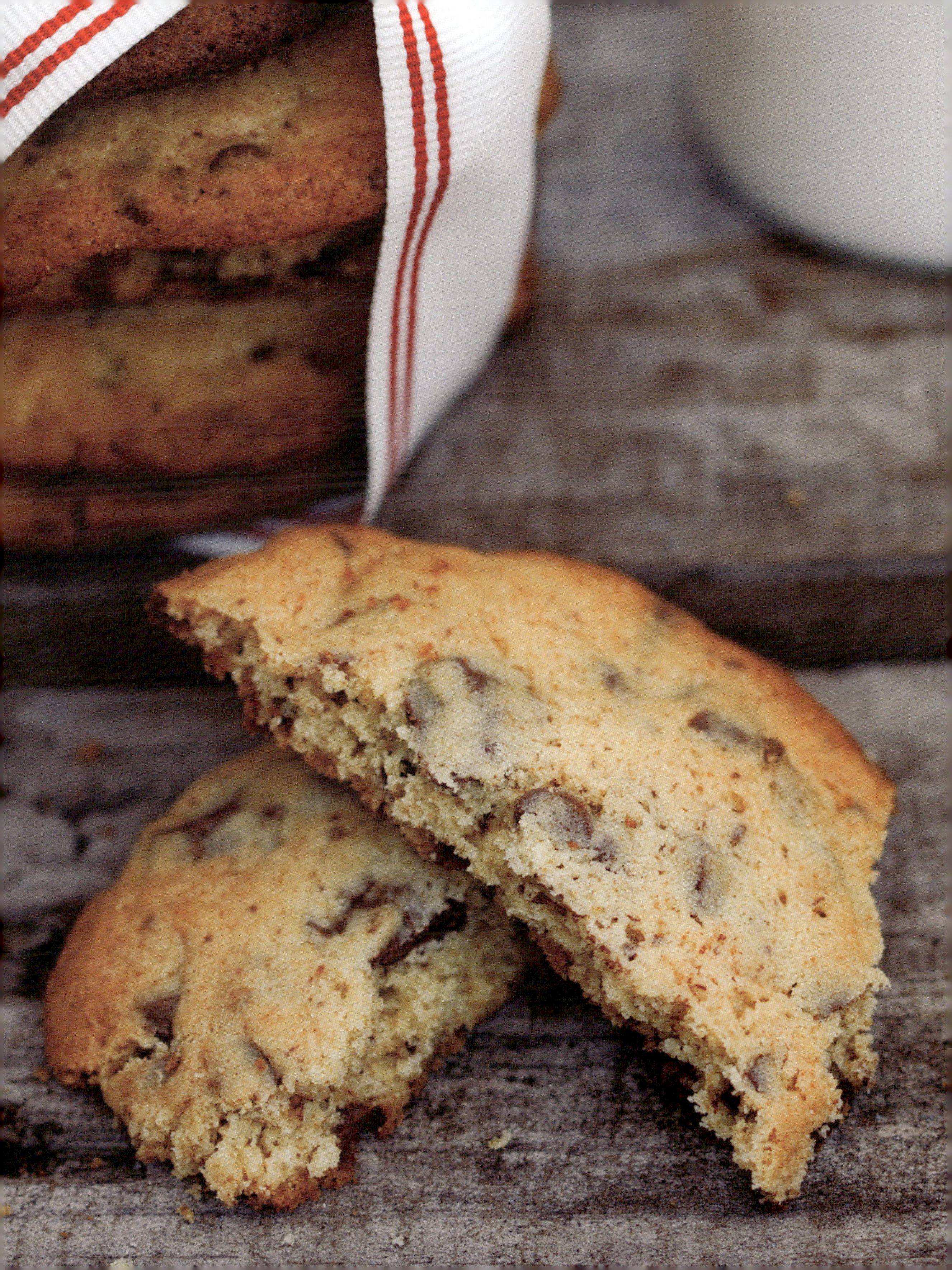

Red velvet cake has become so popular over the last few years and I don't think it's going anywhere soon. People seem to fall over themselves whenever it is served and with good reason. A good red velvet recipe will result in a delicately flavoured, delicious moist cake with a tangy cream cheese frosting. What's not to love?

RED VELVET CUPCAKES

Makes 12 cupcakes

350 g flour
2–3 tablespoons cocoa powder
pinch of salt
325 g sugar
350 ml canola oil
1 teaspoon vanilla extract
2 eggs
1 cup buttermilk
½ teaspoon red colouring

Cream cheese frosting

50 g cream cheese, room temperature
150 g unsalted butter, room temperature
400 g icing sugar, sifted
1 teaspoon vanilla extract
2 tablespoons milk

1. Pre-heat the oven to 180 °C. Line a 12-hole muffin tray with cupcake cases.
2. Sift the flour, cocoa powder, salt and sugar into a large mixing bowl.
3. Mix together the oil, vanilla extract, eggs, buttermilk and red food colouring and pour into the dry ingredients.
4. Mix well until smooth and well combined.
5. Pour the mixture into the cupcake cases, filling them three quarters full.
6. Place in the oven and bake for 15–20 minutes until a skewer inserted comes out clean.
7. Remove from the oven and allow to cool completely before frosting.
8. To make the cream cheese frosting, beat the cream cheese and butter together until light and fluffy.
9. Add the sifted icing sugar and beat until the mixture is thick and smooth.
10. Add the vanilla extract and if necessary, thin out slightly with the milk.
11. Pipe or spread the frosting over the cooled cupcakes.

Baking a cake with polenta might sound odd to you, but it works. I promise!

This cake is intensely lemony, rich and buttery at the same time, which is just perfection in my opinion. I especially love serving it in winter, when all you need to cheer you up is something sunshiny yellow. This cake is just that.

And don't think of serving it with anything other than a good cup of strong coffee or espresso.

LEMON POLENTA CAKE

Makes one single layer cake

- 150 g fine polenta (not the quick-cooking variety)
- 150 g ground almonds
- 15 ml baking powder
- 250 g butter, softened
- 200 g caster sugar
- 3 large, free-range eggs
- zest of 2 lemons
- juice of 1 lemon

Lemon glaze
- 100 g icing sugar, sifted
- juice of 1 lemon

1. Pre-heat the oven to 180 °C. Lightly grease a cake tin of approximately 30 cm and line with baking paper.
2. Mix the dry ingredients together and set aside.
3. Cream the butter and sugar until light and fluffy.
4. Add the eggs and dry ingredients, alternating and mixing well after each addition. Start with an egg and end with the dry ingredients.
5. Add the lemon zest and juice and mix well.
6. Transfer the mixture to the lined cake tin and bake for 40–50 minutes until a skewer inserted comes out clean.
7. Allow to cool completely in the tin before removing.
8. To make the lemon glaze, combine the icing sugar and lemon juice and mix well. Pour over the cooled cake.

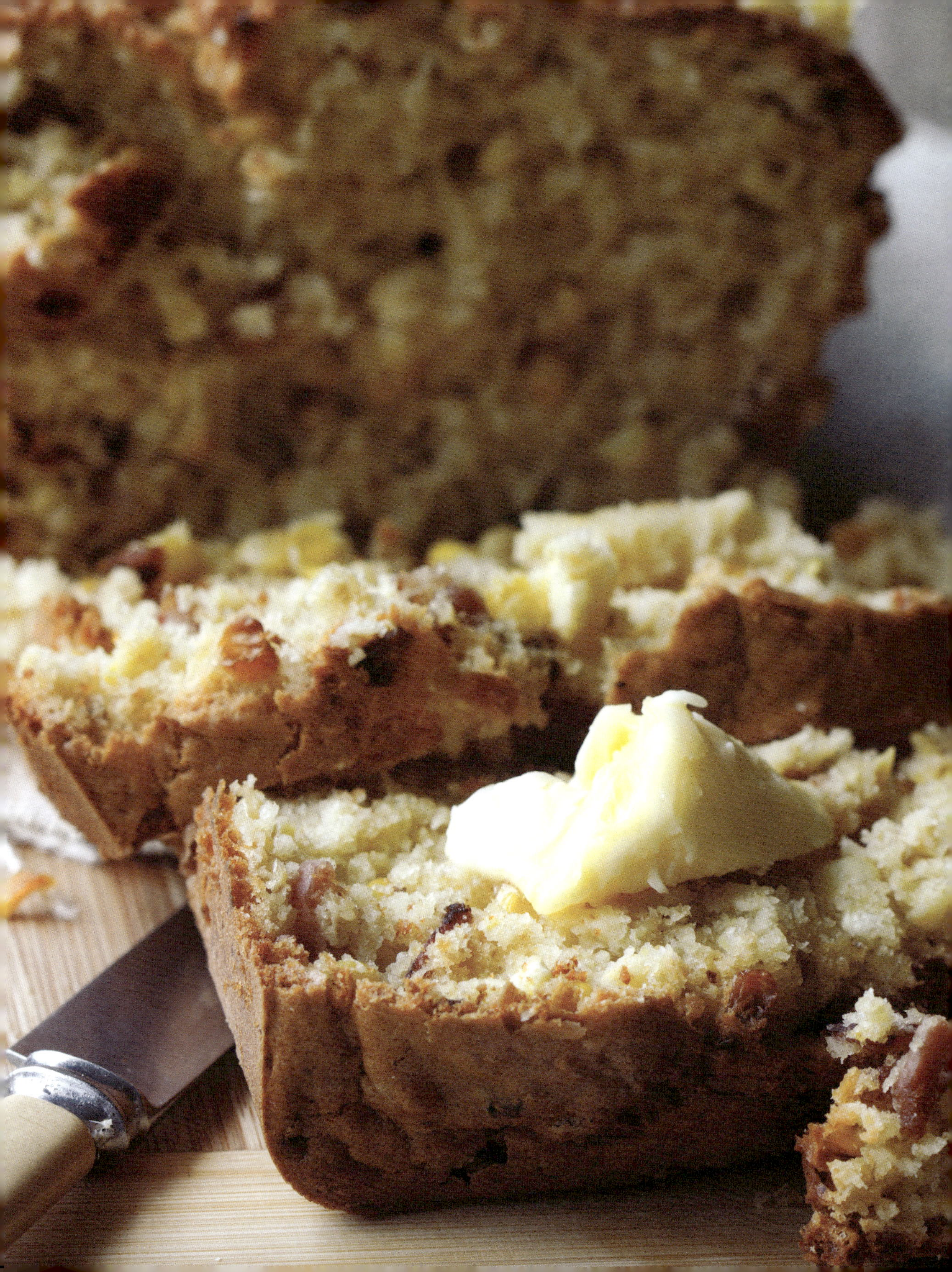

Corn bread with bacon? Who could resist that? A slice of this bread topped with a fried egg is one of the most delicious breakfasts you can have, but if like me, restraint is not in your vocabulary, simply serve it in thick slices spread with lashings of farm-fresh butter.

CORN AND BACON BREAD

Makes 1 standard loaf

- 250 g bacon, diced
- 2½ cups flour
- 2 teaspoons baking powder
- 1 tablespoon sugar
- 1 teaspoon salt
- 4 large eggs
- ½ cup butter, melted
- 1 cup milk
- 1 tin (410 g) whole corn kernels
- ½ tin (about 200 g) creamed sweetcorn
- 1 cup grated Cheddar cheese

1. Pre-heat the oven to 180 °C and grease a standard size loaf tin.
2. Fry the diced bacon in a very hot pan until slightly crisp.
3. Meanwhile, sift all the dry ingredients into a large mixing bowl.
4. Beat together the eggs, butter and milk and pour into the dry ingredients. Mix well.
5. Fold in the corn and bacon and pour into the prepared loaf tin. Sprinkle the grated cheese over the loaf and place in the oven.
6. Bake for 60–75 minutes until the loaf is golden brown and a skewer inserted comes out clean. If the loaf is browning too fast, turn the heat down.
7. Remove from the oven and allow to cool down for 5 minutes before removing from the tray.

Savoury muffins are one of my absolute favourite things to have around the house. They make for great lunchbox fillers and snacks and my kids just love them. These spinach and feta muffins have so much fresh spinach in them that my kids call them 'green muffins'. If you don't want to add quite as much spinach, feel free to reduce the quantity because this will have no effect on the end result, perhaps just the colour. You could also add more or less cheese and even add different cheeses as you prefer. A great idea is to bake double or triple the amount you need and freeze the baked muffins. This way you always have them around and you can quickly defrost them in the microwave or normal oven for super-fast lunches or snacks, plus they'll taste freshly baked.

SPINACH AND FETA MUFFINS

Makes 12 standard muffins

- 1 small onion, finely chopped
- 1 garlic clove, crushed
- 250 g baby spinach, washed and chopped
- ½ teaspoon salt
- ½ teaspoon grated nutmeg
- 1 teaspoon paprika
- 250 g cake flour
- 1 tablespoon baking powder
- 1 egg
- 1 cup milk
- 100 g butter, melted
- 150 g feta cheese, crumbled

1. Pre-heat the oven to 180 °C. Place disposable muffin cups or cupcake cups in a standard 12-hole muffin tray.
2. In a frying pan, sauté the onion, garlic and spinach in 1 tablespoon olive oil until soft and cooked (5–7 minutes). Add the salt, nutmeg and paprika and stir to combine. Remove from the pan and allow to cool slightly.
3. Sift the cake flour and baking powder into a bowl.
4. Combine the egg, milk and melted butter and mix into the dry ingredients.
5. Fold in the crumbled feta cheese and spoon the mixture into the muffin cases. I like to fill them almost to the top with this mixture.
6. Bake for 20–25 minutes until a skewer inserted comes out clean.
7. Remove from the baking tray and allow to cool.

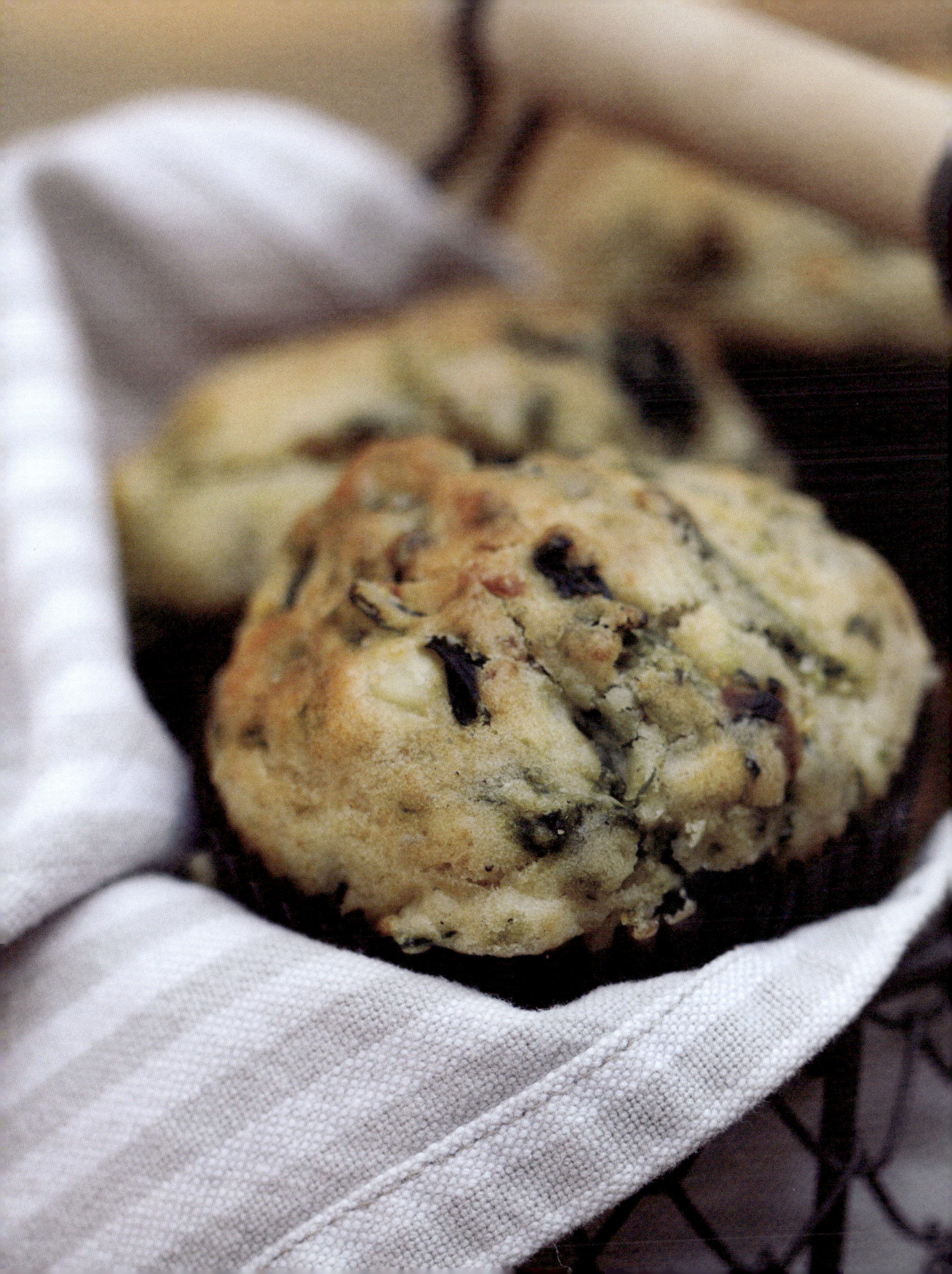

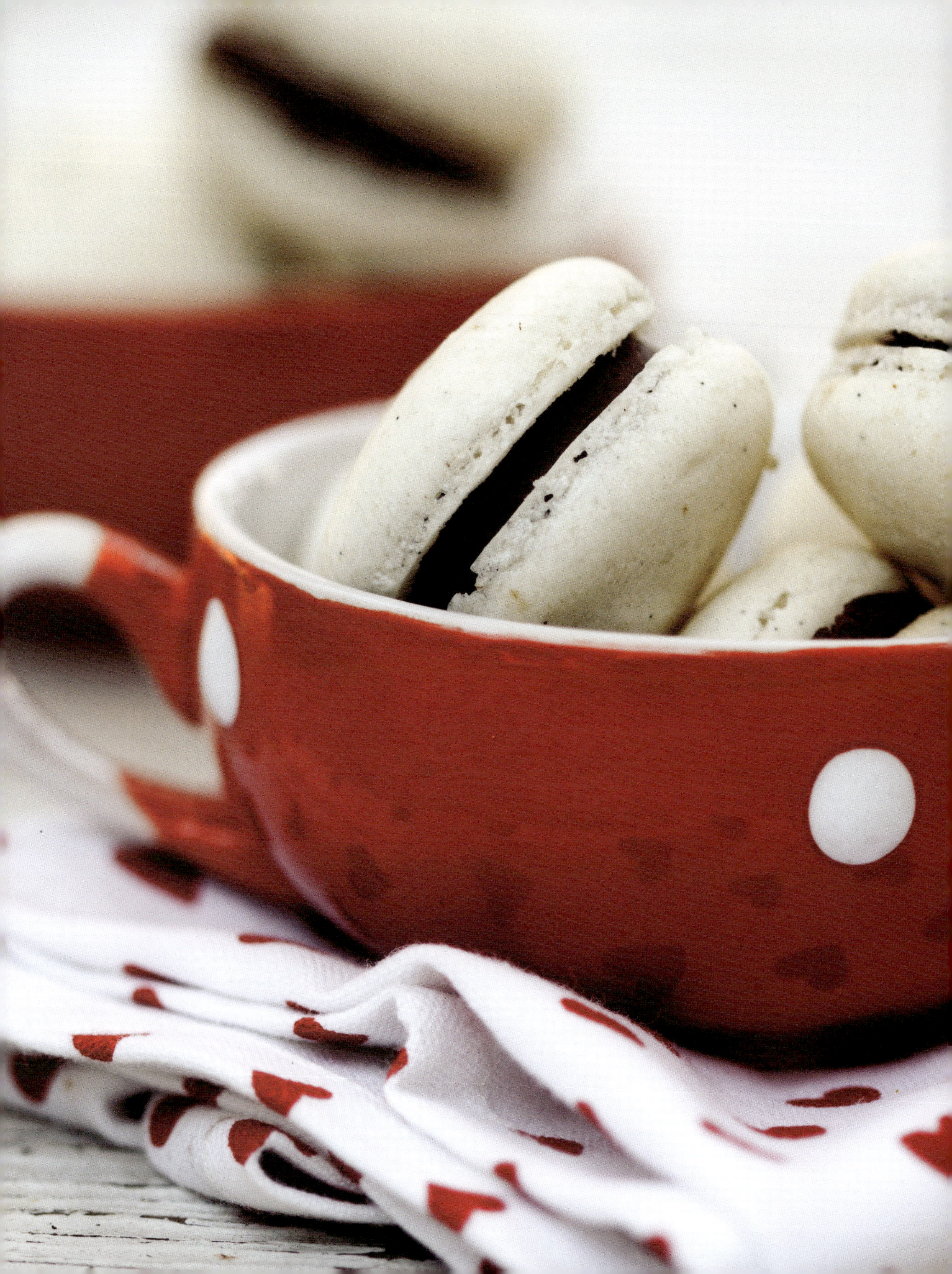

It's not necessary to treat the macaroon mixture too gently when you are mixing it. You want to deflate the mixture slightly. When you pipe the mixture it needs to ooze out of the bag, but it should also not be too runny or it won't hold its shape when piped. This is the tricky part. When I add the ground almond mixture to the whipped egg whites, I fold between 30 and 35 times to make sure the mixture is still thick and luscious but not too airy. It really is all about trial and error as you might fold more or less vigorously than I do. By the third or fourth time you've made these, you will know exactly what works for you. And that's where the fun starts, as you can then start experimenting with different flavours.

VANILLA MACAROONS WITH CHOCOLATE GANACHE FILLING

Makes approximately 36 macaroons

250 g icing sugar
120 g ground almonds
150 g egg whites (approximately 4 extra-large egg whites), room temperature
70 g caster sugar
seeds from 1 vanilla pod

Chocolate ganache

200 g dark chocolate, chopped
200 ml cream

1. Pre-heat the oven to 140 °C and line 2–3 baking trays with baking paper.
2. Combine the icing sugar and the ground almonds in a food processor and pulse until well combined.
3. Sieve the mixture twice. Set aside.
4. Beat the egg whites until soft peaks form.
5. Gradually add the caster sugar until the mixture is stiff and glossy.
6. Slit the vanilla pod lengthwise, scrape out the seeds and add them.
7. Add the ground almond mixture to the egg whites and fold in.
8. Place the mixture in a piping bag and pipe circles of about 2–3 cm onto the baking paper.
9. Place in the oven and bake for 12–15 minutes until they are crisp but still chewy in the middle.
10. Remove the trays from the oven and allow to cool completely. Work very gently when removing them from the trays as they are quite fragile.
11. To make the chocolate ganache, heat the cream and pour over the chopped chocolate. Stir until the chocolate is melted and then place in the refrigerator until set.
12. Pipe or spoon the ganache onto half of the macaroons and sandwich with another half.

BANANA CAKE WITH PEANUT BUTTER FROSTING

Serves 8–10

2 eggs

1 teaspoon vanilla extract

200 ml buttermilk

100 g sugar

240 g cake flour, sifted

1 teaspoon bicarbonate of soda

1 teaspoon baking powder

pinch of salt

100 g butter, room temperature

225 g banana, mashed (weighed with skin off, approximately 4 large bananas)

Frosting

50 g butter, room temperature

75 g smooth peanut butter

400 g icing sugar, sifted

1 tablespoon milk

handful chopped pecans

1. Preheat the oven to 180 °C and grease a 25–30 cm cake tin.
2. Combine all the cake ingredients in a large mixing bowl and beat for 2 minutes until the mixture is smooth and thick.
3. Pour into a well-greased cake tin and bake for 30 minutes or until a skewer inserted comes out clean.
4. Remove the cake from the oven and allow to cool in the tin for 10 minutes before turning it out onto a cooling rack to cool completely.
5. For the icing, cream the butter and peanut butter together until pale and fluffy. Add the sifted icing sugar and beat until incorporated. If necessary, thin out with some of the milk. Spread liberally over the cake and top with the chopped pecans.

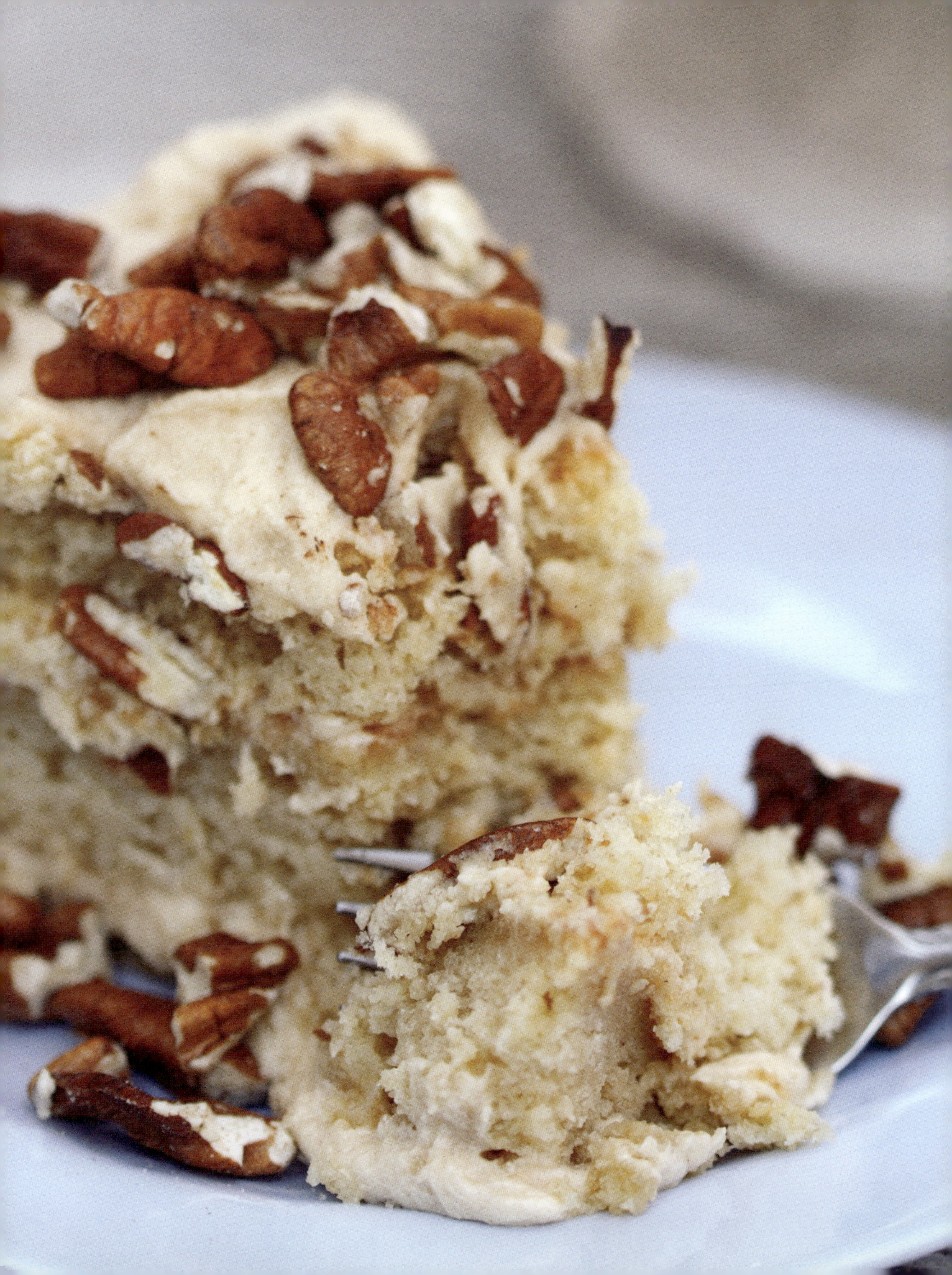

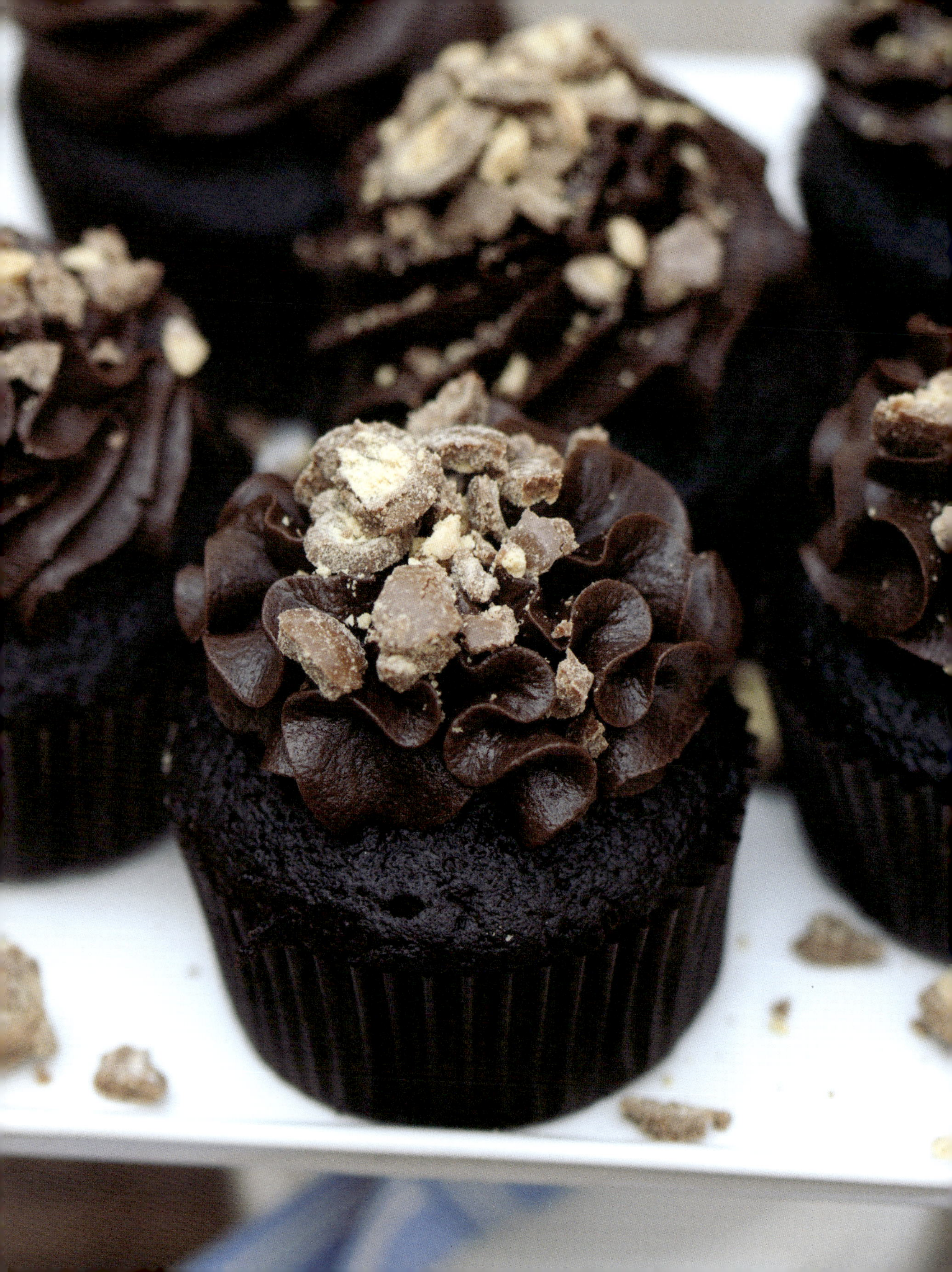

I couldn't have crammed more chocolate into these cupcakes if I tried, and believe me I made a good effort! Even people who say they don't like chocolate will wolf these down and ask for more. They are incredibly rich, deliciously moist and absolutely decadent. Everything I want from a chocolate cupcake.

DEATH BY CHOCOLATE CUPCAKES

Makes 12 cupcakes

200 g caster sugar
175 g cake flour
50 g cocoa powder
1½ teaspoons baking powder
½ teaspoon salt
1 extra-large egg
½ cup milk
75 ml melted unsalted butter
1 teaspoon vanilla extract
½ cup hot water (you could also use strong coffee)

Chocolate icing

100 g unsalted butter, room temperature
400 g icing sugar, sifted
100 g melted dark chocolate, cooled slightly
1 tablespoon cold, strong coffee
chocolate shavings or crushed chocolate malt balls, for decorating

1. Pre-heat the oven to 180 °C. Grease and line a 12-hole muffin tray with cupcake liners.
2. Sift all the dry ingredients into a large bowl.
3. Mix the egg, milk, melted butter and vanilla extract and combine with the dry ingredients. Beat until the mixture is smooth.
4. Slowly add the hot water or coffee and mix until combined. The batter will be very runny.
5. Distribute the batter between the cupcake liners and place in the oven.
6. Bake for 20–25 minutes until a skewer inserted comes out clean.
7. Remove from the oven and allow to cool completely before icing.
8. For the icing, beat the butter and sugar together until thick and fluffy. Slowly pour in the cooled melted chocolate and cold coffee. Mix until you have smooth and thick chocolate icing. If the chocolate is still too hot the butter will melt. If this happens, simply place the bowl in the fridge for 15–20 minutes until the butter firms up again and then beat until light and fluffy.
9. Pipe or spread the icing onto the cooled cupcakes and decorate with chocolate shavings or crushed chocolate malt balls.

I don't know about you but when I read baking recipes without key ingredients such as flour, eggs or sugar, I get a bit nervous. I imagine it will mean I have to work harder or source ingredients I will never find. With this cake, there is none of that. The ingredients are things you have in your kitchen already and all you need is a mixer or a very strong arm.

I also find that with special dietary recipes, people often have the pre-conceived idea that it's going to taste bland or strange. I can debunk that myth too because there are very few chocolate cakes as delicious as this one. No one will guess it has no flour and the intense chocolate taste together with the moist, moreish texture will have them coming back for more.

FLOURLESS CHOCOLATE CAKE

Makes one 30 cm cake

- 300 g chocolate
- 100 g butter
- 1 teaspoon vanilla extract
- 6 eggs
- 150 g caster sugar
- 50 g cocoa powder
- pinch of salt
- extra cocoa powder, to serve
- crème fraîche, to serve

1. Pre-heat the oven to 180 °C. Prepare a 27 cm springform cake pan by greasing it with soft butter and lining it with baking paper.
2. In a double boiler, melt together the chocolate and butter. Add the vanilla and stir.
3. Beat the eggs and sugar until thick and pale.
4. Add the chocolate mixture to the egg mixture and sift in the cocoa powder and pinch of salt.
5. Fold everything together.
6. Pour the mixture into the prepared cake pan and place in the oven.
7. Bake for 25 minutes until the cake has risen and feels slightly firm. If you would like it to be very moist, only bake it for 17–20 minutes.
8. Remove from the oven and allow to cool completely in the tin. Remove from the tin and serve with a dusting of cocoa powder and a dollop of crème fraîche.

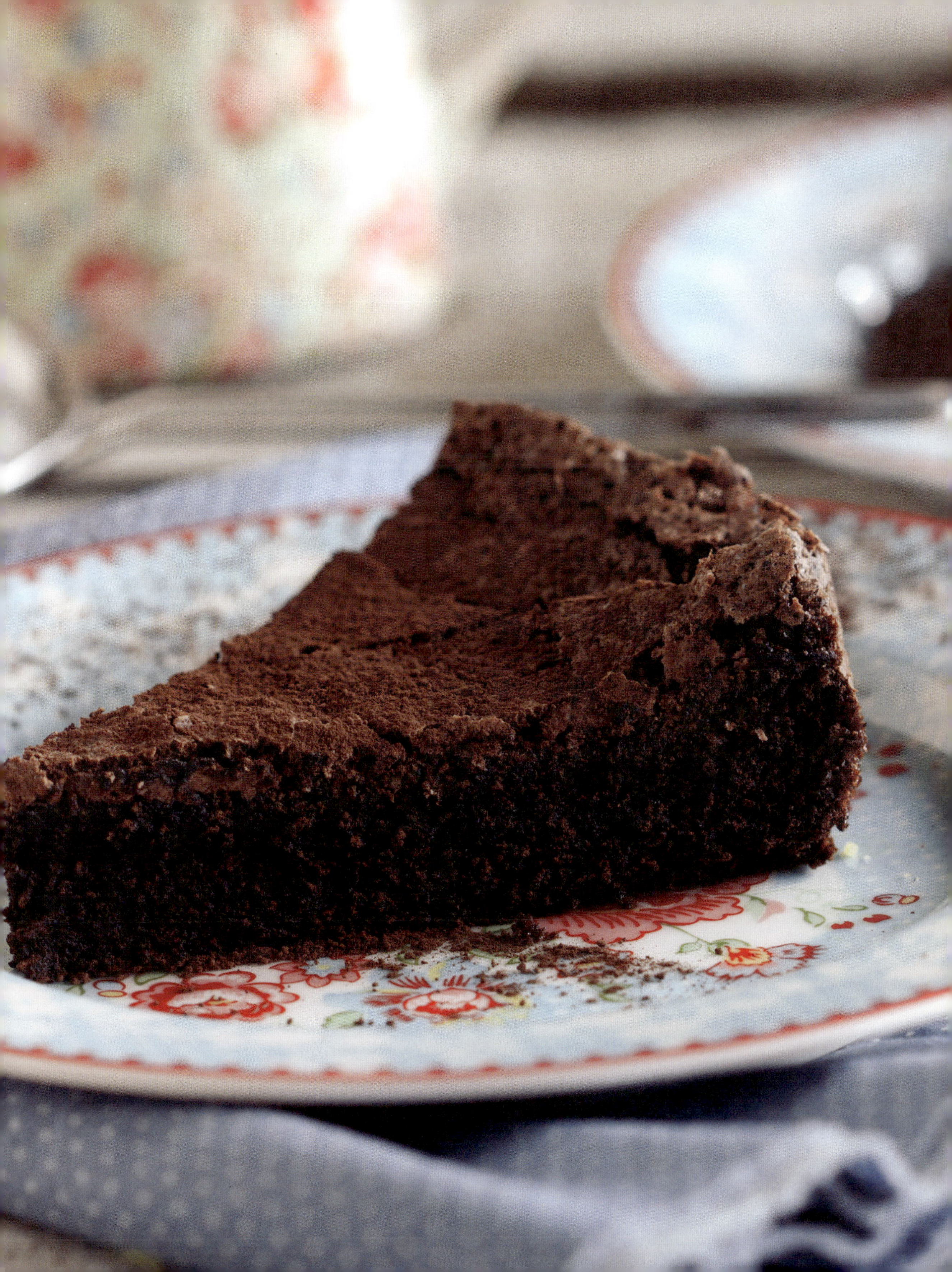

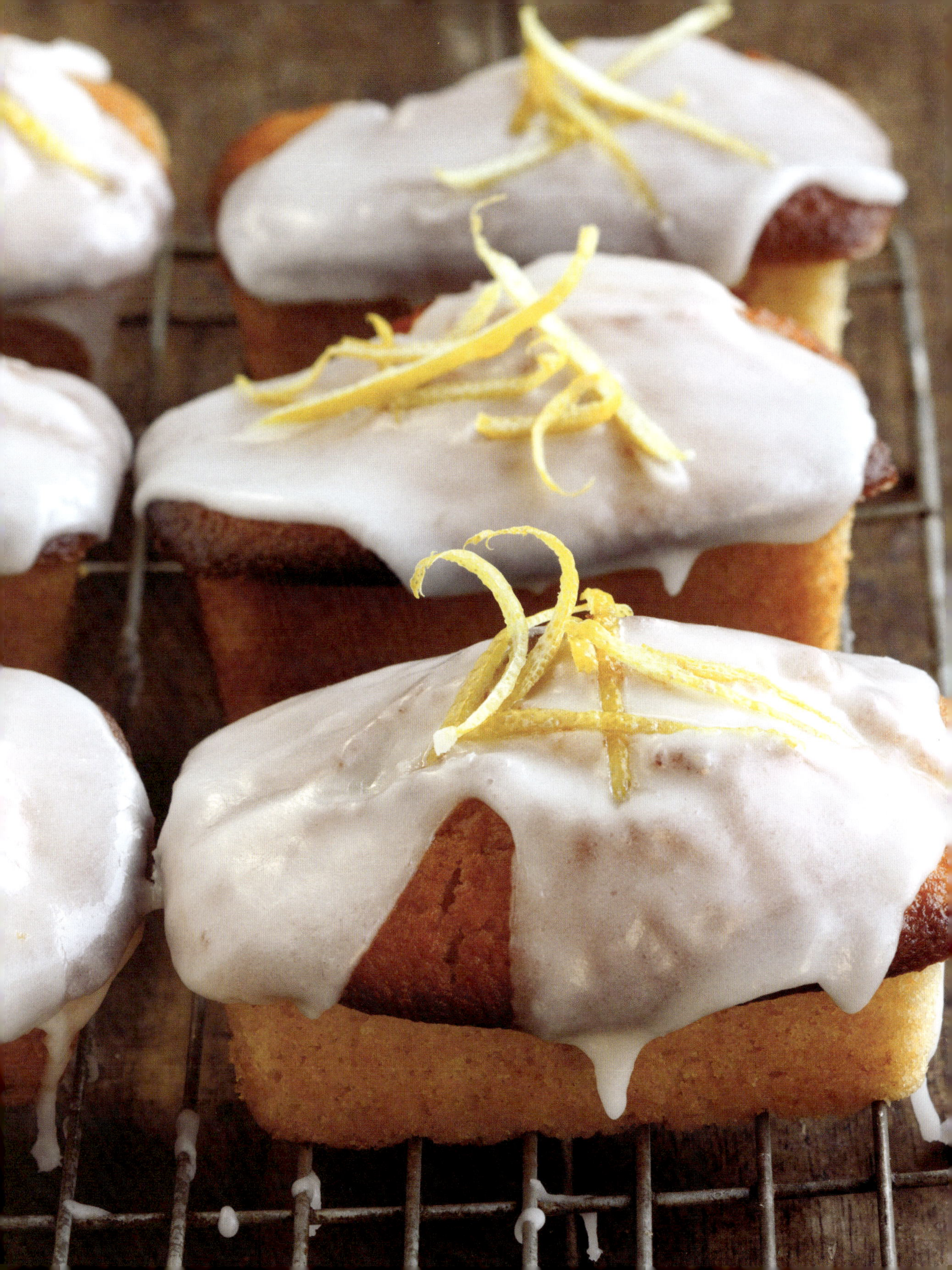

This is by far one of my favourite cake recipes. Not only is it super easy and the result delicious every single time, but it's also lower in fat (especially saturated fats) than most cakes. This is because instead of butter, fat-free yoghurt and canola oil are used to keep it soft and moist.

I've adapted this recipe for cupcakes, sheet cakes and stacked round cakes and have tried it with almost every different flavouring, and it always comes out beautifully, but the little loaf cakes will always be tops for me. I love the simplicity of the lemon glaze but you could also frost the cake with cream cheese frosting (see page 178), which would be equally delicious.

LEMON YOGHURT MINI LOAF CAKES

Makes 6 mini loaf cakes or 1 standard loaf cake

200 g cake flour
2 teaspoons baking powder
½ teaspoon salt
1 cup plain, fat-free yoghurt
200 g caster sugar
3 large eggs
½ teaspoon vanilla extract
½ cup canola oil
zest of 1 lemon

Lemon glaze

250 g icing sugar, sifted
juice of 1–2 lemons (depending on how thick you want the glaze)

1. Pre-heat the oven to 180 °C and grease 6 mini loaf tins.
2. Sift together the cake flour, baking powder and salt and set aside.
3. In a separate bowl, combine the remaining ingredients and mix well.
4. Pour the egg and oil mixture into the dry ingredients and mix to combine.
5. Pour the batter into the loaf tins and bake for 20–25 minutes until a skewer inserted comes out clean.
6. Remove from the oven and allow to cool completely before removing the cakes from the tins.
7. To make the glaze, mix together the icing sugar and lemon juice.
8. Top the cakes with the glaze and extra lemon zest.

Everyone I know loves pecan pie and it's not hard to see why. It's so easy to make, it's shameful that we have to pay so much for it in the shops. And like everything else, home-made always tastes better, plus you have the added bonus of your friends and family thinking you're a kitchen god or goddess!

PECAN PIE

Makes one 30 cm pie/tart

1 roll ready-rolled shortcrust pastry

Filling

200 g pecan nuts, roasted and roughly chopped

4 eggs

50 g butter, melted

1 cup golden syrup

100 g brown sugar

100 g white sugar

1/3 teaspoon salt

1 teaspoon vanilla extract

1. Pre-heat the oven to 160 °C.
2. Roll out the pastry to fit into a 30 cm pie dish or tart tin. Press the pastry into the tin and scatter over the roughly chopped pecan nuts.
3. Stir together the eggs and melted butter.
4. Beat in the syrup, sugars, salt and vanilla.
5. Pour the mixture over the pecans.
6. Place in the pre-heated oven and bake for 45–60 minutes until the filling is set around the edges but still has a slight 'jiggle' in the centre.
7. Remove from the oven and allow to cool completely before serving (it's even better the next day).

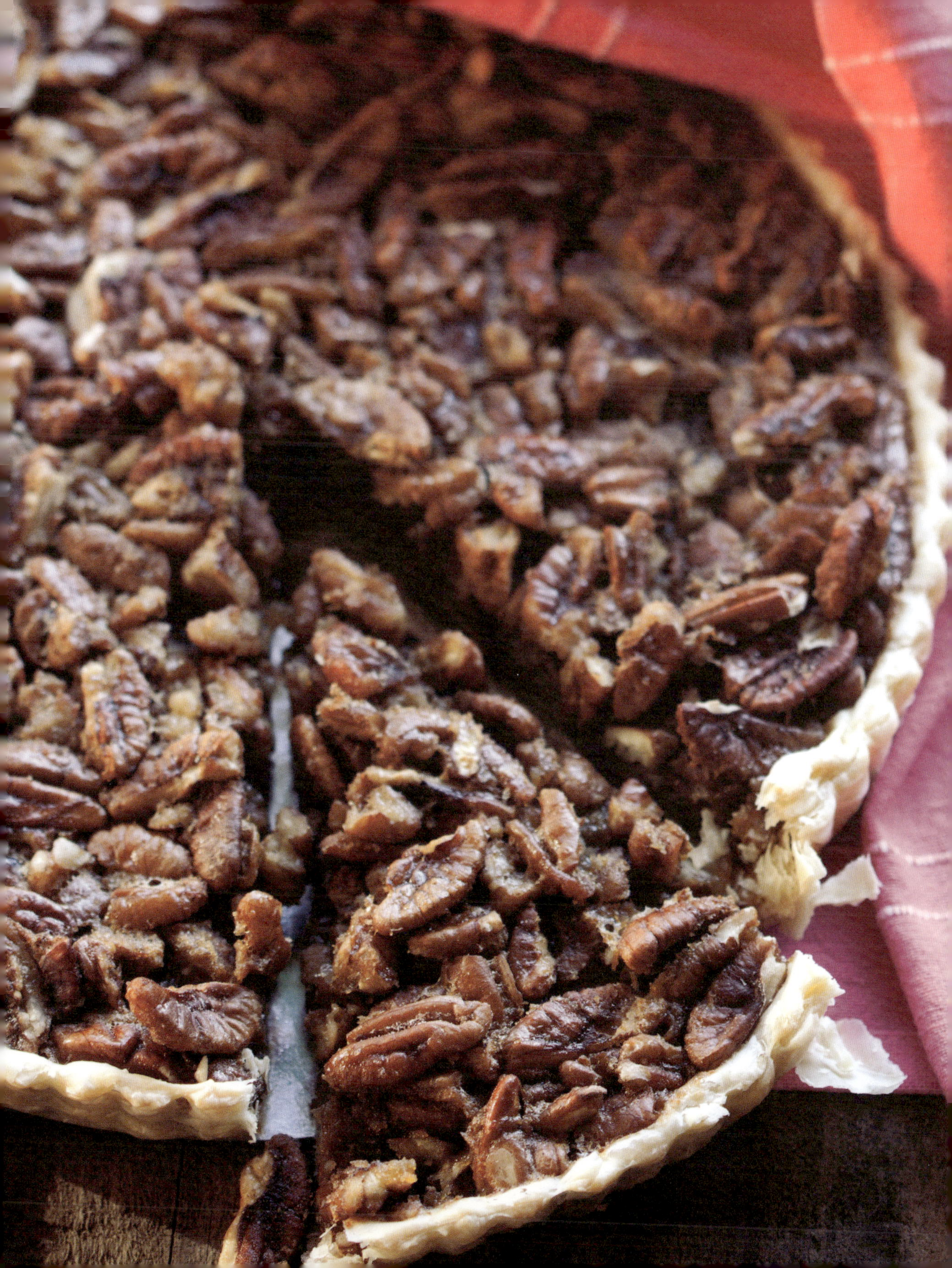

I know, I know. You know someone who has the best recipe for brownies, or that person is you. I know that because before I had my own brownie recipe, I would've defended my friend Nicole's brownies to the death. There's something about brownies that makes people intensely defensive and sometimes quite aggressive. And oh, so opinionated. Especially women. I guess it's quite understandable though. Who doesn't love an ooey-gooey chocolate-packed brownie?

With nuts, without nuts, with icing, without icing, served with ice cream, served with cream. Eaten standing up in the kitchen in your pyjamas. I am most definitely not going to tell you how to enjoy a brownie, but I am going to tell you that I by no means think that my recipe is the best because I've tasted some awesome brownies, but I do think that my recipe is pretty darn good.

Adding unsweetened, desiccated coconut to my recipe results in a brownie that tastes of both a brownie and a very moist and rich lamington, which in my books is not a bad thing. And before you say you don't like coconut, let me assure you that even my coconut-hating husband gobbles these up as quickly as I put them down in front of him.

CHOCOLATE BROWNIES WITH COCONUT

Makes 8–12 brownies

- 250 g butter
- 100 g cocoa powder
- 500 g sugar
- 4 eggs, beaten
- 100 g flour
- 50 g desiccated coconut
- 1 teaspoon baking powder
- 1 teaspoon vanilla
- 100 g toasted pecan nuts, roughly chopped
- 100 g dark chocolate

1. Preheat the oven to 180 °C.
2. In a large pot, combine the butter, cocoa and sugar and allow the mixture to melt together. Stir to combine and allow to cool slightly. Add the eggs slowly, beating very well while doing so (I do this with my hand mixer to stop the eggs from curdling).
3. Add the flour, coconut, baking powder and vanilla and mix well. Add the nuts and stir through.
4. Pour the batter into a well-greased, rectangular or square baking tray or dish of approximately 20–25 cm. Make sure that the batter is 2–4 cm deep in the pan.
5. Bake for 20–25 minutes. The brownies should be firm but squidgy in the middle.
6. Melt the chocolate and pour onto the brownies. Allow to set slightly before slicing.
7. Serve with vanilla ice cream.

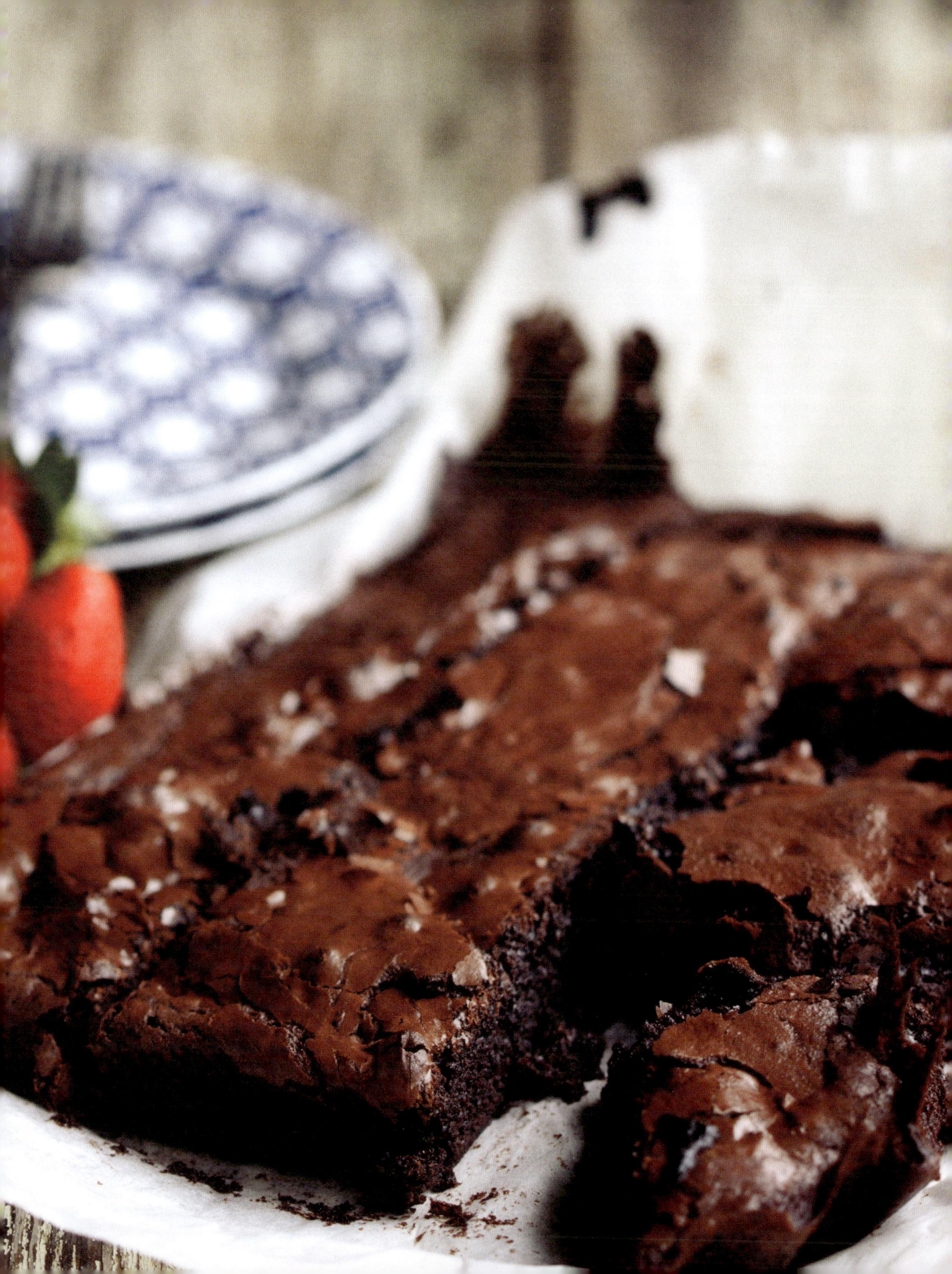

CONVERSION CHART

1 teaspoon (tsp) = 5ml
1 tablespoon (tbsp) = 15ml
1 cup = 250ml

Liquid Conversions

Metric	Imperial	US cups
30 ml	1 fl oz	⅛ cup
60 ml	2 fl oz	¼ cup
80 ml	2¾ fl oz	⅓ cup
125 ml	4 fl oz	½ cup
185 ml	6 fl oz	¾ cup
250 ml	8 fl oz	1 cup
375 ml	12 fl oz	1½ cups
500 ml	16 fl oz	2 cups
500 ml	20 fl oz	2½ cups
750 ml	24 fl oz	3 cups
1 litre	32 fl oz	4 cups

Cup Measures

1 cup butter	220 g	7 oz
1 cup breadcrumbs, fresh	50 g	3½ oz
1 cup sugar, brown	200 g	6½ oz
1 cup sugar, white	225 g	7 oz
1 cup caster sugar	200 g	6½ oz
1 cup icing sugar	125 g	4 oz
1 cup rice, uncooked	220 g	7 oz
1 cup couscous, uncooked	180 g	6 oz
1 cup polenta, uncooked	180 g	6 oz
1 cup parmesan, finely grated	100 g	3½ oz
1 cup of flour	125 g	4½ oz

Ingredients

Aubergine	Eggplant/ brinjal
Bicarbonate of soda	Baking soda
Biscuits	Cookies
Cake/ plain flour	All purpose flour
Caster sugar	Super fine sugar
Courgette	Zucchini/ baby marrow
Coriander	Cilantro
Icing sugar	Confectioner's sugar/ powdered sugar

Weights

Imperial	Metric
½ oz	10 g
¾ oz	20 g
1 oz	25 g
1½ oz	40 g
2 oz	50 g
2½ oz	60 g
3 oz	75 g
4 oz	110 g
4½ oz	125 g
5 oz	150 g
6 oz	175 g
7 oz	200 g
8 oz	225 g
9 oz	250 g
10 oz	275 g
12 oz	350 g
1 lb	450 g
1 lb 8 oz	700 g
2 lb	900 g
3 lb	1.35 kg

Oven Temperatures

°C	Gas Mark	°F
140	1	275
150	2	300
170	3	325
180	4	350
190	5	375
200	6	400
220	7	425
230	8	450
240	9	475

INDEX

A
aubergine parmigiana 148

B
baguette with grilled vegetables and chevin 144
baking 170–197
   banana cake with peanut butter frosting 186
   choc-chunk cookies 176
   chocolate brownies with coconut 196
   corn and bacon bread 182
   death by chocolate cupcakes 189
   flourless chocolate cake 190
   lemon polenta cake 179
   lemon yoghurt mini loaf cakes 193
   millionaire's shortbread 175
   pecan pie 194
   red velvet cupcakes 178
   spinach and feta muffins 182
   strawberry and cream cupcakes 172
   vanilla macaroons with chocolate ganache filling 185
banana
   cake with peanut butter frosting 186
   caramel tartlettes 163
basil pesto 5
beef
   my ultimate steak sandwich 103
   slow braised oxtail 99
   stroganoff with mixed mushrooms 88
   Thai beef and noodle salad 95
biltong and blue cheese quiche 18
black forest trifle 155
Bollywood lamb chops with cucumber salad 86
bruschetta with fresh tomatoes 6
butter chicken bunny chow 52
butternut
   creamy, baked 136
   gnocchi with sage cream 41
   risotto with feta and chilli 133

C
Cajun
   prawn salad with aioli 24
   roast fish with courgette salad 117
cauliflower soup with bacon 15

cheese
   cheesy meatballs baked in tomato sauce 45
   fried mozzarella with roasted tomato sauce 2
   four-cheese mac 'n cheese 31
chicken 50–78
   and asparagus pasta 39
   and potato salad, warm with pesto dressing 76
   bacon and cheese stuffed breasts 67
   biryani 56
   butter chicken bunny chow 52
   crispy chicken burgers with home-made aioli 70
   home-made chicken nuggets 72
   lemon roasted chicken 61
   liver pâté 9
   livers in creamy mushroom sauce 62
   mini chicken burgers with sweet potato fries 78
   Moroccan chicken on butternut couscous 69
   pie 64
   roast breasts on barley risotto 75
   roulade with smoked mozzarella and rocket 55
   spicy chicken soup with avocado salsa 59
chocolate
   brownies with coconut 196
   cake, flourless 190
   choc-chunk cookies 176
   truffles 164
   white chocolate mousse with fresh pineapple 167
corn
   and clam chowder 110
   and bacon bread 182
courgette fritters with tzatziki 139
cupcakes
   death by chocolate 189
   red velvet 178
   strawberry and cream 172
curry
   butter chicken bunny chow 52
   crab curry 113
   lamb, empanadas 91
   vegetable and coconut curry 143

D
desserts 149–169
   banana caramel tartlettes 163
   black forest trifle 155

chocolate truffles 164
flapjacks with mascarpone and blueberries 160
malva pudding 157
millefeuille with white chocolate cream and berries 159
*mini pavlovas with roasted pears and
    chocolate cream* 165
my gran's pumpkin fritters in caramel sauce 152
Peppermint Crisp mess 156
poached nectarines with mascarpone 150
tiramisu 169
white chocolate mousse with fresh pineapple 167

E
eggs en cocotte, with leeks and bacon 19

F
fettuccini, with prawns and courgettes 37
flapjacks, with mascarpone and blueberries 160
flourless chocolate cake 190
fritters
    courgette, with tzatziki 139
    pumpkin, in caramel sauce 152

H
huevos rancheros 21

L
lamb
    Bollywood lamb chops with cucumber salad 86
    curry empanadas 91
    korma 96
    *roast lamb with 3-hour potatoes, crème fraîche-
        smothered green beans and
        honey-roasted carrots* 84
    shank pies 80
lemon
    yoghurt mini loaf cakes 193
    polenta cake 179
linguini with garlic and mushrooms 46

M
meat 79–103
malva pudding 157
Moroccan chicken on butternut couscous 69
millionaire's shortbread 175

millefeuille with white chocolate cream and berries 159
mini
    lemon yoghurt loaf cakes 193
    pavlovas with roasted pears and chocolate cream 165
muffins, spinach and feta 182
mushrooms, stuffed 137
mussel soup 16

N
nectarines, poached with mascarpone 150

O
oxtail, slow-braised 99

P
pasta 26–29
    *baked penne with aubergine, courgette and sun-dried
        tomatoes* 36
    butternut gnocchi with sage cream 41
    cheesy meatballs baked in tomato sauce 45
    chicken and asparagus pasta 39
    fettuccini with prawns and courgettes 37
    four-cheese mac 'n cheese 31
    linguini with garlic and mushrooms 46
    *pasta with roasted cherry tomatoes,
        ricotta and pesto* 28
    spaghetti arrabiata 25
    spaghetti with clams and cream 49
    summer vegetable pasta with poached eggs 32
    vegetable-loaded spaghetti Bolognese 42
pâté
    chicken liver 9
Peppermint Crisp mess 156
pesto, basil 5
pie
    chicken 64
    lamb shank 80
    pecan 194
    spinach and feta pies 146
pork
    and apple burgers 92
    chops with mustard sauce 98
    kebabs on spicy tomato orzo 83
    steaks with balsamic onions 100
potato and taleggio frittata 134
prawn and pea risotto 118
pumpkin fritters in caramel sauce 152

Q
quesadillas with cheese, corn and kidney beans 140
quiche, biltong and blue cheese 18

R
risotto
    butternut with feta and chilli 133
    prawn and pea 118
    spicy with crispy calamari 109
    tomato and basil 130

S
salad
    Cajun prawn salad with aioli 24
    Thai beef and noodle salad 95
    warm chicken and potato salad with pesto dressing 76
    warm spring vegetable salad 23
seafood 104–127
baked seafood rice 106
    Cajun roast fish with courgette salad 117
    crab curry 113
    corn and clam chowder 110
    fish tacos with fresh coriander and lime 126
    grilled fish skewers with garlic butter 111
    oven-roasted prawns with peri-peri sauce 114
    prawn and pea risotto 118
    salt and peper squid 125
    seafood 'stoup' 122
    spicy risotto with crispy calamari 109
    teriyaki salmon 119
    Thai fried rice with calamari 121
    smoked salmon cream cheese rolls 12
soup
    cauliflower with bacon 15
    mussel 16
    seafood 'stoup' 122
spicy chicken with avocado salsa 59
spaghetti
    arrabiata 25
    with clams and cream 49
    vegetable-loaded spaghetti Bolognese 42
spinach
    and feta pies 146
    and feta muffins 182
squid, salt and pepper 125
starters 1–25
    basil pesto 5
    biltong and blue cheese quiche 18
    bruschetta with fresh tomatoes 6
    Cajun prawn salad with aioli 24
    caramelised onion and goat's cheese tarts 11
    cauliflower soup with bacon 15
    chicken liver pâté 9
    eggs en cocotte with leeks and bacon 19
    fried mozzarella with roasted tomato sauce 2
    huevos rancheros 21
    smoked salmon cream cheese rolls 12
    tomato and pesto tart 8
    mussel soup 16
    warm spring vegetable salad 23
strawberry and cream cupcakes 172
summer vegetable pasta with poached eggs 32

T
teriyaki salmon 119
tart
    banana caramel tartlettes 163
    tomato and pesto 8
    caramelised onion and goat's cheese 11
Thai
    beef and noodle salad 95
    fried rice with calamari 121
    tiramisu 169
tomato and basil risotto 130

V
vanilla macaroons with chocolate ganache filling 185
vegetable and coconut curry 143
vegetarian 128–148
    aubergine parmigiana 148
    baguette with grilled vegetables and chevin 144
    butternut risotto with feta and chilli 133
    courgette fritters with tzatziki 139
    creamy baked butternut 136
    potato and taleggio frittata 134
    quesadillas with cheese, corn and kidney beans 140
    spinach and feta pies 146
    stuffed mushrooms 137
    tomato and basil risotto 130
vegetable and coconut curry 143

W
white chocolate mousse with fresh pineapple 167